THE
100 BEST
MUTUAL
FUNDS
YOU CAN BUY
2002

Also by Gordon K. Williamson
First Time Investor
Big Decisions, Small Investor
Low Risk Investing
Making the Most of Your 401(k)

THE

100

BEST

MUTUAL
FUNDS
YOU CAN BUY
2002

Gordon K. Willamson

Adams Media Corporation
Avon, Massachusetts

Published by Adams Media Corporation
57 Littlefield Street, Avon, MA 02322
www.adamsmedia.com

ISBN: 1-58062-535-5

Printed in Canada.

J I H G F E D C B A

This publication is designed to provide accurate and authoritative information with
regard to the subject matter covered. It is sold with the understanding that the publisher
is not engaged in rendering legal, accounting, or other professional advice. If legal
advice or other expert assistance is required, the services of a competent professional
person should be sought.
—From a *Declaration of Principles* jointly adopted by a Committee of the
American Bar Association and a Committee of Publishers and Associations

While due care has been taken to ensure accurate and current data, the ideas, principles,
conclusions, and general suggestions contained in this volume are subject to the laws
and regulations of local, state, and federal authorities, as well as to court cases and any
revisions of court cases. Due to the magnitude of the database and the complexity of
the subject matter, occasional errors are possible; the publisher assumes no liability
direct or incidental for any actions or investments made by readers of this book, and
strongly suggests that readers seek consultation with legal, financial, or accounting professionals before making any investment.

The data used to analyze the funds is current through time of publication.

This book is available at quantity discounts for bulk purchases.
For information, call 1-800-872-5627.

Visit our exciting small business Web site at businesstown.com

Dedication
This book is dedicated to all of my clients.
I would be nowhere without their trust and support.

Acknowledgments
Special thanks to Cynthia Shaffer for her computer skills.
This is a truly thankless job, and I appreciate everything she has done.

Contents

I.
About This Book

There are roughly 6 million business entities operating in the United States; close to 15,000 of these businesses are publicly held (meaning they have issued stock to the public). Of the 15,000 publicly traded companies, fewer than 4,000 are listed on the New York Stock Exchange (NYSE). The world's total stock market capitalization is approximately $20 trillion, one-half of which is represented by domestic equities.

There are over 13,000 mutual funds. There are well over three times as many mutual funds as there are stocks listed on the NYSE! The mutual fund industry is now the second largest financial institution in the nation, with assets exceeding $8 trillion, up from $1 trillion in 1991. By the beginning of the year 2000, U.S. households held 81 percent of mutual fund assets, up from 74 percent in 1990. Individual stocks and mutual funds accounted for 38 percent of U.S. households' financial assets, surpassing the previous all-time high of 34 percent in 1968. Just under 49 million households own shares of one or more mutual funds, up from 4.6 million in 1980.

Mutual funds are the *best* investment vehicle that has been developed in the twentieth century. When properly selected, these vehicles combine professional management, ease of purchase and redemption, simple record keeping, risk reduction, and superb performance, all in one type of investment. There are dozens of other types of investments, but none match the overall versatility of mutual funds.

A mutual fund is simply one method of investing. When you invest in a fund, your money is pooled with thousands of other investors' monies. This large pool of money is overseen by the fund's management. These managers invest this pool of money in one or more types of investments. The universe of investments includes common stocks, preferred stocks, corporate bonds, tax-free municipal bonds, U.S. government obligations, zero-coupon bonds, convertible securities, gold, silver, foreign securities, and even real estate. The amount of money invested in one or more of these categories depends upon the fund's objectives and restrictions and on the management's perception of the economy.

The beauty of mutual funds is that once the investor decides on the *type* of investment desired, there are several funds that fulfill that criterion. As an example, someone who needs current income would be attracted to bond funds (or a series of equity-oriented funds coupled with what is known as a "systematic withdrawal plan"—a monthly income program described in Appendix D). A person interested in appreciation would focus on an aggressive growth, growth and income, and/or international stock fund. A person who wanted some current income plus some growth to offset the effects of inflation should consider a balanced fund.

The track records of these funds can easily be obtained, as contrasted to the track records of stockbrokers, who are not ranked at all. A few mutual fund sources even look at a fund's risk-adjusted return, a standard of measurement that has not been sufficiently emphasized in the past.

This book was written to fill a void. There are already several mutual fund books and directories, but none deal exclusively with the very best funds. More important, *none of these publications measure risk properly*.

This is the twelfth edition of this book. If you have read one or more of the previous editions, you will notice that this edition includes many funds not previously listed and that several of the *previous* "100 Best" are not included here. This does not mean that you should sell or transfer from a previous recommendation to one that appears in this edition. For the most part, mutual funds described in past editions are still excellent choices and should not be moved. There are a number of reasons a fund no longer appears in this, or previous, editions. These reasons will be detailed in Chapter 10.

Moving from one fund to another can often spell trouble. Consider a Morningstar study that compared the performance of its growth fund index with the average investor's return during the five-year period ending May 31, 1994. While the overall market gained, on average, 12.5 percent a year, the average investor *lost* 2.5 percent a year. From 1984 through 2000, the S & P 500 averaged 16.3% a year; the typical stock investor earned only 5.3% a year during the same period. The conclusion is simple: By jumping from one investment to another, investors lose out on the solid performance they are seeking. Volatility can make it easy for investors to forget about the long-term case for stocks. In the third quarter of 1999, when the market suffered, the possibility of choosing a stock that dropped 20 percent or more in value was one in four, versus one in a thousand for a mutual fund.

Speaking of performance, unusually high stock returns during the 1990s have caused investor expectations to soar. Recent chart-toppers have threatened to raise expectations even higher: 177 funds posted 1999 returns of more than 100 percent. From 1989 to 1998, only ten funds could claim an annual return that high.

Other sources give almost endless numbers and performance statistics for hundreds and hundreds of mutual funds, leaving readers to draw their own conclusions as to what are the best funds. This book will save you a great deal of time because it has taken the over 13,000 existing funds and narrowed them down to the best 100, ranked by specific category and risk level. Even money market funds are included, a category rarely covered by any other publication.

Investors and financial advisors are not concerned with mediocre or poor performers; they simply want the best funds, *given certain parameters*. Personal investment considerations should include (in order of priority) your time horizon, risk tolerance, financial goals, existing portfolio, and tax bracket. Parameters within a given fund category include risk, performance, and consistency.

Current books and periodicals that cover funds focus on how a fund has performed in the past. Studies clearly point out that a fund whose performance is in the top half one year has a 50–50 chance of being in the bottom half the next year, or the year after that. Since there is little correlation between the past and the future when it comes to market returns, this book concentrates on consistency in management and the amount of risk assumed.

The model used to rank the 100 best is fully described in a later chapter. It is a logical, common sense approach that cuts through the statistical jargon; it is also easy to understand. As my dad used to say, "There is nothing as uncommon as common sense."

II.
What Is a Mutual Fund?

A mutual fund is an investment company—an entity that makes investments on behalf of individuals and institutions that share common financial goals. The fund pools the money of many people, each with a different amount to invest. Professional money managers then use the pool of money to buy a variety of stocks, bonds, or money market instruments that, in their judgment, will help the fund's shareholders achieve their financial objectives.

Each fund has an investment objective, described in the fund's prospectus, that is important to both the manager and the potential investor. The fund manager uses it as a guide when choosing investments for the fund's portfolio. Prospective investors use it to determine which funds are suitable for their own needs. Mutual funds' investment objectives cover a wide range. Some follow aggressive investment policies, involving greater risk, in search of higher returns; others seek current income from more conservative investments.

When the fund earns money, it distributes the earnings to its shareholders. Earnings come from stock dividends, interest paid by bonds or money market instruments, and gains from the sale of securities in the fund's portfolio. Dividends and capital gains produced are paid out in proportion to the number of fund shares owned. Thus, shareholders who invest a few hundred dollars get the same investment return per dollar as those who invest hundreds of thousands.

Mutual funds remain popular because they are convenient and efficient investment vehicles that give all individuals—even those with small sums to invest—access to a splendid array of opportunities. Mutual funds are uniquely democratic institutions. They can take a portfolio of giant blue-chip companies like IBM, General Electric, and General Motors and slice it into small enough pieces so that almost anyone can buy.

Mutual funds allow you to participate in foreign stock and bond markets that might otherwise demand too much time, expertise, or expense to be worthwhile. International funds make investing across national borders no more difficult than investing across state lines. Over the next decade, as securities markets develop in the former Iron Curtain countries, mutual funds will no doubt give investors many opportunities to participate in those markets as well.

Mutual funds have opened up a world of fixed-income investing to people who, until recently, had few choices apart from passbook accounts and savings bonds. Through bond funds, shareholders can tap into the interest payments from any kind of fixed-income security you can imagine—and many you have never heard of. The range goes from U.S. Treasury bonds (T-bonds) to collateralized mortgage obligations

(CMOs), adjustable-rate preferred stock, floating-rate notes, and even to other countries' debts—denominated both in U.S. dollars and in other currencies.

What is heavily marketed is not necessarily what is appropriate for you to invest in. A global biotechnology fund may be a great investment, but it may not be the right mutual fund for you. Buying what is "hot" rather than what is appropriate is one of the most common mistakes made by investors and an issue that is addressed throughout this book.

A reason to invest is to offset the effects of inflation. Over time, inflation can erode individuals' purchasing power. Mutual funds that invest primarily in common stocks may help keep you ahead of inflation over the long term.

	year	amount
a gallon of milk	2018	$5.16
	1998	$2.88
	1978	$1.42
a new car	2018	$33,271
	1998	$18,565
	1978	$6,478
a gallon of gasoline	2018	$1.90
	1998	$1.06
	1978	$0.67

Source: Economic and Statistic Administration, U.S. Bureau of Economic Analysis.

III.
How to Invest in a Mutual Fund

Investing in a mutual fund means buying shares of the fund. An investor becomes an owner of shares in the fund just as he or she might be an owner of shares of stock in a large corporation. The difference is that a fund's only business is investing in securities, and the price of its shares is directly related to the value of the securities held by the fund.

Mutual funds continually issue new shares for purchase by the public. The price per share for existing fund investors is not decreased by the ongoing issuance of new shares because each share created is offset by the amount of new money coming in. Phrased another way, new money that comes into the fund is used to purchase additional securities in order not to dilute the income or value for existing shareholders.

A fund's share price can change from day to day, depending on the daily value of the securities held by the fund. The share price is called the net asset value (NAV), which is calculated as follows. The total value of the fund's investments at the end of the day, after expenses, is divided by the number of shares outstanding.

Newspapers report mutual fund activity every day. An example from the *Wall Street Journal* is shown here.

Everett Funds:

Evrt r	12.38	NL	−.01
MaxRtn	18.39	NL	+.06
ValTr	12.33	NL	−.01
LtdSl	17.71	NL	−.14
ExtrMid	2.82	2.95	−.02
ExJY p	7.24	7.60	+.01
FBK Gth t	11.06	11.06	..

FJA Funds:

Capit f	14.67	15.69	−.02
NwHrz	9.65	10.10	..
Permt	12.91	13.81	..
Perrin	20.96	22.42	−.02

The first column in the table is the fund's abbreviated name. Several funds under a single heading indicate a family of funds.

The second column is the net asset value per share as of the close of the preceding business day. In some newspapers, the NAV is identified as the sell or the bid price—the amount per share you would receive if you sold your shares. Each mutual fund determines its net asset value every business day by dividing the market value of its total assets, less liabilities, by the number of shares outstanding. On any given day, you can determine the value of your holdings by multiplying the NAV by the number of shares you own.

The third column is usually the offering price or, in some papers, the buy or the asked price—the price you would pay if you purchased shares. The buy price is the NAV plus any sales charges. If there are no sales charges, an NL for no load appears in this column. In such a case, the buy price would be the same as the NAV.

The next column shows the change, if any, in the NAV from the preceding quotation—in other words, the change over the most recent one-day trading period. Thus, if you see a "+.06" in the newspaper next to your fund, *each* of your shares in the fund went up in value by six cents during the previous day.

A *p* following the abbreviated name of the fund denotes a fund that charges a fee that is subtracted from assets for marketing and distribution costs, also known as a 12b-1 plan (named after the federal government rule that permits such an expense). If the fund name is followed by an *r*, the fund has a contingent deferred sales load (CDSL) or a redemption fee. A CDSL is a charge incurred if shares are sold within a certain period; a redemption fee is a cost you would pay *whenever* shares are sold. An *f* indicates a fund that habitually enters the previous day's prices, instead of the current day's. A *t* designates a fund that has both a CDSL or a redemption fee and a 12b-1 plan.

IV.
How a Mutual Fund Operates

A mutual fund is owned by all of its shareholders, the people who purchased shares of the fund. The day-to-day operation of a fund is delegated to a management company.

The management company, often the organization that created the fund, may offer other mutual funds, financial products, and financial services as well. The management company usually serves as the fund's investment advisor.

The investment advisor manages the fund's portfolio of securities. The advisor is paid for its services in the form of a fee that is based on the total value of the fund's assets; fees average 0.5 percent. The advisor employs professional portfolio managers who invest the fund's money by purchasing a number of stocks or bonds or money market instruments, depending on what type of fund it is.

These fund professionals decide where to invest the fund's assets. The money managers make their investment decisions based on extensive, ongoing research into the financial performance of individual companies, taking into account general economic and market trends. In addition, they are backed up by economic and statistical resources. On the basis of their research, money managers decide what and when to buy, sell, or hold for the fund's portfolio, in light of the fund's specific investment objective.

In addition to the investment advisor, the fund may also contract with an underwriter that arranges for the distribution of the fund's shares to the investing public. The underwriter may act as a wholesaler, selling fund shares to security dealers, or it may retail directly to the public.

V.
Different Categories of Mutual Funds

Aggressive Growth. The investment objective of aggressive growth funds is max-imum capital gains, with little or no concern for dividends or income of any kind. What makes this category of mutual funds unique is that fund managers often have the ability to use borrowed money (leverage) to increase positions. Sometimes they deal in stock options and futures contracts (commodities). These trading techniques sound, and can be, scary, but such activities represent only a minor portion of the funds' holdings.

Because of their bullish dispositions, these funds will usually stay fully invested in the stock market. For investors, this means better-than-expected results during good (bull) markets and worse-than-average losses during bad (bear) market periods. Fortunately, the average bull market is almost four times as long as the typical bear market.

Do not be confused by economic conditions and stock market performance. There have been eight recessions since World War II. During seven of those eight recessions, U.S. stocks went up. During all eight recessions, stocks posted impressive gains in the second half of every recession. By the same token, do not underestimate the impact of a loss. A 20 percent decline means that you must make 25 percent to break even. A loss of 20 percent does not happen very often to aggressive growth funds, particularly on a calendar year basis, but you should be aware that such extreme downward moves are possible. Often brokers like to focus on the +45 percent and +50 percent years, such as 1980 and 1991, while glossing over a bad year, such as 1984, when aggressive growth funds were down almost 13 percent on average.

One of the great wonders of the stock market is how volatility of returns is reduced when one's holding period is increased. Because of this, aggressive growth funds should only be owned by one of two kinds of investors: those who can live with high levels of daily, monthly, quarterly, and/or annual price per share fluctuations, and those who realize the importance of a diversified portfolio that cuts across several investment categories—the investor who looks at how the entire package is performing, not just one segment.

The typical price-earnings (p/e) ratio for stocks in this category is 30, a figure that is about 7 percent lower than the S & P 500 Index (which has an average p/e ratio of 32). This group of funds has an average beta of 1.0, making its *market-related* risk the same as that of the S & P 500 (which always has a beta of 1.0, no matter what market conditions or levels are).

The standard deviation for aggressive growth funds is 34.4 percent. This means that one's expected return for any given year may vary either way by 34.4

percent. In other words, since aggressive growth funds have averaged 11.1 percent over the past three years, annual returns are expected to range from -23.3 percent (11.1 - 34.4) to 45.4 percent (11.1 + 34.4). This would represent one standard deviation (39 percent in the case of aggressive growth funds). A single standard deviation accounts for what you can expect two out of every three months (67 percent of the time or roughly two out of every three years). If you are looking for greater assurance, then two standard deviations must be used (multiply 34.4 percent times 2 in this case). This means that returns for about 95 percent of the months (two standard deviations) would be 11.1 percent plus or minus 68.8 percent. In other words, a range of -57.7 percent to 79.9 percent.

Small-company stocks have an average p/e ratio of 32. (The price-earnings ratio refers to the selling price of a stock in relation to its annual earnings. Thus a fund category that has a p/e ratio of, say, 10 is comprised of mutual funds whose typical stock in the portfolio is selling for ten times what the corporation's earnings are for the year.) Small-company stock funds have a standard deviation of 33 percent and a beta of 0.8 percent, figures that support the view that this category is less volatile than aggressive growth funds.

Historical returns over the past 3, 5, 10, and 15 years for aggressive growth and small-company stock funds are shown here. All of the figures shown are average *annual* rates of return (all periods ending March 31, 2001).

category	3 years	5 years	10 years	15 years
aggressive growth	16%	16%	17%	13%
small-company stocks	10%	14%	17%	13%
S & P 500	12%	18%	17%	16%
T-bills	5%	5%	5%	5%
CPI (rate of inflation)	3%	3%	3%	3%

The aggressive growth fund category is dominated by technology and service stocks. Technology alone represents close to 48 percent of the typical aggressive growth fund's portfolio, followed by 20 percent in service and 9 percent in health stocks. Small-company stocks are also dominated by technology (33 percent) and service issues (19 percent).

Balanced. This kind of fund invests in common stocks and corporate bonds. The weighting given to stocks depends on the fund manager's perception of, or belief in, the market. The more bullish the manager is, the more likely the portfolio will be loaded up with equities. Yet no matter how strongly management feels about the stock market, it would be very rare to see stocks equal more than 67 percent of the portfolio. Similarly, no matter how bearish one becomes, it would be unlikely for a balanced fund to have more than 67 percent of its holdings represented by bonds. Often a fund's prospectus will outline the weighting ranges: The fund's managers must stay within these wide boundaries at all times. A small portion of these funds is made up of cash equivalents (T-bills, CDs, commercial paper, etc.), with a very small amount sometimes dedicated to preferred stocks and convertible securities.

Three other categories—"multi-asset global," "convertible," and "asset allocation"—have been combined with balanced funds for the purposes of this book. This grouping together is logical; because overall objectives are largely similar, general portfolio composition can be virtually identical in many cases, and the fund managers in each of these categories have the flexibility to load up heavily on stocks, bonds, preferreds, or convertible securities.

Multi-asset global funds typically emphasize bonds more than stocks or cash. It is not uncommon to see a multi-asset global fund that has 60 percent of its holdings in bonds, with 10 to 20 percent in stocks, and the remainder in foreign equities, preferred stocks, and cash. For the *stock* portion of this category, the p/e ratio is 35 and the standard deviation is 14 percent. On the bond side, the average maturity of debt instruments in the portfolio is ten years.

Convertible funds, as the name implies, are made up mostly of convertible preferred stocks and convertible bonds. The conversion feature allows the owner, the fund in this case, to convert or exchange securities for the corporation's common stock. Conversion and price appreciation take place during bull-market periods. Uncertain or down markets make conversion much less likely; instead, management falls back on the comparatively high dividend or interest payments that convertibles enjoy. The typical convertible fund has somewhere between two-thirds and three-quarters of its holdings in convertibles; the balance is in cash, stocks, and preferreds. For the stock portion of this category, the p/e ratio is 34 and the standard deviation is 17 percent. On the bond side, the average maturity of debt instruments in the portfolio is seven years.

Asset allocation funds, like other categories that fall under the broad definition of "balanced," are hybrid in nature—part equity and part debt. These funds have a tendency to emphasize stocks over bonds. A fund manager who wants to take a defensive posture may stay on the sidelines by converting moderate or large parts of the portfolio into cash equivalents. The average asset allocation fund has somewhere between 50 and 65 percent of its portfolio in common stocks, with the remainder in bonds, foreign stocks, and cash. For the stock portion of this category, the p/e ratio is 34 and the standard deviation is 13 percent. On the bond side, the average maturity of debt instruments in the portfolio is nine years.

The typical price-earnings (p/e) ratio for stocks in this category is 33, a figure that is lower than that of the S & P 500. This group of funds has an average beta of 0.6, making its *market–related risk* 40 percent less than the S & P 500. Keep in mind that beta refers to a portfolio's *stock market–related* risk—it is not a meaningful way to measure bond or foreign security risk. The typical bond in these funds has an average maturity of nine years.

The standard deviation for balanced funds is 12 percent, approximately one-fourth the level of aggressive growth funds. This means that one's expected return for any given year will vary by 12 percent. (For example, if you were expecting an annualized return of 14 percent, your actual return would range from 2 percent to 26 percent most of the time.)

Historical returns over the past 3, 5, 10, and 15 years for balanced, multi-asset global, convertible, and asset allocation funds are shown on page 11. All of the figures shown are average *annual* rates of return (all periods ending March 31, 2001).

category	3 years	5 years	10 years	15 years
balanced	8%	11%	12%	11%
multi-asset global	8%	8%	9%	7%
convertible	11%	13%	15%	11%
asset allocation	8%	11%	11%	9%
Corp./Gov't Bond Index	6%	6%	8%	9%

The equity portion of the balanced fund category is dominated by technology and service stocks. These two groups represent over one-third of the typical balanced fund's stock portfolio. The other three top equity sectors are financials, industrial cyclicals, and health stocks.

Like other hybrid funds, balanced funds provide an income stream. The average yield of balanced, multi-asset global, and asset allocation funds is under 2.5 percent. The typical yield for convertible securities funds is about 2.8 percent. High-tax-bracket investors who want to invest in these funds should consider using tax-sheltered money, if possible. Balanced, multi-asset global, asset allocation, and convertible bond funds are particularly attractive within an IRA, other qualified retirement plans, or variable annuities. (For more information about both fixed-rate and variable annuities, see two of my other books, *The 100 Best Annuities* and *Getting Started in Annuities*.)

Corporate Bonds. These funds invest in debt instruments (IOUs) issued by corporations, governments, and agencies of the U.S. government. Perhaps the typical corporate bond fund should be called a "government-corporate" fund. Bond funds have a wide range of maturities. The name of the fund will often indicate whether it is made up of short-term or medium-term obligations. If the name of the fund does not include the words "short-term" or "intermediate," then the fund most likely invests in bonds with average maturities over ten years. The greater the maturity, the more the fund's share value can change. There is an inverse relationship between interest rates and the value of a bond; when one moves up, the other goes down.

The weighted maturity date of the bonds within this group averages eight years, with a typical coupon rate of 6.9 percent. (The coupon rate represents what the corporation or government pays out annually on a per-bond basis.) All bonds have a maturity date—a date when the issuer (the government, municipality, or corporation) pays back the *face value* of the bond (which is almost always $1,000 per bond) and stops paying interest. There are often hundreds of different securities in any given bond fund. Each one of these securities (bonds in this case) has a maturity date; these maturity dates can range anywhere from a few days to up to thirty years. "Weighted maturity" refers to the time left until the average bond in the portfolio comes due (matures).

The standard deviation for corporate bonds is 3 percent, less than one-third of that found with balanced funds. This means that one's expected return for any given month, quarter, or year will be more predictable than almost any other category of mutual funds.

Using a beta measurement for bonds is of little value, because beta defines *stock market* risk and has nothing to do with interest-rate or financial risk. Historical returns over the past 3, 5, 10, and 15 years for corporate bond funds are shown here. All of the figures shown are average *annual* rates of return (all periods ending March 31, 2001).

category	3 years	5 years	10 years	15 years
corporate bond funds	5%	5%	7%	8%
government bond funds	5%	5%	7%	7%
municipal bond funds	3%	4%	6%	7%
world bond funds	3%	5%	5%	8%
CPI (rate of inflation)	3%	3%	3%	3%

Like income funds, corporate funds provide a high yield that is fully taxable and should be sheltered whenever possible. The average yield of these bond funds is just over 6 percent.

Global Stock. This category of mutual funds invests in equities issued by domestic and foreign firms. Fifteen of the twenty largest corporations in the world are located outside the United States. It makes sense to be able to invest in these and other corporations and industries—to be able to take advantage of opportunities wherever they appear. Global, also known as world, stock funds have the ability to invest in any country. The more countries a fund is able to invest in, the lower its overall risk level will be; often return potential will also increase.

For the purposes of this book, the global stock category includes foreign and international equity funds. When it comes to investing in mutual funds, the words "foreign" and "international" are interchangeable. A foreign, or international, fund invests in securities outside the United States. Some foreign funds are broadly diversified, including stocks from European as well as Pacific Basin economies. Other international funds specialize in a particular region or country. A global fund invests in domestic as well as foreign securities. The portfolio manager of a global fund generally has more latitude in the securities selected, since either domestic or foreign securities can end up representing 50 percent or more of the portfolio, depending on management's view of the different markets, whereas a foreign or international fund may not be allowed to invest in U.S. stocks or bonds.

The typical price-earnings (p/e) ratio for stocks in this category is 36, a figure that is virtually identical to that of the S & P 500. This group of funds has an average beta of 0.8, meaning that its *U.S. market–related* risk is about 20 percent less than that of the general market, as measured by the S & P 500. The standard deviation for global stock funds is 24 percent, versus 27 percent for growth funds.

Foreign stock funds, which are exclusive of U.S. investments, have a p/e ratio of 37. Their standard deviation over the past three years has been 24 percent. Pacific Basin funds, a more narrowly focused type of foreign fund, have an average p/e ratio of 36 and a standard deviation of 36 percent. European funds, another type of specialized international fund, have a price-earnings ratio of 35 and a standard deviation of 25 percent.

Historical returns over the past 3, 5, 10, and 15 years for global stocks are shown here. All of the figures shown are average *annual* rates of return (all periods ending March 31, 2001).

category	3 years	5 years	10 years	15 years
global stock funds	22%	20%	13%	15%
foreign stock funds	10%	9%	10%	12%
emerging markets funds	4%	8%	9%	11%
Pacific Basin funds	5%	4%	4%	10%
European funds	12%	16%	12%	10%

The four areas that dominate world stock funds are the United States (36 percent of a typical fund's holdings), Europe (35 percent), Japan (10 percent), and the Pacific Rim (6 percent).

Government Bonds. These funds invest in securities issued by the U.S. government or one of its agencies (or former affiliates), such as GNMA, FHLMC, or FNMA. Investors are attracted to bond funds of all kinds for two reasons. First, bond funds have monthly distributions; individual bonds pay interest only semiannually. Second, effective management can control interest-rate risk by varying the average maturity of the fund's portfolio. If management believes that interest rates are moving downward, the fund will load up heavily on long-term obligations. If rates do decline, long-term bonds will appreciate more than their short- and medium-term counterparts. Conversely, if the manager anticipates rate hikes, average portfolio maturity can be pared down so that there will be only modest principal deterioration if rates do go up.

Bond funds have portfolios with a wide range of maturities. Many funds use their names to characterize their maturity structure. Generally, "short term" means that the portfolio has a weighted average maturity of less than five years. "Intermediate" implies an average maturity of five to ten years, and "long term" is over ten years. The longer the maturity, the greater the change in the fund's price per share (your principal) when interest rates change. Longer-term bond funds are riskier than short-term funds but tend to offer higher yields. The top holdings of government bond funds are GNMAs and U.S. Treasury notes (T-notes) of varying maturities.

The weighted maturity date of the bonds within this group averages just under nine years, with a typical coupon rate of 7 percent (the coupon rate represents what is paid out annually on a per-bond basis)—figures that are virtually identical to the corporate bond category. These funds have a standard deviation of 3 percent—again the figure is almost identical to that for corporate bonds. This means that corporate and government bonds have similar volatilities.

Historical returns over the past 3, 5, 10, and 15 years for government bond funds are shown on page 14. All of the figures shown are average *annual* rates of return (all periods ending March 31, 2001).

category	3 years	5 years	10 years	15 years
government bond funds	5%	5%	7%	7%
high-yield bond funds	-2%	3%	10%	8%
CPI (rate of inflation)	3%	3%	3%	3%
utility funds	13%	15%	14%	13%
convertible bond funds	11%	13%	15%	11%

Like corporate bond funds, government funds provide a high yield that is fully taxable on the federal level and should be sheltered whenever possible. Interest from direct obligations of the U.S. government—T-bonds, T-notes, T-bills, EE bonds, and HH bonds—are exempt from state and local income taxes. This means that a part of the income you receive from funds that include such securities is exempt from *state* taxes.

Corporate bonds are rated as to their safety. The two major rating services are Moody's and Standard and Poor's. By reading the fund's prospectus or by telephoning the mutual fund company, you can find out how safe a corporate bond fund is. The vast majority of these funds are extremely conservative and safety (default) is not really an issue. U.S. government bonds are not rated since it is believed that there is no chance of default—unlike a corporation, the federal government can print money.

Growth. These funds seek capital appreciation with dividend income as a distant secondary concern. Indeed, the average annual income stream from growth funds is just 1.3 percent. Investors who are attracted to growth funds are aiming to sell stock at a profit; they are not normally income oriented. If you are interested in current income you will want to look at Appendix D: Systematic Withdrawal Plan.

Growth funds are attracted to equities from large, well established corporations. Unlike aggressive growth funds, growth funds may end up holding large cash positions during market declines or when investors are nervous about recent economic or market activities. The typical price-earnings (p/e) ratio for stocks in this category is 38, compared to 37 for the S & P 500. This group of funds has an average beta of 0.9, which is roughly 10 percent less than the S & P 500.

The standard deviation for growth funds is 27 percent. This means that one's expected return for any given year will vary by 27 percentage points. As an example, if you were expecting a 15 percent annual return, annual returns would probably range between negative 12 percent and positive 42 percent (15 percent plus or minus 27 percent).

Historical returns over the past 3, 5, 10, and 15 years for growth and small-company stock funds are shown here. All of the figures shown are average *annual* rates of return (all periods ending March 31, 2001).

category	3 years	5 years	10 years	15 years
growth funds	14%	17%	17%	14%
small-company stock funds	10%	14%	17%	13%
S & P 500	12%	18%	17%	16%
growth & income funds	9%	15%	15%	13%
global stock funds	9%	8%	10%	12%

Technology (33 percent of the typical portfolio), service (17 percent), financial (12 percent), and health stocks (10 percent) dominate growth funds.

Growth and Income. With a name like this, one would think that this category of mutual funds is almost equally as concerned with income as it is with growth. The fact is, growth and income funds have an average dividend yield of just 1.25 percent. This boost in income is due to the small holdings in bonds and convertibles possessed by most growth and income funds.

The typical price-earnings (p/e) ratio for stocks in this category is 32, versus 37 for the S & P 500. This group of funds has an average beta of 0.9, meaning that its *market-related risk* is 10 percent less than that of the general market, as measured by the S & P 500.

The standard deviation for growth and income funds is 21 percent, about 20 percent less than that found with the average growth fund. This means that, as a group, growth and income funds have slightly more predictable returns than growth funds.

For the purposes of this book, a second category, "equity-income funds," has been combined with growth and income. Equity-income funds have a lower standard deviation (18 percent compared to 21 percent for growth and income funds), a higher yield (1.6 percent compared to 1.2 percent), and a lower beta (0.8 percent compared to 0.9 percent for growth and income funds).

The typical growth and income fund is divided as follows: 90 percent in common stocks (4 percent of which is in foreign stock), 4 percent in cash, 2 percent in bonds, and 4 percent in other assets. The average equity-income fund is divided as follows: 84 percent in common stocks (5 percent of which is in foreign stock), 5 percent in bonds, 3 percent in cash, and 3 percent in other assets. The typical price-earnings (p/e) ratio for stocks in this category is 25.

Historical returns over the past 3, 5, 10, and 15 years for growth and income funds are shown here. All of the figures shown are average *annual* rates of return (all periods ending March 31, 2001).

category	3 years	5 years	10 years	15 years
growth and income funds	9%	15%	15%	13%
equity-income funds	7%	14%	14%	13%
growth funds	14%	17%	17%	14%
balanced funds	8%	11%	12%	11%
foreign stock funds	10%	9%	10%	12%

Technology, financial, and service stocks dominate growth and income funds, representing over half of the typical portfolio. Industrial cyclicals, health, and energy stocks represent the other major industry groups for this category.

High-Yield. These funds generally invest in lower-rated corporate debt instruments. Bonds are characterized as either "bank quality," also known as "investment grade," or "junk." Investment-grade bonds are bonds rated AAA, AA, A, or BAA; junk bonds are instruments rated less than BAA: BA, B, CCC, CC, C, and D. High-yield bonds, also referred to as junk bonds, offer investors higher yields in exchange for the additional risk of default. High-yield bonds are subject to less *interest-rate risk* than regular corporate or government bonds. However, when the economy slows or people panic, these bonds can quickly drop in value.

The average weighted maturity date of the bonds within this group is seven years, a figure similar to that for high-quality corporate and government bond funds. The typical coupon rate is 9 percent. (The coupon rate represents what the corporation pays out annually on a per-bond basis.) When it comes to high-yield bonds, investors would be wise to accept a lower yield in return for more stability of principal and appreciation potential. As with income funds, corporate funds provide a high yield that is fully taxable and should be sheltered whenever possible.

The standard deviation for high-yield bond funds is 8 percent, a figure that is more than twice the rate of corporate and government bond funds as a whole but 4 percent less than balanced and 5 percent less than global bond funds. Historical returns over the past 3, 5, 10, and 15 years for high-yield corporate bond funds are shown here. All of the figures shown are average *annual* rates of return (all periods ending March 31, 2001).

category	3 years	5 years	10 years	15 years
high-yield bond funds	-2%	3%	10%	8%
corporate bond funds	5%	5%	7%	8%
government bond funds	5%	5%	7%	7%
world bond funds	3%	5%	5%	8%
balanced funds	8%	11%	12%	11%

Metals and Natural Resources. Metals funds invest in precious metals and mining stocks from around the world. The majority of these stocks are located in North America; South Africa and Australia are the only other major players. Most of these companies specialize in gold mining. Some funds own gold and silver bullion outright. Direct ownership of the metal is considered to be a more conservative posture than owning stocks of mining companies; these stocks are more volatile than the metal itself.

Metals funds, also known as gold funds, are the most speculative group represented in this book. They are considered to be a sector or specialty fund in that they are only able to invest in a single industry or country. Metals funds enjoy international diversification but are still narrowly focused; the limitations of the fund are what make it so unpredictable. Usually, fund management can invest in only three things: mining stocks, direct metal ownership (bullion or coins), and cash equivalents.

Despite their volatile nature, gold funds are included in the book because they can actually reduce portfolio risk. Why? Because gold and other investments often move in opposite directions. For example, when government bonds are moving down in value, gold funds often increase in value. What could otherwise be viewed as a wild investment becomes somewhat tame when included as part of a diversified portfolio.

The typical dividend for metal funds is 0.5 percent. The typical price-earnings (p/e) ratio for stocks in this category is 31, about 20 percent less than the p/e ratio for the S & P 500.

This group of funds has an average beta of 0.7, meaning that its stock market–related risk is modest—but do not let this fool you. We are only talking about *stock market risk*. Beta focuses on that portion of risk that investors cannot reduce by further diversification in U.S. stocks. Metals funds, as shown by their wild track record, are anything but conservative. A 0.7 beta indicates that movement in this category has a fair amount to do with the direction of the S & P 500; therefore, risk can be reduced by further diversification. The standard deviation for metals funds is 36 percent, versus a standard deviation of 63 percent for technology funds and 35 percent for emerging markets funds.

Another category, natural resources, has been combined with metals funds for this book. As the name implies, natural resources funds are commodity-driven, just as metals funds are heavily influenced by two commodities: gold and silver. In the case of natural resources funds, the prices of oil, gas, and timber are the driving force. Natural resources funds invest in companies that are involved with the discovery, exploration, development, refinement, storage, and transportation of one or more of these three natural resources. The standard deviation for this group is 30 percent, beta is 0.8, and the p/e ratio is 34.

Historical returns over the past 3, 5, 10, and 15 years for metals and natural resources funds are shown here. All of the figures shown are average *annual* rates of return (all periods ending March 31, 2001).

category	3 years	5 years	10 years	15 years
metals funds	-9%	-14%	-5%	-1%
aggressive growth funds	16%	16%	17%	13%
natural resources funds	7%	11%	11%	10%
European funds	12%	16%	12%	10%
CPI (rate of inflation)	3%	3%	3%	3%

Money Market. These funds invest in short-term money market instruments such as bank CDs, T-bills, and commercial paper. By maintaining a short average maturity and investing in high-quality instruments, money market funds are able to maintain a stable $1 net asset value. Since money market funds offer higher yields than a bank's insured money market deposit accounts, they are a very attractive haven for savings or temporary investment dollars. Like bond funds, money market funds come in both taxable and tax-free versions. Reflecting their tax-free status, municipal money market funds pay lower *before-tax* yields than taxable money market funds but can offer higher returns on an *after-tax* basis.

Since the price per share of taxable money market funds always stays at $1, interest is shown by the accumulation of additional shares. (For example, at the beginning of the year you may have 1,000 shares, and by the end of the year 1,050. The fifty-share increase, or $50, represents interest.) There are no such things as capital gains or unrecognized gains in a money market fund. The entire return, or yield, is fully taxable (except in the case of a tax-free money market fund where your gain or return would always be exempt from federal taxes and possibly state income taxes as well).

These funds are designed as a place to park your money for a relatively short period of time, in anticipation of a major purchase such as a car or house, or until conditions appear more favorable for stocks, bonds, and/or real estate. There has only been one money market fund, now defunct, that has ever lost money for its investors (most of whom were bankers).

There are approximately 900 taxable money market funds and 450 tax-exempt money funds. By far the largest money market fund is the Merrill Lynch CMA Money Fund ($68 billion). As of March 31, 2000, the ten largest money market funds controlled close to $350 billion and had an average maturity of fifty-eight days. The five highest-yielding taxable money market funds as of the middle of 2000 were Strong Investors Money Fund (5.6 percent over the past twelve months), Scudder Premium Money Market Shares (5.5 percent), OLDE Premium Plus MM Series (5.4 percent), Zurich YieldWise Government Money Fund (5.4 percent), and Aon Money Market Fund (5.4 percent).

The standard deviation for money market funds is lower than any other category of mutual funds. Historical returns over the past 3, 5, 10, and 15 years for taxable and tax-free money market funds are shown here. All of the figures shown are average *annual* rates of return (all periods ending March 31, 2001).

category	3 years	5 years	10 years	15 years
money market funds	5%	5%	5%	6%
tax-free money market funds	3%	3%	3%	4%
gov't money market funds	5%	5%	5%	6%
government bond funds	5%	5%	7%	7%
CPI (rate of inflation)	3%	3%	3%	3%

Municipal Bonds. Also known as tax-free, these funds are made up of tax-free debt instruments issued by states, counties, districts, or political subdivisions. Interest from municipal bonds is normally exempt from federal income tax. In almost all states, interest is also exempt from state and local income taxes if the portfolio is made up of issues from the investor's state of residence, a U.S. territory (Puerto Rico, the U.S. Virgin Islands, etc.), or the District of Columbia.

Until the early 1980s, municipal bonds were almost as sensitive to interest rate changes as corporate and government bonds. During the last several years, however, tax-free bonds have taken on a new personality. Now when interest rates change, municipal bonds exhibit only one-half to one-third the price change that occurs with similar funds comprised of corporate or government issues. This decreased volatility is due to a smaller supply of municipal bonds and the elimination of almost all tax shelters, which has increased the popularity of tax-free bonds.

Three kinds of events may result in tax liability for every mutual fund except money market funds. The first two events described here cannot be controlled by the investor. The final event is determined solely by you, the shareholder (investor).

First, when bonds or stocks are sold in the fund portfolio for a profit (or loss), a capital gain (or capital loss) occurs. These gains and losses are passed down to the shareholder. Tax-free bond funds are not immune from capital gains taxes (or capital losses).

Second, interest and/or dividends paid by the securities within the fund are also passed on to shareholders (investors). As already mentioned, interest from municipal bonds is free from federal income taxes and, depending on the fund, may also be exempt from state income taxes. Municipal bond funds do not own stocks or convertibles, so they never throw off dividends.

Third, a taxable event may occur when you sell or exchange shares of a fund for cash or to go into another fund. As an example, suppose you bought into the fund at X dollars and cents per share. If shares are sold (or exchanged) by you for X plus Y, then there will a taxable gain (on Y, in this example). If shares are sold or exchanged for a loss $(X$ minus $Y)$, then there will be a capital loss. Municipal bond funds are subject to such capital gains or losses. Fortunately, you are never required to sell off shares in any mutual fund; the decision as to when and how much is always yours.

The standard deviation for municipal bond funds is 3 percent, meaning that this category's volatility is virtually identical to corporate bonds and government securities. Historical returns over the past 3, 5, 10, and 15 years for municipal funds are shown here. All of the figures shown are average *annual* rates of return (all periods ending March 31, 2001).

category	3 years	5 years	10 years	15 years
municipal bond funds	3%	4%	6%	7%
CA municipal bond funds	4%	5%	7%	7%
NY municipal bond funds	4%	5%	7%	7%
government bond funds	5%	5%	7%	7%
muni bonds (single state)	3%	4%	6%	7%

Technology. It is difficult to identify a segment of the economy that has not been profoundly influenced by technology. From traditional manufacturers developing e-commerce strategies to emerging companies with revolutionary new products, technology is changing businesses and creating unprecedented opportunities for investors. Technology represents nearly half of all business equipment spending by U.S. companies. Consumer spending on information technology as a percentage of disposable income has nearly tripled in the past twelve years. Today, nearly one-third of the S & P 500 Index is made up of technology stocks, up from just 7 percent in 1990.

Because of this sector's volatility, most investors historically have considered the technology sector a "speculative sector play" and consequently either have limited their holdings in this area to a small portion of their overall portfolios or avoided them altogether. In light of the astonishing returns achieved by many technology fund managers in 1999, some investors may have forgotten that the technology market itself returned 116 percent. These funds invest in common stocks of all aspects of technology, including computer hardware and software, telecommunications, semiconductor, networking, data storage, data security, fiber optics, wireless, and the Internet.

Technology is changing the way we work, live, and think. As the computer revolution evolves into the Internet revolution and then the wireless revolution, technology continues to amaze and dazzle us. This is true for investors in technology stocks as well. The technology sector of the stock market, as measured by the S & P

500 Technology Index, has outperformed the general stock market, as measured by the S & P 500, over the past 1-, 3-, 5-, and 10-year periods—by a wide margin.

Annualized Returns: Technology Stocks vs. the S & P 500
(all periods ending June 30, 2001)

category period	technology sector	S & P 500
1 year	44.5%	7.3%
3 years	47.4%	19.7%
5 years	42.1%	23.8%
10 years	28.1%	17.8%

The typical price-earnings (p/e) ratio for stocks in this category is 55, versus 37 for the S & P 500. This group of funds has an average beta of 1.1, meaning that its *market-related risk* is 10 percent greater than that of the general market, as measured by the S & P 500. This statement is misleading due to the category's extremely high standard deviation (see next paragraph).

The standard deviation for technology funds is 63 percent, a figure that is significantly higher than any other category in the book. The next closest category, aggressive growth funds, has a standard deviation of 39. This means that, as a group, technology funds are expected to have less predictable returns than any other fund or category in the book.

Historical returns over the past 3, 5, 10, and 15 years for technology funds are shown here. All of the figures shown are average *annual* rates of return (all periods ending March 31, 2001).

category	3 years	5 years	10 years	15 years
technology funds	69%	44%	31%	25%
aggressive growth funds	16%	16%	17%	13%
growth funds	14%	17%	16%	14%
S & P 500	12%	18%	17%	16%
utility funds	13%	15%	14%	13%

Utilities. These funds invest in common stocks of utility companies. A small percentage of the funds' assets are invested in bonds. Investors opposed to or in favor of nuclear power can seek out funds that avoid or buy into such utility companies by reviewing a fund's semiannual report or by telephoning the fund using its toll-free phone number.

If you like the usual stability of a bond fund but want more appreciation potential, then utility funds are for you. Since these funds are interest-rate sensitive, their performance somewhat parallels that of bonds but is also influenced by the stock market. The large dividend stream provided by utility funds makes them less risky than other categories of stock funds. Recession-resistant demand for electricity, gas, and other utilities translates into a comparatively steady stream of returns.

Since a healthy portion of the total return for utility funds (dividends) cannot be controlled by the investor, these funds are best suited for retirement plans or as part of some other tax-sheltered vehicle. But even if you do not have a qualified retirement plan such as an IRA, pension plan, or TSA, utility funds can be a wise choice to lower overall portfolio volatility. The average p/e (price-earnings) ratio for this category is 27. The standard deviation for utility funds is 17 percent, a figure that is about 20 percent lower than that of growth and income funds. Utility funds have a beta of 0.5.

Historical returns over the past 3, 5, 10, and 15 years for utilities funds are shown here. All of the figures shown are average *annual* rates of return (all periods ending March 31, 2001).

category	3 years	5 years	10 years	15 years
utility funds	13%	15%	14%	13%
convertible funds	11%	13%	15%	11%
multi-asset global funds	8%	8%	9%	7%
asset allocation funds	8%	11%	11%	9%
balanced funds	8%	11%	12%	11%

World Bonds. Although the United States leads the world in outstanding debt, other countries and foreign corporations also issue IOUs as a way of financing projects and operations. As high as our debt seems, it is not out of line when compared to our GNP (now called GDP—gross domestic product). The ratio of our debt to GDP is lower than any other member of the group of seven. (The other G-7 members are Germany, Japan, Canada, Italy, the United Kingdom, and France.)

International, also known as foreign, bond funds invest in fixed-income securities outside the United States. Global, or world, bond funds invest around the world, including the United States. Foreign bond funds normally offer higher yields than their domestic counterparts but also provide additional risk. Global bonds, on the other hand, provide less risk than a pure U.S. bond portfolio and also enjoy greater rates of return.

Global diversification reduces risk because the major economies around the world do not move up and down at the same time. As we climb out of a recession, Japan may be just entering one, and Germany may still be in the middle of one. When Italy is trying to stimulate its economy by lowering interest rates, Canada may be raising its rates in order to curtail inflation. By investing in different world bond markets, you ensure that you will not be at the mercy of any one country's political environment or fiscal policy.

The weighted maturity date of the bonds within this group is eight years, about one year less than U.S. government bond funds. Global bond funds have an average coupon rate of 7 percent. As with any investment that throws off a high current income, global and foreign bond funds should be part of a qualified retirement plan or variable annuity whenever possible.

The standard deviation for world bond funds is 9 percent, a low figure but one that is still about three times as great as the typical U.S. government bond fund. Historical returns over the past 3, 5, 10, and 15 years for world bond funds are shown on page 22. All of the figures shown are average annual rates of return (all periods ending March 31, 2001).

category	3 years	5 years	10 years	15 years
world bond funds	3%	5%	5%	8%
government bond funds	5%	5%	7%	7%
corporate bond funds	5%	5%	7%	8%
high-yield bond funds	-2%	3%	10%	8%
CPI (rate of inflation)	3%	3%	3%	3%

All Categories. An inescapable conclusion drawn from these different tables is that patience usually pays off. The single-digit performers over the past fifteen years have been corporate bonds, government bonds, high-yield bonds, metals (the only negative performer), money market, municipal bonds, and natural resources. The most important thing left out of all of these tables is risk. However, one could make the case that stocks are not much riskier than bonds when one's holding period is ten to fifteen years. The tables also do not take into account the tax advantages of certain investments. Government bonds are exempt from state and local income taxes. (Note: This is only true with direct obligations of the United States, it does not apply to GNMAs, FNMAs, or other government-agency issues.) Municipal bonds are exempt from federal income taxes and, depending on the type of tax-free fund as well as your state of residency, may also be exempt from any state or local taxes.

Money market funds should never be considered an investment. Money market funds, T-bills, and bank CDs should be viewed as places to park your money temporarily. Such accounts are best used to earn interest before you make a major purchase, while you are becoming educated about investing in general, or until market conditions change. Metals funds should be avoided by almost all investors. The track record of this category is wild and usually negative. It is doubtful that a strong case can be made for metals. Diversification and risk reduction can be accomplished by owning other categories such as money market, one or more of the bond categories, and even possibly natural resources.

Average Annual Returns for the 15-Year Period Ending March 31, 2001

category	15 years	category	15 years
aggressive growth	13%	growth & income	13%
asset allocation	9%	high-yield	8%
balanced	11%	metals (only)	-1%
convertible bond	11%	money market	6%
corporate bond	8%	multi-asset global	7%
equity-income	13%	municipal bond	7%
European stocks	10%	natural resources	11%
foreign	12%	small company	13%
global equity	12%	technology	20%
government bond	7%	utilities	13%
growth	14%	world bond	8%
		average for all categories	10%

A common theme throughout this book is that, given time, equity (the different stock categories) always outperforms debt (the different bond categories). This does not mean that all of your money should be in the equity categories. Not everyone has the same level of patience or time horizon. It does mean that the great majority of investors need to review their portfolios and perhaps begin to emphasize domestic and foreign stocks more.

VI.
Which Funds Are Best for You?

When asked what they are looking for, investors typically say "I want the best." This could mean that they are looking for the most safety and greatest current income or the highest total return. There is no single "best" fund. The top-performing fund may have incredible volatility, causing shareholders to redeem their shares at the first sign of trouble. The "safest" fund may be devastated by risks not previously thought of: inflation and taxes.

As you have already seen, there are several different categories of mutual funds, ranging from tax-free money market accounts to precious metals. During one period or another, each of these categories has dominated some periodical's "ten best funds" list. These impressive scores may only last a quarter, six months, or a year. The fact is that no one knows what will be the *next* best-performing category or individual fund.

For some fund groups, such as international stocks, growth, growth and income, and aggressive growth, the reign at the top may last for several years. For other categories, such as money market, government bond, and precious metals, the glory may last a year or even less. Trying to outguess, chart, or follow a financial guru in order to determine the next trend is a fool's paradise. The notion that anyone has special insights into the marketplace is sheer nonsense. Countless neutral and lengthy studies attest to this fact. If this is the case, what should we do?

Step 1: Categories That Have Historically Done Well
First, we should look at those generic categories of investments that have historically done well over long periods of time. A time frame of at least fifteen or twenty years is recommended. True, your investment horizon may be a fraction of this, but keep in mind two points. First, fifteen or twenty years includes good as well as bad times. Second, bad results cannot be hidden when you are studying the long term. Even the investor looking at a one- or two-year holding period should ask, "Do I want something that does phenomenally well one out of every five years, or do I want something that has a very good return in eight or nine out of every ten years?" Unless you are a gambler, the answer is obvious.

All investments can be categorized as either debt or equity instruments. Debt instruments in this book include corporate bonds, government bonds, high-yield bonds, international bonds, money market accounts, and municipal bonds. Equity instruments include growth, growth and income, international stocks, metals, and utility funds. Four other categories are hybrid instruments: asset allocation, balanced, convertible, and multi-asset global funds. In this book, these four categories are combined under the heading "balanced."

Throughout history, *equity has outperformed debt*. The longer the time frame reviewed, the better equity vehicles look. Over the past half century, the worst fifteen-year holding period performance for stocks (+4.3 percent a year) was very similar to the average fifteen-year holding period performance for long-term government bonds (+4.9 percent a year). For twenty-year holding periods, the worst period for common stocks has been more than 40 percent better than the average for long-term government bonds. Indeed, stocks have outperformed bonds in every decade. Look at it this way: would you rather have loaned Henry Ford or Bill Gates the money to start their companies, or would you rather have given them money in return for a piece of the action?

Step 2: Review Your Objectives

Decide what you are trying to do with your portfolio. Everyone wants one of the following: growth, current income, or a combination of growth and income. Don't assume that if you are looking for current income your money should go into a bond or money market fund. There is a way to set up an equity fund so that it will give you a high monthly income. This is known as a "systematic withdrawal program" and is discussed in Appendix D. The growth-oriented investor, on the other hand, should consider certain categories of debt instruments or hybrid securities to help add more stability to a portfolio.

Objectives are certainly important, but so is the element of time. The shorter the time frame and the greater the need for assurances, the greater the likelihood that debt instruments should be used. A growth investor who is looking at a single-year time frame and wants a degree of safety is probably better off in a series of bond and/or money market accounts. On the other hand, the longer the commitment, the better equities look. Thus, even a cautious investor who has a life expectancy (or whose spouse has a life expectancy) of ten years or more should seriously consider having at least a moderate portion of his or her portfolio in equities.

A retired couple in their sixties should realize that one or both of them will probably live at least fifteen more years. Since this is the case, and since we know that equities have almost always outperformed bonds when looking at a horizon of ten years or more, their emphasis should be in this area.

The conservative investor may say that stocks are too risky. True, the day-to-day or year-to-year volatility of equities can be quite disturbing. However, it is also true that the medium- and long-term effects of inflation and the resulting diminished purchasing power of a fixed-income investment are even more devastating. At least with an equity there is a better than 50–50 chance that it will go up in value. In the case of inflation, what do you think are the chances that the cost of goods and services will go *down* during the next 1, 3, 5, or 10 years? The answer is "not likely."

Step 3: Ascertain Your Risk Level

No investment is worthwhile if you stay awake at night worrying about it. If you do not already know or are uncertain about your risk level, contact your financial advisor. These professionals usually have some kind of questionnaire that you can answer. Your responses will give a good indication of which investments are proper for you and which should be avoided. If you do not deal with a financial advisor, try the following test. Your score, and what it means, are shown at the end of the questionnaire.

Test for Determining Your Risk Level

1. "I invest for the long term, five to ten years or more. The final result is more important than daily, monthly, or annual fluctuations in value."

(10) Totally disagree. (20) Willing to accept some volatility, but not loss of principal. (30) Could accept a moderate amount of yearly fluctuation in return for a good *total* return. (40) Would accept an *occasional* negative year if the final results were good. (50) Agree.

2. Rank the importance of current income.

(10) Crucial, the exact amount must be known. (20) Important, but I am willing to have the amount vary each period. (30) Fairly important, but other aspects of investing are also of concern. (40) Only a modest amount of income is needed. (50) Current income is unimportant.

3. Rank the amount of loss you could tolerate in a single *quarter*.

(10) None. (20) A little, but over a year's time the total value of the investment should not decline. (30) Consistency of total return is more important than trying to get big gains. (40) One or two quarters of negative returns are the price you must pay when looking at the total picture. (50) Unimportant.

4. Rank the importance of beating inflation.

(10) Factors such as preservation of principal and current income are much more important. (20) I am willing to have a slight variance in my returns, *on a quarterly basis only*, in order to have at least a partial hedge against inflation. (30) Could accept some annual volatility in order to offset inflation. (40) I consider inflation to be important, but have mixed feelings about how much volatility I could accept from one year to the next. (50) The long-term effects of inflation are devastating and should not be ignored by anyone.

5. Rank the importance of beating the stock market over any given two-to-three-year period.

(10) Irrelevant. (20) A small concern. (30) Fairly important. (40) Very important. (50) Absolutely crucial.

Add up your score from questions 1 through 5. Your risk, as defined by your total point score, is as follows: 0–50 points = extremely conservative; 50–100 points = somewhat conservative; 100–150 points = moderate; 150–200 points = somewhat aggressive; 200–250 points = very aggressive.

Step 4: Review Your Current Holdings

Everyone has heard the expression, "Don't put all your eggs in one basket." This advice also applies to investing. No matter how much we like investment X, if a third of our net worth is already in X, we probably should not add any more to this investment. After all, there is more than one good investment.

Since no single investment category is the top performer every year, it makes sense to diversify into several *fundamentally* good categories. By using *proper* diversification, we have an excellent chance of being number one with a portion of our portfolio every year. Babe Ruth may have hit more home runs than almost anyone, but he also struck out more. As investors, we should be content with consistently hitting doubles and triples.

Trying to hit a homer every time may result in financial ruin. Never lose track of the fact that losses always have a greater impact than gains. An investment that goes up 50 percent the first year and falls 50 percent the next year still has a net loss of 25 percent. This philosophy is emphasized throughout the book.

Step 5: Implementation

There is no such thing as the perfect time to invest. No matter how strongly you or some "expert" individual or publication believes that the market is going to go up or down, no one actually knows.

Once you have properly educated yourself, *now* is the right time to invest. If you are afraid to make the big plunge, consider some form of dollar-cost averaging (see Appendix C). This is a disciplined approach to investing; it also reduces your risk exposure significantly.

Reading investment books and attending classes are encouraged, but some people may be tempted to remain on the sidelines indefinitely. For such people, there is no perfect time to invest. If the stock market drops 200 points, they are waiting for the next hundred-point drop. If stocks or bonds are up 15 percent, they say things are peaking and they will invest as soon as it drops by 10 percent. If the stock or bond market does drop by that magical figure, these same investors are now certain that it will drop another 10 percent.

This "strategy" described is frustrating. More important, it is wrong. One can look back in history and find lots of reasons not to have invested. But the fact is that all of the investments in this book have gone up almost every year. The "wait and see" approach is a poor one; the same reasons for not investing will still exist in the present and throughout the future.

Remember, your money is doing something right now. It is invested somewhere. If it is under the mattress, it is being eaten away by inflation. If it is in a "risk-free" investment, such as an insured savings account, bank CD, or U.S. Treasury bill, it is being subjected to taxation and the cumulative effects of reduced purchasing power. Do not think you can hide by having your money in some safe haven. Once you understand that there can be things worse than market swings, you will become an educated investor who knows there is no such thing as a truly risk-free place or investment.

If you are still not convinced, consider the story of Louie the Loser. There is only one thing you can say about Louie's timing: It is *always* awful. So it is no surprise that when he decided to invest $10,000 a year in a fund featured in this book, he managed to pick the *worst* possible times. *Every year* for the past twenty years (1980–1999), he has invested on the very day that the stock market *peaked*. How has he done? He has over $1,123,000, which means his money has grown at an average rate of 16.2 percent a year (a cumulative investment of $200,000; twenty years times $10,000 invested each year).

Yet even by picking the *worst* possible days, Louie still came out way ahead of the $379,000 he would have had if he had put his money in U.S. Treasury bills twenty years ago. Even though his timing was terrible, he still fared much better than if he had done what many people are doing today: waiting for the "perfect" time to invest.

After asking you a series of questions, your investment advisor can give you a framework within which to operate. Investors who do not have a good adviser may wish to look at the different sample portfolios shown here. These general recommendations will provide you with a sense of direction.

The Conservative Investor
15 percent balanced
10 percent utilities
15 percent growth & income
10 percent world bond
10 percent international equities
10 percent money market or short-term bonds
30 percent intermediate-term municipal or government bonds
    (depending on your tax bracket)

This portfolio would give you a weighting of 43 percent in equities (stocks) and 57 percent in debt instruments (bonds and cash equivalents). Investors who are not in a high federal income tax bracket may wish to avoid municipal bonds completely and use government bonds instead.

If your tax bracket is such that you are not sure whether you should own tax-free or taxable bonds (if, that is, the after-tax return on government bonds is similar to what a similarly maturing, high-quality municipal bond pays), lean toward a municipal bond fund—they are almost always less volatile than a government bond fund that has the same or a similar average maturity.

The Moderate Investor
10 percent small-company growth
 5 percent balanced/convertibles
15 percent growth
20 percent growth & income
10 percent high-yield bond
10 percent world bond
15 percent global equities
10 percent technology
 5 percent natural resources

This portfolio would give you a weighting of 80 percent in equities (common stocks) and 20 percent in debt instruments. The figures are a little misleading since high-yield bonds are more of a hybrid investment—part stock and part bond. The price, or value, of high-yield bonds is influenced by economic (macro and micro) news as well as interest rate changes. Whereas government, municipal, and high-quality corporate bonds often react favorably to bad economic news such as a recession, increases in the jobless rate, a slowdown in housing starts, and so on, high-yield bonds have a tendency to view such news positively. Thus, taking into account that high-yield bonds are about halfway between traditional bonds and stocks, the weighting distribution is more in the range of 85 percent equities and 15 percent bonds.

The Aggressive Investor
15 percent aggressive growth
20 percent small-company growth
20 percent growth
10 percent growth & income
15 percent international equities
20 percent technology

This portfolio would give you a weighting of 100 percent in equities. Bond fund categories, with the possible exception of high-yield and international, are not recommended for the aggressive investor because they usually do not have enough appreciation potential.

Readers of the previous editions of this book may notice that this edition weighs equities (the different stock categories) more heavily than it has in the past. This is because bonds cannot experience the appreciation or total return for the balance of the 1990s that they saw in the 1980s and very early 1990s. For the most part, bonds increase in value because of falling interest rates. In 1981, the prime interest rate briefly peaked at 21.5 percent; for more than a dozen years this benchmark figure dropped. During the balance of the 1990s, it would be literally impossible for the prime interest rate to drop thirteen points (it cannot drop below zero).

Stocks, on the other hand, could end up doing worse than bonds, the same, or better. At least conceptually, however, equities have the possibility of exceeding their performance over the past ten years. The 1980s or 1990s were not the best ten years in a row for stocks. It is certainly possible that the next ten years, or the ten years beginning in 2003 or 2004, will be the best; the downturn in 2000 and the first half of 2001 actually increases the odds of very positive returns in the future. When you look at the state of the world, the conditions certainly seem more favorable now for tremendous economic and stock market growth for the next several decades.

Step 6: Review
After implementation, it is important that you keep track of how you are doing. One of the beauties of mutual funds is that, if you choose a fund with good management, managers will do their job and you can spend your time on something

else. Nevertheless, review your situation at least quarterly. Once you feel comfortable with your portfolio, only semiannual or annual reviews are recommended.

Daily or weekly tracking is pointless. If a particular investment goes up or down 5 percent, that does not mean you should rush out and buy more or sell off. That same investment may do just the opposite the following week or month. By watching your investments too closely, you will be defeating a major attribute of mutual funds: professional management. Presumably these fund managers know a lot more about their particular investments than you do. If they do not, you should either choose another fund or start your own mutual fund.

Step 7: Relax

If you do your homework by reading this book, you will be in fine shape. There are several thousand mutual funds. Some funds are just plain bad. Most mutual funds are mediocre. And, as with everything else in this world, a small portion are truly excellent. This book has taken those thousands of funds and eliminated all of the bad, mediocre, and fairly good. What are left are only excellent mutual funds.

If you would like help in designing a portfolio or picking a specific fund, telephone the Institute of Business & Finance (800-848-2029). The institute will be able to give you the names and telephone numbers of Certified Fund Specialists (CFS) in your area. To become a CFS, one must complete a rigorous one-year educational program, pass a comprehensive exam, adhere to a professional code of ethics, and meet annual continuing education requirements.

VII.
Fund Features

Advantages of Mutual Funds

This chapter lists some of the features of mutual funds—advantages not found in other kinds of investments.

Ease of Purchase. Mutual fund shares are easy to buy. For those who prefer to make investment decisions themselves, mutual funds are as close as the telephone or the mailbox. Those who would like help in choosing a fund can draw upon a wide variety of sources.

Many funds sell their shares through stockbrokers, financial planners, or insurance agents. These representatives can help you analyze your financial needs and objectives and recommend appropriate funds. For these professional services, you may be charged a sales commission, usually referred to as a "load." This charge is expressed as a percentage of the total purchase price of the fund shares. In some cases, there is no initial sales charge, or load, but there may be an annual fee and/or another charge if shares are redeemed during the first few years of ownership.

Other funds distribute their shares directly to the public. They may advertise in magazines and newspapers; most can be reached through toll-free telephone numbers. Because there are no sales agents involved, most of these funds, often called "no loads," charge a much lower fee or no sales commission at all. With these funds it is generally up to you to do your investment homework.

In order to attract new shareholders, some funds have adopted 12b-1 plans (named after a federal government rule). These plans enable the fund to pay its own distribution costs. Distribution costs are those costs associated with marketing the fund, either through sales agents or through advertising. The 12b-1 fee is charged against fund assets and is paid indirectly by existing shareholders. Annual distribution fees of this type usually range between 0.1 percent and 1.25 percent of the value of the account.

Fees charged by a fund are described in the prospectus. In addition, a fee table listing all transactional fees and all annual fund expenses can be found at the front of the prospectus.

Access to Your Money (Marketability). Mutual funds, by law, must stand ready on any business day to redeem any or all of your shares at their current net asset value (NAV). Of course, the value may be greater or less than the price you originally paid, depending on the market.

To sell shares back to the fund, all you need to do is give the fund proper notification, as explained in the prospectus. Most funds will accept such notification by telephone; some funds require a written request. The fund will then send your check promptly. In most instances the fund will issue a check when it receives the notification; by law it must send you the check within seven business days. You receive the price your shares are worth *on the day* the fund gets proper notice of redemption from you. If you own a money market fund, you can also redeem shares by writing checks directly against your fund balance.

Disciplined Investment. The majority of funds allow you to set up what is known as a "check-o-matic plan." Under such a program a set amount of money is automatically deducted from your checking account each month and sent directly to the mutual fund of your choice. Your bank (or credit union) will not charge you for this service. Mutual funds also offer such programs free of charge. Automatic investment plans can be changed or terminated at any time, again at no charge.

Exchange Privileges. As the economy or your own personal circumstances change, the kinds of funds you hold may no longer be the ones you need. Many mutual funds are part of a "family of funds" and offer a feature called an exchange privilege. Within a family of funds there may be several choices, each with a different investment objective, varying from highly conservative funds to more aggressive funds that carry a higher degree of risk. An exchange privilege allows you to transfer all or part of your money from one of these funds to another. Exchange policies vary from fund to fund. The fee for an exchange is nominal, $5 or less. For the specifics about a fund's exchange privilege, check the prospectus.

Automatic Reinvestment. You can elect to have any dividends and capital gains distributions from your mutual fund investment turned back into the fund, automatically buying new shares and expanding your current holdings. Most shareholders opt for the reinvestment privilege. There is usually no cost or fee involved.

Automatic Withdrawal. You can make arrangements with the fund to automatically send you, or anyone you designate, checks from the fund's earnings or principal. This system works well for retirees, families who want to arrange for payments to their children at college, or anyone needing monthly income checks. See Appendix D for a more detailed example as to how a systematic withdrawal plan (SWP) works.

Detailed Record Keeping. The fund will handle all the paperwork and record keeping necessary to keep track of your investment transactions. A typical statement will note such items as your most recent investment or withdrawal and any dividends or capital gains paid to you in cash or reinvested in the fund. The fund will also report to you on the tax status of your earnings. If you lose any paperwork, the fund will send you copies of current or past statements.

Retirement Plans. Financial experts have long viewed mutual funds as appropriate vehicles for retirement investing; indeed, they are quite commonly used for this purpose. For retirees over the age of seventy and a half, mutual fund companies will recompute the minimum amount that needs to be taken out each year, as dictated by the IRS. Mutual funds are ideal for Keoghs, IRAs, 401(k) plans, and other employer-sponsored retirement plans. Many funds offer prototype retirement plans and standard IRA agreements. Having your own retirement plan drafted by a law firm would cost you thousands of dollars, not to mention what you would be charged for the updates that would be needed every time the laws change. Mutual funds offer these plans and required updates for free.

Accountability. There are literally dozens of sources that track and monitor mutual funds. It is easy for you to determine a fund's track record and volatility over several different time periods. Federal regulatory bodies such as the NASD (National Association of Securities Dealers) and SEC (Securities and Exchange Commission) have strict rules concerning performance figures and what appears in advertisements, brochures, and prospectuses.

Flexibility. Investment choices are almost endless: domestic stocks, foreign debt, international equities, government obligations, money market instruments, convertible securities, short- and intermediate-term bonds, real estate, gold, and natural resources. Your only limitation is the choices offered by the fund family or families you are invested in. And because you can move part or all of your money from one mutual fund to another fund within the same family, usually for only a minimal transfer fee, your portfolio can become more aggressive, conservative, or moderate with a simple phone call.

Economies of Scale. As a shareholder (investor) in a fund, you automatically get the benefit of reduced transaction charges. Since a fund is often buying or selling thousands of shares of stock at a time, it is able to conduct its transactions at dramatically reduced costs. The fees a fund pays are far lower than what you would pay even if you were buying several hundred shares of a stock from a discount broker. The same thing is true when it comes to bonds. Funds are able to add them to their portfolio without any markup. When you buy a bond through a broker, even a discounter, there is always a markup; it is hidden in the price you pay and sell the bond for. The savings for bond investors ranges anywhere from less than 1 percent all the way up to 5 percent.

Risk Reduction: Importance of Diversification
If there is one ingredient to successful investing that is universally agreed upon, it is the benefit of diversification. This concept is also backed by a great deal of research and market experience. The benefit provided by diversification is risk reduction. Risk to investors is frequently defined as volatility of return—in other words, how much an investment's return might vary. Investors prefer returns that are relatively predictable; that is to say, less volatile. On the other hand, they want returns to be high. Diversification eliminates most of the risk without reducing potential returns.

A fund's portfolio manager(s) will normally invest the fund's pool of money in fifty to 150 different securities to spread the fund's holdings over a number of investments. This diversification is an important principle in lessening the fund's overall investment risk. Such diversification is typically beyond the financial capacity of most individual investors. The following table shows the relationship between diversification and investment risk, defined as the variability of annual returns of a stock portfolio.

number of stocks	risk ratio
1	6.6
2	3.8
4	2.4
10	1.6
50	1.1
100	1.0

Note that the variability of return, or risk, associated with holding just one stock is more than six times that of a 100-stock portfolio. Yet the *increased* potential return found in a portfolio made up of a small number of stocks is minimal.

VIII.
Reading a Mutual Fund Prospectus

The purpose of the fund's prospectus is to provide the reader with full and complete disclosure. The prospectus covers the following key points:

- The fund's investment objective: what the managers are trying to achieve
- The investment methods it uses in trying to achieve this objective
- The name and address of its investment adviser and a brief description of the advisor's experience
- The level of investment risk the fund is willing to assume in pursuit of its investment objective
- Any investments the fund will *not* make (for example, real estate, options, or commodities)
- Tax consequences of the investment for the shareholder
- How to purchase shares of the fund, including the cost of investing
- How to redeem shares
- Services provided, such as IRAs, automatic investment of dividends and capital gains distributions, check writing, withdrawal plans, and any other features
- A condensed financial statement (in tabular form, covering the last ten years or the period the fund has been in existence if less than ten years) called "Per Share Income and Capital Changes" (The fund's performance may be calculated from the information given in this table)
- A tabular statement of any fees charged by the fund and their effect on earnings over time

IX.
Commonly Asked Questions

Q. Are mutual funds a new kind of investment?

No. In fact, they have roots in eighteenth-century Scotland. The first U.S. mutual fund was organized in Boston in 1924. This fund, Massachusetts Investors Trust, is still in existence today. Several mutual fund companies have been in operation for over half a century.

Q. How much money do you need to invest in a mutual fund?

Literally anywhere from a few dollars to several million. Many funds have no minimum requirements for investing. A few funds are open to large institutional accounts only. The vast majority of funds require a minimum investment of between $250 and $1,000.

Q. Do mutual funds offer a fixed rate of return?

No. Mutual funds invest in securities such as stocks, bonds, and money market accounts whose yields and values fluctuate with market conditions.

Mutual funds can make money for their shareholders in three ways. First, they pay their shareholders dividends earned from the fund's investments. Second, if a security held by a fund is sold at a profit, funds pay their shareholders capital gains distributions. And third, if the value of the securities held by the fund increases, the value of each mutual fund share also increases.

In none of these cases, however, can a return be guaranteed. In fact, it is against the law for a mutual fund to make a claim as to its future performance. Ads quoting returns are based on past performance and should not be interpreted as a fixed-rate yield. Past performance should not be taken as a predictor of future earnings.

Q. What are the risks of mutual fund investing?

Mutual funds are investments in financial securities with fluctuating values. The value of the securities in a fund's portfolio, for example, will rise and fall according to general economic conditions and the fortunes of the particular companies that issue those securities. Even the most conservative assets, such as U.S. government obligations, will fluctuate in value as interest rates change. These are risks that investors should be aware of when purchasing mutual fund shares.

Q. How can I evaluate a fund's long-term performance?

You can calculate a fund's performance by referring to the section in the prospectus headed "Per Share Income and Capital Changes." This section will give you the figures needed to compute the annual rates of return earned by the fund each year for the past ten years (or for the life of the fund if less than ten years). There are also several periodicals that track the performance of funds on a regular basis. You can also telephone the fund and they will give you performance figures.

Q. What's the difference between *yield* and *total return*?

Yield is the income per share paid to a shareholder from the dividends and interest over a specified period of time. Yield is expressed as a percentage of the current offering price per share.

Total return is a measure of the per-share change in total value from the beginning to the end of a specified period, usually a year, including distributions paid to shareholders. This measure includes income received from dividends and interest, capital gains distributions, and any unrealized capital gains or losses. Total return looks at the whole picture: appreciation (or loss) of principal plus any dividends or income. Total return provides the best measure of overall fund performance; *do not be misled by an enticing yield*.

Q. How much does it cost to invest in a mutual fund?

A mutual fund normally contracts with its management company to provide for most of the needs of a normal business. The management company is paid a fee for these services, which usually include managing the fund's investments.

In addition, the fund may pay directly for some of its costs, such as printing, mailing, accounting, and legal services. Typically, these two annual charges average 1.5 percent. In such a fund you would be paying $10 to $15 a year on every $1,000 invested.

Some fund directors have adopted plans (with the approval of the fund's shareholders) that allow them to pay certain distribution costs (the costs of advertising, for example) directly from fund assets. These costs may range from 0.1 percent to 1.25 percent annually.

There may also be other charges involved—for example, in exchanging shares. Some funds may charge a redemption fee when a shareholder redeems his or her shares, usually within five years of purchasing them. All costs and charges assessed by the fund organization are disclosed in its prospectus.

Q. Is the management fee part of the sales charge?

No, the management fee paid by the fund to its investment advisor is for services rendered in managing the fund's portfolio. An average fee ranges from 0.5 percent to 1 percent of the fund's total assets each year. As described earlier, the management fee and other business expenses generally total somewhere between 1 percent and 1.5 percent. These expenses are paid from the fund's assets and are reflected in the price of the fund shares. In contrast, most sales charges are deducted from your initial investment.

Q. Is my money locked up for a certain period of time in a mutual fund?

Unlike some other types of financial accounts, mutual funds are liquid investments. That means that any shares an investor owns may be redeemed freely on any day the fund is open for business. Since a mutual fund stands ready to buy back its shares at their current net asset value, you always have a buyer for your shares at current market value.

Q. How often do I get statements from a mutual fund?

Mutual funds ordinarily send immediate confirmation statements when an investor purchases or redeems (sells) shares. Statements alerting shareholders to reinvested dividends are sent out periodically. At least semiannually, investors also receive statements on the status of the fund's investments. Tax statements, referred to as "substitute 1099s," are mailed annually. Some funds automatically send out quarterly reports.

Q. I've already purchased shares of a mutual fund. How can I tell how well my investment is doing?

Figuring out how well your fund is faring is a two-step procedure. First, you need to know how many shares you *now* own. The "now" is emphasized because if you have asked the fund to plow any dividends and capital gains distributions back into the fund for you, it will do so by issuing you more shares, thereby increasing the value of your investment. Once you know how many shares you own, look up the fund's net assets value (sometimes called the sell or bid price) in the financial section of a major metropolitan daily newspaper. Next, multiply the net asset value by the number of shares you own to figure out the value of your investment as of that date. Compare today's value against your beginning value.

You will need to keep the confirmation statements you receive when you first purchase shares and as you make subsequent purchases in order to compare present value to the original purchase value. You will also need these statements for tax purposes.

Q. Do investment experts recommend mutual funds for IRAs and other qualified plans?

Financial experts view many mutual funds as compatible with the long-term objectives of saving for retirement. Indeed, fund shareholders cite this reason for investing more than any other. Many kinds of funds work best when allowed to ride out the ups and downs of market cycles over long periods of time.

Funds can also offer the owner of an IRA, Keogh, pension plan, 401(k), or 403(b) flexibility. By using the exchange privilege within a family of funds, the investor can shift investments from one kind of security to another in response to changes in personal finances or the economic outlook, or as retirement approaches.

Q. Are money market funds a good investment?

No. If I were to recommend an investment to you that lost money in seventeen of the last twenty-five calendar years (adjusted for income taxes and inflation), you would probably balk. Yet this is the track record of CDs, money market accounts, and T-bills. Money market funds are an excellent place to park your money for the short term—some period less than two years.

Q. Why don't more people invest in foreign (international) securities?

Ignorance. The reality is that foreign securities (stocks and bonds), when added to domestic investments, actually reduce the portfolio's level of risk. Stock and bond markets around the world rarely move up and down at the same time. This random correlation is what helps lower risk and volatility: When U.S. stocks (or bonds) are going down, securities in other parts of the world may well be moving sideways or going up.

Q. Is standard deviation the correct way to measure risk?

No. Standard deviation measures volatility (or predictability) of returns. The standard deviation for each of the mutual funds in this book is ranked under the star system next to the heading "predictability of returns." The system used in this book for measuring risk is different, punishing funds for performance that is less than that offered by T-bills, a figure commonly referred to as the "risk-free rate of return." To me this makes more sense than a system that punishes a fund for volatility by translating its high standard deviation figure as "high risk." This is what most financial writers do, whether the volatility the fund experienced was upward or downward volatility. I have yet to meet an investor who is upset that he or she did better than expected. No one minds *upward* volatility.

Q. Why not simply invest in those funds that were the best performers over the past 1, 3, 5, or 10 years?

This would be a big mistake. There is little relationship (or correlation) between the performance of one fund or fund category from one year to the next. This, by the way, is the way most investors and advisors select investments—making this one of the biggest and costliest mistakes one could make. Unfortunately, no one knows what the next best performing fund or category will be.

Q. Speaking of common stocks, what are the odds of making money in the market?

If you think investing in the market is too risky, what are the odds that:

You will win a state lottery?	1 in 4 million
You will be dealt a royal flush poker hand?	1 in 649,739
The Earth will be struck by a huge meteor during your lifetime?	1 in 9,000
You will be robbed this year?	1 in 500
The airlines will lose your luggage?	1 in 186
You will be audited by the IRS?	1 in 100
You will roll dice and get snake eyes?	1 in 36
You will go to Disney World this year?	1 in 9
The next bottled water you buy will be nothing more than tap water?	1 in 4
You will eat out today?	1 in 2
An investment in stocks will make money in any given year?	7 in 10

Source: *What the Odds Are*, Les Krantz (Harper Perennial, 1992)

X.
How the 100 Best Funds Were Determined

With an entry field that numbers over 13,000, it is no easy task to determine the 100 best mutual funds. Magazines and newspapers report on the "best" by relying on performance figures over a specific period, usually 1, 3, 5, or 10 years. Investors often rely on these sources and invest accordingly, only to be disappointed later.

Studies from around the world bear out what investors typically experience: that there is no correlation between the performance of a stock or bond from one year to the next. The same can be said for individual money managers—and sadly, for most mutual funds.

The criteria used to determine the 100 best mutual funds are unique and far-reaching. In order for a fund to be considered for this book, it must pass several tests. First, all stock and bond funds that have had managers for less than five years were excluded; in the case of money market funds, the only remaining category, the criterion was liberalized since overhead costs have a much greater bearing on net returns than management's expertise.

This first step alone eliminated well over half the contenders. The reasoning for the cutoff is simple: A fund is often only as good as its manager. An outstanding ten-year track record may be cited in a periodical, but how relevant is this performance if the manager who oversaw the fund left a year or two ago? This criterion was liberalized in selecting money market funds because this category of funds normally requires less expertise.

Second, any fund that places in the bottom (worst) half of its *category's* risk ranking is excluded. No matter how profitable the finish line looks, the number of investors will be sparse if the fund demonstrates too much negative activity. In most cases, a little performance was gladly given up if a great deal of risk was eliminated. This reflects the book's philosophy that returns must be viewed in relation to the amount of risk that was taken. In most cases the funds described in the book possess outstanding risk management. Those few selected funds where risk control has been less than stellar have shown tremendous performance, and their risky nature has been highlighted to warn the reader.

Virtually all sources measure risk by something known as *standard deviation*. Determining an investment's standard deviation is not as difficult as you might imagine. First, you calculate the asset's average annual return. Usually, the most recent three years are used, updated each quarter. Once an average annual rate of return is determined, a line is drawn on a graph, representing this return.

Next, the monthly returns are plotted on the graph. Since three years is a commonly accepted time period for such calculations, a total of thirty-six individual points are plotted—one for each month over the past three years. After all of these points are plotted, the standard deviation can be determined. Quite simply, standard deviation measures the variance of returns from the norm (the line drawn on a graph).

There is a problem in using standard deviation to determine the risk level of any investment, including a mutual fund. The shortcoming of this method is that standard deviation punishes *good* as well as bad results. An example will help expose the problem.

Suppose there were two different investments, X and Y. Investment X went up almost every month by exactly 1.5 percent but had a few months each year when it went down 1 percent. Investment Y went up only 1 percent most months, but it always went up 6 percent for each of the final months of the year. The standard deviation of Y would be substantially higher than X. It might be so high that we would avoid it because it was classified as "high risk." The fact is that we would love to own such an investment. No one ever minds *upward* volatility or surprises; it is only negative or downward volatility that is cause for alarm.

The system used for determining risk in this book is not widely used, but it is certainly a fairer and more meaningful measurement. The book's method for determining risk is to see how many months over the past three years a fund underperformed what is popularly referred to as a "risk-free vehicle," something like a bank CD or U.S. Treasury bill. The more months a fund falls below this safe return, the greater the fund will be punished in its risk ranking.

Third, the fund must have performed well for the past three and five years. A one- or two-year time horizon could be attributed to luck or nonrecurring events. A ten- or fifteen-year period would certainly be better, if not for the reality that the overwhelming majority of funds are managed by a different person today than they were even six years ago.

Finally, the fund must either possess an excellent risk-adjusted return or have had superior returns with no more than average levels of risk. It is assumed that most readers are equally concerned with risk and reward. Thus, the foundation of the text is based on which mutual funds have the best *risk-adjusted returns*.

Sadly, some funds were excluded, despite their superior performance and risk control, because they were either less than five years old, had new management, or were closed to new investors.

XI.
The 100 Best Funds

This section describes the 100 very best funds. As discussed, the methodology used to narrow down the universe of funds is based on performance, risk, and management.

Every one of these 100 funds is a superlative choice. However, there must still be a means to compare and rank each of the funds within its peer group. Each one of the 100 funds is first categorized by its investment objective. The category breakdown is as follows:

category of mutual fund	number
aggressive growth	8
balanced	10
corporate bond	8
global equity	10
government bond	5
growth	9
growth & income	9
health care	2
high-yield bond	4
metals/natural resources	2
money market	10
municipal bond	10
technology	4
utilities	5
world bond	4
total	**100 funds**

There are five areas to be ranked: (1) total return, (2) risk/volatility, (3) management, (4) tax minimization (current income in the case of bond, hybrid, and money market funds), and (5) expense control. Of these five classifications, management, risk/volatility, and total return are the most important.

The track record of a fund is only as good as its management, which is why extensive space is given to this section for each fund. The areas of concern are the length of time the manager, or team, has overseen the fund and the management's background and investment philosophy.

The risk/volatility of the fund is the second biggest concern. Investors like to be in things that have somewhat predictable results—that aren't up 60 percent one year and down 25 percent the next. A few such highly volatile funds are included, but the risk associated with such a fund is clearly highlighted, informing the prospective investor.

Total return was the third concern. When all is said and done, people like to make lots of money with an acceptable level of risk, or at least get decent returns by taking little, if any, risk. This is also known as the *risk-adjusted return*. So, although the very safest funds within each category were preferred, this safety had to be combined with impressive returns.

The fourth category, current income, was of lesser importance. Income is important to a lot of people but often gets in the way of selecting the proper investment; preservation of capital should also be considered. There is a better way to get current income than to rely on monthly dividend or interest checks. This is known as a systematic withdrawal plan (SWP). A sixty-six-year example of a SWP is shown in Appendix D. Current-income-oriented investors will truly be amazed when they see how such a system works.

In the case of equity funds, "tax minimization" was substituted for the category "current income." This was done for two reasons. First, there is no reason a fund whose objective is capital appreciation should be punished simply because it does not throw off a high dividend. Once you are familiar with the benefits of using a systematic withdrawal plan, you will no longer care whether a certain aggressive growth or even a growth and income fund pays much in the form of dividends. Second, unless your money is sheltered in a qualified retirement plan (IRA, pension plan, etc.), income taxes are a real concern. Funds should be rewarded for minimizing shareholder tax liability. This is why every mutual fund in the book is rated, one way or another, when it comes to personal income taxes.

Tax-conscious investors want to downplay current income as much as possible. For them, a high current income simply means paying more in taxes. For other categories, such as growth and income, utilities, and balanced, a healthy current income stream often translates into lower risk. And for still other categories, such as corporate bonds, government bonds, international bonds, money market, and municipal bonds, current income is, and rightfully should be, a major determinant for selection.

The final category, expenses, rates how effective management is in operating the fund. High expense ratios for a given category mean that the advisors are either too greedy or simply do not know or care about running an efficient operation. The actual expenses incurred by a fund are not directly seen by the client, but such costs are deducted from the portfolio's gross returns, which is important.

In addition to looking at the expense ratio of a fund, the turnover rate is studied. The turnover rate shows how often the fund buys and sells its securities. There is a real cost when such a transaction occurs. These transaction costs, also known as commissions, are borne by the fund and eat into the gross return figures. Expense ratios do not include transaction costs incurred when management decides to replace or add a security. Thus, expense ratios do not tell the whole story. By scrutinizing the turnover rate, the rankings take into account excessive trading. A fund's turnover rate may represent a larger true cost to the investor than the fund's expense ratio.

Each fund is ranked in each one of these five categories. The rating ranges from zero to five points (stars) in each category. The points can be transcribed as follows: zero points = poor, one point = fair, two points = good, three points = very good, four points = superior, and five points = excellent.

All of the rankings for each fund are based on how such a fund fared against its peer group category in the book. Thus, even though a given rating may only be fair or even poor, it is within the context of the category and its peers that have made the book—a category that only includes the very best. There is a strong likelihood that a fund in the book that is given a low score in one category would still rate as great when compared to the entire universe of funds or even compared to other funds within the same category but not included in this book.

Do not be fooled by a low rating for any fund in any of the five areas. All 100 of these funds are true winners. Keep in mind that only about one in one hundred funds can appear in the book. The purpose of the ratings is to show the best of the best.

Aggressive Growth Funds

These funds focus strictly on appreciation, with no concern about generating income. Aggressive growth funds strive for maximum capital growth, frequently using such trading strategies as leveraging, purchasing restricted securities, or buying stocks of emerging growth companies. Portfolio composition is almost exclusively U.S. stocks.

Aggressive growth funds can go up in value quite rapidly during favorable market conditions. These funds will often outperform other categories of U.S. stocks during bull markets but suffer greater percentage losses during bear markets.

Over the past fifteen years (ending 12/31/00), small stocks, which are included in the aggressive growth category, have *underperformed* common stocks by 4.4 percent per year, as measured by the Standard & Poor's 500 Stock Index. From 1986 through 2000, small stocks averaged 11.6 percent, while common stocks averaged 16.0 percent compounded per year. A $10,000 investment in small stocks grew to $51,580 over the past fifteen years; a similar initial investment in the S & P 500 grew to $92,670.

During the past twenty years, there have been sixteen 5-year periods (1981–1985, 1982–1986, etc.). The Small Stock Index, made up from the smallest 20 percent of companies listed on the NYSE, as measured by market capitalization, outperformed the S & P 500 in just five of those sixteen 5-year periods. During these same twenty years, there have been eleven 10-year periods (1981–1999, 1982–1991, etc.). The Small Stock Index never outperformed the S & P 500 during any of those eleven 10-year periods.

During the past thirty years, there have been eleven 20-year periods (1971–1990, 1972–1991, etc.). The Small Stock Index outperformed the S & P 500 in nine of those eleven 20-year periods.

Over the past fifty years, there have been forty-six 5-year periods (1951–1955, 1952–1955, etc.). The Small Stock Index outperformed the S & P 500 in twenty-eight of those forty-six 5-year periods. Over the past fifty years, there have been forty-one 10-year periods (1951–1956, 1952–1961, etc.). The Small Stock Index outperformed the S & P 500 in twenty-seven of those forty-one 10-year periods, the last such period being 1991–2000.

A dollar invested in small stocks for the past fifty years grew to $738 by the end of 2000 (versus $407 for $1 invested in the S & P 500). For small stocks, this translates into an average compound return of 14.1 percent per year. Over the past fifty years, the worst year for small stocks was 1973, when a loss of 31 percent was suffered. Two years later these same stocks posted a gain of almost 53 percent in one year. The best year so far has been 1967, when small stocks posted a gain of 84 percent. The best five years in a row for this category were 1975 to 1979, when

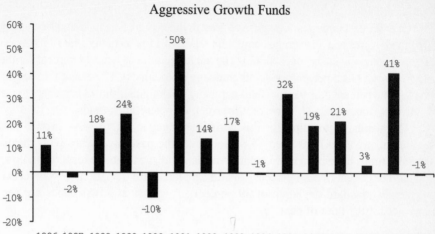

Aggressive Growth Funds

the rate of return averaged 40 percent per year. The worst five-year period over the past half century has been 1969 to 1973, when this group lost an average of 12.25 percent per year. For ten-year periods, the best has been 1975 to 1984 (30 percent per year); the worst has been 1965 to 1974 (3.2 percent per year).

In order to obtain the kinds of returns described here, investors would have needed quite a bit of patience and understanding. During the 1990s, small-company stocks had a standard deviation (variation of return) of 20.2 percent, compared to 15.8 percent for common stocks and 8.9 percent for long-term government bonds.

During the past three years, aggressive growth funds have underperformed the S & P 500 by -1.2 percent per year. Over the past five years, this fund category has underperformed the S & P 500 by an average of 4.1 percent per year. Average turnover during the past three years has been 110 percent.

The p/e ratio is 30 for the typical aggressive growth fund, versus 32 for the S & P 500. The typical stock in these portfolios is only 8 percent the size of the average stock in the S & P 500. The average beta is 1.0, which means the group has a market-related risk that is almost identical to that of the S & P 500. There is over $360 billion in all aggressive growth funds combined. The average aggressive growth fund throws virtually no annual income stream. The typical annual expense ratio for this group is 1.6 percent.

The p/e ratio for the typical small-company fund is 27, a figure about 15 percent lower than the S & P 500. Yet the typical stock in these portfolios is only about 3 percent the size of the average stock in the S & P 500. The average beta is 1.0, which means the group's market-related risk is the same as the S & P 500. There is about $200 billion in all small-company funds combined. The average small-company growth fund throws off an income stream of close to zero annually. The typical annual expense ratio for this group is 1.6 percent.

There are 230 funds that make up the aggressive growth category. The small-company stock category, which has 790 funds, has been combined with aggressive growth. Thus, for this section, there were a total of 1,020 possible candidates. Total market capitalization of these two categories combined is $375 billion.

Over the past three years, aggressive growth funds (which include small-company stock funds) have had an average compound return of 11 percent per year (9.9 percent for small-company stock funds alone). The annual return has been 14 percent for the past five years (13.8 percent for small-company stock funds), 17 percent for the past decade (16.8 percent per year for small-company stock funds), and 13 percent per year for the past fifteen years (13.3 percent for small-company stock funds).

The standard deviation for this combined category (aggressive growth and small-company stock) has been 34 percent over the past three years. This means that these funds have been more volatile than any other category except technology (standard deviation of 63.6 percent), health care (standard deviation of 38 percent), and metals (standard deviation of 39 percent). Aggressive growth funds are certainly not for the faint of heart.

Bridgeway Aggressive Growth

5615 Kirby Drive, Suite 518
Houston, TX 77005
(800) 661-3550
www.bridgewayfund.com

total return	★★★★★
risk reduction	★★
management	★★★★
tax minimization	★★★★★
expense control	★★★
symbol BRAGX	19 points
up-market performance	excellent
down-market performance	very good
predictability of returns	poor

Total Return ★★★★★

Over the past five years (ending 12/31/00), Bridgeway Aggressive Growth has taken $10,000 and turned it into $46,530 ($29,860 over three years). This translates into an annualized return of 36 percent over the past five years and 44 percent over the past three years. Over the past five years, this fund has outperformed 99 percent of all mutual funds; within its general category, it has done better than 99 percent of its peers. Aggressive growth funds have averaged 14 percent annually over these same five years.

Risk/Volatility ★★

Over the past five years, Bridgeway has been safer than 45 percent of all aggressive growth funds. Over the past decade, the fund has had no negative years, while the S & P 500 has had one (off 9 percent in 2000); the Russell 2000 fell three times (off 2 percent in 1994, 3 percent in 1998, and 3 percent in 2000). The fund has underperformed the S & P 500 and the Russell 2000 once in the past ten years.

	past 5 years		past 10 years	
worst year	14%	2000	14%	2000
best year	121%	1999	121%	1999

In the past, Bridgeway has done better than 95 percent of its peer group in up markets but outperformed just 20 percent of its competition in down markets. Consistency, or predictability, of returns for Bridgeway Aggressive Growth can be described as poor. This fund's risk-related return is excellent.

Management ★★★★

There are sixty-five stocks in this $110 million portfolio. The average aggressive growth fund today is $360 million in size. Close to 98 percent of the fund's holdings are in stocks, the balance is in cash. The stocks in this portfolio have an average price-earnings (p/e) ratio of 24 and a median market capitalization of $2.5 billion. The portfolio's equity holdings can be categorized as mid-cap and a blend of growth and value stocks. The fund's categorization is somewhat misleading since close to half of the portfolio is in small-cap issues and almost a third is in large-cap equities; less than 10 percent of the holdings are mid-cap.

John Montgomery, a graduate of MIT and Harvard, has managed this fund for the past seven years. John also manages two small-cap and one large-cap fund. Montgomery currently favors technology, durables, energy, and retail stocks. There are four funds besides Aggressive Growth within the Bridgeway family. Overall, the fund family's risk-adjusted performance can be described as good.

Tax Minimization ★★★★★
During the past five years, a $10,000 initial investment grew to $43,610 after taxes, assuming a 39.6 percent income tax bracket (state and federal combined) and a capital gains rate of 28 percent. This means that investors in this fund were able to preserve 92 percent of their total returns. Compared to other equity funds, this fund's tax savings are considered to be excellent.

Expenses ★★★
Bridgeway Aggressive Growth's expense ratio is 1.3 percent; it has averaged 1.4 percent annually over the past three calendar years. The average expense ratio for the 1,050 funds in this category is 1.6 percent. This fund's turnover rate over the past year has been 200 percent, while its peer group average has been 110 percent.

Summary
Bridgeway Aggressive Growth is the number one performer in its category for the past three and five years. It has ranked in the top half of its category for each of the past five years, often in the top quartile. Over the past three and five years, the fund's performance has ranked in the top 1 percent for all mutual funds as well as within its category, mid-cap growth. Returns have been extremely high while risk exposure has only been average; risk-adjusted returns have been exceptional over the past three and five years. The fund ranks in the top quintile when it comes to growth persistence: the ability to consistently outperform equity funds over the previous five years. This fund is a number one choice for an investor looking for a blend of value and growth as well as small and large issues.

Profile

minimum initial investment $2,000	IRA accounts available . . . . yes
subsequent minimum investment . . $500	IRA minimum investment $2,000
available in all 50 states. . . . . yes	date of inception . . . . Aug. 1994
telephone exchanges. . . . . yes	dividend/income paid . . . . annually
number of funds in family 5	largest sector weighting . . . technology

Citizens Emerging Growth Fund
230 Commerce Way, Suite 300
Portsmouth, NH 03801
(800) 223-7010
www.citizensfunds.com

total return	★★★★
risk reduction	★★★
management	★★★
tax minimization	★★★★
expense control	★★
symbol WAEGX	16 points
up-market performance	excellent
down-market performance	excellent
predictability of returns	good

Total Return   ★★★★
Over the past five years (ending 12/31/00), Citizens Emerging Growth Fund has taken $10,000 and turned it into $31,950 ($23,830 over three years). This translates into an annualized return of 26 percent over the past five years and 34 percent over the past three years. Over the past five years, this fund has outperformed 99 percent of all mutual funds; within its general category, it has done better than 94 percent of its peers. Aggressive growth funds have averaged 14 percent annually over these same five years.

Risk/Volatility   ★★★
Over the past five years, Citizens has been safer than 75 percent of all aggressive growth funds. Over the past decade, the fund has had one negative year, while the S & P 500 has also had one (off 9 percent in 2000); the Russell 2000 fell three times (off 2 percent in 1994, 3 percent in 1998, and 3 percent in 2000). The fund has underperformed the S & P 500 once and the Russell 2000 once in the past ten years.

	past 5 years		past 10 years	
worst year	-1%	2000	-1%	2000
best year	68%	1999	68%	1999

In the past, Citizens has done better than 95 percent of its peer group in up markets and outperformed 80 percent of its competition in down markets. Consistency, or predictability, of returns for Citizens Emerging Growth Fund can be described as good. This fund's risk-related return is excellent.

Management   ★★★
There are thirty-five stocks in this $370 billion portfolio. The average aggressive growth fund today is $360 million in size. Close to 90 percent of the fund's holdings are in stocks. The stocks in this portfolio have an average price-earnings (p/e)

ratio of 29 and a median market capitalization of $4 billion. The fund does not own companies that are involved with weapons, tobacco, or alcohol. The portfolio's equity holdings can be categorized as mid-cap and growth-oriented issues.

Richard D. Little has managed this fund for the past seven years. He and comanager Ron Jacks are particularly attracted to companies with upward earnings revisions, earnings surprises, as well as accelerating earnings. There are seven funds besides Emerging Growth within the Citizens family. Overall, the fund family's risk-adjusted performance can be described as very good.

Tax Minimization   ★★★★
During the past five years, a $10,000 initial investment grew to $28,000 after taxes, assuming a 39.6 percent income tax bracket (state and federal combined) and a capital gains rate of 28 percent. This means that investors in this fund were able to preserve 82 percent of their total returns. Compared to other equity funds, this fund's tax savings are considered to be very good.

Expenses   ★★
Citizens Emerging Growth Fund's expense ratio is 1.8 percent; it has averaged 1.9 percent annually over the past three calendar years. The average expense ratio for the 1,050 funds in this category is 1.6 percent. This fund's turnover rate over the past year has been 205 percent, while its peer group average has been 110 percent.

Summary
Citizens Emerging Growth Fund is only one of two funds in its category that does a superb job during bear as well as bull markets. Within its category, it is the second-best performer when it comes to up- and down-market returns; its combined results easily make it the number one choice. The fund's turnover rate is quite high, but management's ability to outperform 99 percent of all mutual funds as well as 94 percent of its peers makes this offering a compelling choice. Investors would be wise to check out other offerings from the Citizens family of funds.

Profile
minimum initial investment $2,500
subsequent minimum investment . . . $50
available in all 50 states. . . . . yes
telephone exchanges. . . . . yes
number of funds in family 8

IRA accounts available . . . . yes
IRA minimum investment $1,000
date of inception . . . . Feb. 1994
dividend/income paid . . . . annually
largest sector weighting . . . technology

INVESCO Dynamics Fund-Investor Shares
P.O. Box 173706
Denver, CO 80217
(800) 525-8085
www.invescofunds.com

total return	★★★
risk reduction	★★★
management	★★★
tax minimization	★★★★
expense control	★★★★
symbol FIDYX	17 points
up-market performance	very good
down-market performance	good
predictability of returns	good

Total Return   ★★★
Over the past five years (ending 12/31/00), INVESCO Dynamics Fund-Investor Shares has taken $10,000 and turned it into $28,030 ($19,530 over three years and $85,120 over the past ten years). This translates into an annualized return of 23 percent over the past five years, 25 percent over the past three years, and 24 percent for the decade. Over the past five years, this fund has outperformed 97 percent of all mutual funds; within its general category, it has done better than 85 percent of its peers. Aggressive growth funds have averaged 14 percent annually over these same five years.

Risk/Volatility   ★★★
Over the past five years, INVESCO has been safer than 70 percent of all aggressive growth funds. Over the past decade, the fund has had two negative years, while the S & P 500 has had one (off 9 percent in 2000); the Russell 2000 fell three times (off 2 percent in 1994, 3 percent in 1998, and 3 percent in 2000). The fund has underperformed the S & P 500 once and the Russell 2000 twice in the past ten years.

	past 5 years		past 10 years	
worst year	-8%	2000	-8%	2000
best year	72%	1999	72%	1999

In the past, INVESCO has done better than 75 percent of its peer group in up markets but outperformed just 40 percent of its competition in down markets. Consistency, or predictability, of returns for INVESCO Dynamics Fund-Investor Shares can be described as good. This fund's risk-related return is excellent.

Management   ★★★

There are 155 stocks in this $7.5 billion portfolio. The average aggressive growth fund today is $360 million in size. Close to 98 percent of the fund's holdings are in stocks. The stocks in this portfolio have an average price-earnings (p/e) ratio of 44 and a median market capitalization of $8 billion. The portfolio's equity holdings can be categorized as mid-cap and growth-oriented issues.

Timothy J. Miller and Thomas R. Wald have managed this fund for the past six years. Management concentrates on issues that have a market capitalization of between $2 and $15 billion. There are fifty-three funds besides Dynamics within the INVESCO family. Overall, the fund family's risk-adjusted performance can be described as very good.

Tax Minimization   ★★★★

During the past five years, a $10,000 initial investment grew to $24,785 after taxes, assuming a 39.6 percent income tax bracket (state and federal combined) and a capital gains rate of 28 percent. This means that investors in this fund were able to preserve 82 percent of their total returns. Compared to other equity funds, this fund's tax savings are considered to be very good.

Expenses   ★★★★

INVESCO Dynamics Fund's expense ratio is 1 percent; it has averaged 1 percent annually over the past three calendar years. The average expense ratio for the 1,050 funds in this category is 1.6 percent. This fund's turnover rate over the past year has been 170 percent, while its peer group average has been 110 percent.

Summary

INVESCO Dynamics Fund-Investor Shares turns in solid results across the board. It has the lowest expense ratio of any aggressive growth or small-cap fund in the book. The fund ranks in the top quintile when it comes to growth persistence: the ability to consistently outperform equity funds over the previous five years. Management has been particularly adept at choosing different industry groups at particularly favorable times, thereby often avoiding the "crash and burn" mentality of many of its peers. Investors would be wise to check out other offerings from the INVESCO family.

Profile

minimum initial investment . . . . . $1,000   *IRA accounts available* . . . . yes
subsequent minimum investment . . . $50   *IRA minimum investment* $250
available in all 50 states . . . . yes   *date of inception* . . . . Sept. 1967
telephone exchanges . . . . yes   *dividend/income paid* . . . . annually
number of funds in family 54   *largest sector weighting* . . . technology

MFS Mid-Cap Growth B
P.O. Box 2281
Boston, MA 02107
(800) 637-2929
www.mfs.com

total return	★★★
risk reduction	★★★
management	★★★
tax minimization	★★★
expense control	★
symbol OTCBX	13 points
up-market performance	excellent
down-market performance	poor
predictability of returns	good

Total Return ★★★
Over the past five years (ending 12/31/00), MFS Mid-Cap Growth B has taken $10,000 and turned it into $29,320 ($22,480 over three years). This translates into an annualized return of 24 percent over the past five years and 31 percent over the past three years. Over the past five years, this fund has outperformed 98 percent of all mutual funds; within its general category, it has done better than 90 percent of its peers. Aggressive growth funds have averaged 14 percent annually over these same five years.

Risk/Volatility ★★★
Over the past five years, MFS has been safer than 65 percent of all aggressive growth funds. Over the past decade, the fund has had no negative years, while the S & P 500 has had one (off 9 percent in 2000); the Russell 2000 fell three times (off 2 percent in 1994, 3 percent in 1998, and 3 percent in 2000). The fund has underperformed the S & P 500 once and the Russell 2000 twice in the past ten years.

	past 5 years		past 10 years	
worst year	7%	2000	3%	1996
best year	77%	1999	77%	1999

In the past, MFS has done better than 98 percent of its peer group in up markets and outperformed 50 percent of its competition in down markets. Consistency, or predictability, of returns for MFS Mid-Cap Growth B can be described as good. This fund's risk-related return is excellent.

Management   ★★★

There are eighty-five stocks in this $650 million portfolio. The average aggressive growth fund today is $360 million in size. Close to 95 percent of the fund's holdings are in stocks. The stocks in this portfolio have an average price-earnings (p/e) ratio of 35 and a median market capitalization of $3.6 billion. The portfolio's equity holdings can be categorized as mid-cap and growth-oriented issues.

A team has managed this fund for the past five years. Management focuses on companies that are representative of the S & P Mid-Cap 400 Index. There are 191 funds besides Mid-Cap Growth B within the MFS B family. Overall, the fund family's risk-adjusted performance can be described as very good.

Tax Minimization   ★★★

During the past five years, a $10,000 initial investment grew to $25,070 after taxes, assuming a 39.6 percent income tax bracket (state and federal combined) and a capital gains rate of 28 percent. This means that investors in this fund were able to preserve 78 percent of their total returns. Compared to other equity funds, this fund's tax savings are considered to be good.

Expenses   ★

MFS Mid-Cap Growth's expense ratio is 2 percent; it has averaged 2.1 percent annually over the past three calendar years. The average expense ratio for the 1,050 funds in this category is 1.6 percent. This fund's turnover rate over the past year has been 130 percent, while its peer group average has been 110 percent.

Summary

MFS Mid-Cap Growth B ranks as the second-best performer in a bull market for its category. Management has a rather eclectic taste when it comes to equity selection; such security selection has benefited investors well over the past several years. When it comes to sheer performance in all market conditions, the fund has outshone 90 percent of its broad group. Investors would be wise to check out other offerings from the MFS group.

Profile

minimum initial investment $1,000	IRA accounts available . . . . yes
subsequent minimum investment . . . $50	IRA minimum investment $250
available in all 50 states. . . . . yes	date of inception. . . . . Dec. 1993
telephone exchanges. . . . . yes	dividend/income paid . . . . annually
number of funds in family 192	largest sector weighting . . . technology

Oppenheimer Capital Appreciation A

P.O. Box 5270
Denver, CO 80217
(800) 525-7048
www.oppenheimerfunds.com

total return	★★★
risk reduction	★★★★
management	★★★★
tax minimization	★★★★
expense control	★★★★★
symbol OPTFX	20 points
up-market performance	good
down-market performance	poor
predictability of returns	very good

Total Return   ★★★

Over the past five years (ending 12/31/00), Oppenheimer Capital Appreciation A has taken $10,000 and turned it into $28,120 ($17,400 over three years and $61,715 over the past ten years). This translates into an annualized return of 23 percent over the past five years, 20 percent over the past three years, and 20 percent for the decade. Over the past five years, this fund has outperformed 97 percent of all mutual funds; within its general category, it has done better than 90 percent of its peers. Aggressive growth funds have averaged 14 percent annually over these same five years.

Risk/Volatility   ★★★★

Over the past five years, Oppenheimer has been safer than 85 percent of all aggressive growth funds. Over the past decade, the fund has had one negative year, while the S & P 500 has also had one (off 9 percent in 2000); the Russell 2000 fell three times (off 2 percent in 1994, 3 percent in 1998, and 3 percent in 2000). The fund has underperformed the S & P 500 once and the Russell 2000 twice in the past ten years.

	past 5 years		past 10 years	
worst year	-1%	2000	-1%	2000
best year	42%	1999	42%	1999

In the past, Oppenheimer has done better than 90 percent of its peer group in up markets but outperformed just 15 percent of its competition in down markets. Consistency, or predictability, of returns for Oppenheimer Capital Appreciation A can be described as very good. This fund's risk-related return is excellent.

Management   ★★★★

There are 140 stocks in this $3.2 billion portfolio. The average aggressive growth fund today is $360 million in size. Close to 93 percent of the fund's holdings are in stocks. The stocks in this portfolio have an average price-earnings (p/e) ratio of 35 and a median market capitalization of $27 billion. The portfolio's equity holdings can be categorized as large-cap and a blend of growth and value stocks.

Jane C. Putnam has managed this fund for the past six years. Management is allowed to invest in companies of any size and may have up to a third of the portfolio's assets in foreign securities; hedging is also permitted. There are 166 funds besides Capital Appreciation A within the Oppenheimer family. Overall, the fund family's risk-adjusted performance can be described as good.

Tax Minimization   ★★★★

During the past five years, a $10,000 initial investment grew to $25,765 after taxes, assuming a 39.6 percent income tax bracket (state and federal combined) and a capital gains rate of 28 percent. This means that investors in this fund were able to preserve 87 percent of their total returns. Compared to other equity funds, this fund's tax savings are considered to be very good.

Expenses   ★★★★★

Oppenheimer Capital Appreciation's expense ratio is 1 percent; it has averaged 1 percent annually over the past three calendar years. The average expense ratio for the 1,050 funds in this category is 1.6 percent. This fund's turnover rate over the past year has been 55 percent, while its peer group average has been 110 percent.

Summary

The fund ranks in the top quintile when it comes to growth persistence: the ability to consistently outperform equity funds over the previous five years. The fund has outperformed 90 percent of its peers and over 95 percent of all portfolios. Oppenheimer Capital Appreciation A has the lowest expense ratio of its category.

Profile

minimum initial investment $1,000	*IRA accounts available* . . . . yes
subsequent minimum investment . . . $25	*IRA minimum investment* $250
available in all 50 states. . . . . yes	*date of inception* . . . . Jan. 1981
telephone exchanges. . . . . yes	*dividend/income paid* . . . . annually
number of funds in family 167	*largest sector weighting* . . . technology

Royce Total Return
1414 Avenue of the Americas
New York, NY 10019
(800) 221-4268
www.roycefunds.com

total return	★
risk reduction	★★★★★
management	★★★★
tax minimization	★★★
expense control	★★★★
symbol RYTRX	17 points
up-market performance	poor
down-market performance	very good
predictability of returns	excellent

Total Return ★
Over the past five years (ending 12/31/00), Royce Total Return has taken $10,000 and turned it into $20,115 ($12,600 over three years). This translates into an annualized return of 15 percent over the past five years and 8 percent over the past three years. Over the past five years, this fund has outperformed 75 percent of all mutual funds; within its general category, it has done better than 85 percent of its peers. Aggressive growth funds have averaged 14 percent annually over these same five years.

Risk/Volatility ★★★★★
Over the past five years, Royce has been safer than 99 percent of all aggressive growth funds. Over the past decade, the fund has had no negative years, while the S & P 500 has had one (off 9 percent in 2000); the Russell 2000 fell three times (off 2 percent in 1994, 3 percent in 1998, and 3 percent in 2000). The fund has underperformed the S & P 500 once and the Russell 2000 three times in the past ten years.

	past 5 years		past 10 years	
worst year	2%	1999	2%	1999
best year	25%	1996	27%	1995

In the past, Royce has done better than 60 percent of its peer group in up markets and outperformed 85 percent of its competition in down markets. Consistency, or predictability, of returns for Royce Total Return can be described as excellent. This fund's risk-related return is very good.

Management   ★★★★

There are 160 stocks in this $270 million portfolio. The average aggressive growth fund today is $360 million in size. Close to 99 percent of the fund's holdings are in stocks. The stocks in this portfolio have an average price-earnings (p/e) ratio of 16 and a median market capitalization of $520 million. The portfolio's equity holdings can be categorized as small-cap and value-oriented issues.

Charles M. Royce has managed this fund for the past eight years. Roughly two-thirds of the fund is always invested in stocks that have a market capitalization of less than $1 billion. Management uses a value-oriented approach to selecting equities. Royce is considered to be a conservative investor as evidenced by his strong preference for dividend-paying issues. There are eleven funds besides Total Return within the Royce family. Overall, the fund family's risk-adjusted performance can be described as very good to excellent.

Tax Minimization   ★★★

During the past five years, a $10,000 initial investment grew to $17,790 after taxes, assuming a 39.6 percent income tax bracket (state and federal combined) and a capital gains rate of 28 percent. This means that investors in this fund were able to preserve 77 percent of their total returns. Compared to other equity funds, this fund's tax savings are considered to be good.

Expenses   ★★★★

Royce Total Return's expense ratio is 1.3 percent; it has averaged 1.3 percent annually over the past three calendar years. The average expense ratio for the 1,050 funds in this category is 1.6 percent. This fund's turnover rate over the past year has been 35 percent, while its peer group average has been 110 percent.

Summary

Royce Total Return is the most predictable of its peer group plus has the lowest risk. This fund is a particularly good choice due to the conservative approach of management risk. Overhead costs have been kept low, partially due to a very low turnover rate. Investors are strongly encouraged to check out other funds from Royce.

Profile

minimum initial investment $2,000	*IRA accounts available* . . . . yes
subsequent minimum investment . . . $50	*IRA minimum investment* $500
available in all 50 states. . . . . yes	*date of inception.* . . . . Dec. 1993
telephone exchanges. . . . . yes	*dividend/income paid* . . . . annually
number of funds in family. 12	*largest sector weighting* indust. cyclicals

Smith Barney Aggressive Growth A
7 World Trade Center, 41st Floor
New York, NY 10048
(800) 451-2010
www.smithbarney.com

total return	★★★★★
risk reduction	★★★★
management	★★★★★
tax minimization	★★★★★
expense control	★★★★★
symbol SHRAX	24 points
up-market performance	excellent
down-market performance	excellent
predictability of returns	good

Total Return ★★★★★
Over the past five years (ending 12/31/00), Smith Barney Aggressive Growth A has taken $10,000 and turned it into $34,360 ($26,280 over three years and $79,260 over the past ten years). This translates into an annualized return of 28 percent over the past five years, 38 percent over the past three years, and 23 percent for the decade. Over the past five years (ending 12/31/00), this fund has outperformed 99 percent of all mutual funds; within its general category, it has done better than 98 percent of its peers. Aggressive growth funds have averaged 14 percent annually over these same five years.

Risk/Volatility ★★★★
Over the past five years, Smith Barney has been safer than 55 percent of all aggressive growth funds. Over the past decade, the fund has had one negative year, while the S & P 500 has also had one (off 9 percent in 2000); the Russell 2000 fell three times (off 2 percent in 1994, 3 percent in 1998, and 3 percent in 2000). The fund has underperformed the S & P 500 once and the Russell 2000 twice in the past ten years.

	past 5 years		past 10 years	
worst year	3%	1996	-2%	1994
best year	64%	1999	64%	1999

In the past, Smith Barney has done better than 95 percent of its peer group in up markets and outperformed 65 percent of its competition in down markets. Consistency, or predictability, of returns for Smith Barney Aggressive Growth A can be described as good. This fund's risk-related return is excellent.

Management   ★★★★★
There are seventy-five stocks in this $1.5 billion portfolio. The average aggressive growth fund today is $360 million in size. Close to 97 percent of the fund's holdings are in stocks. The stocks in this portfolio have an average price-earnings (p/e) ratio of 37 and a median market capitalization of $13 billion. The portfolio's equity holdings can be categorized as large-cap and growth-oriented issues.

Richard A. Freeman has managed this fund for the past eighteen years. He is considered an excellent stock picker and tends to hold onto a security once he buys it. (Note: he has owned Intel since the early 1980s.) Close to half of the portfolio's holdings are represented by fewer than a dozen issues. There are 144 funds besides Aggressive Growth A within the Smith Barney family. Overall, the fund family's risk-adjusted performance can be described as very good.

Tax Minimization   ★★★★★
During the past five years, a $10,000 initial investment grew to $33,875 after taxes, assuming a 39.6 percent income tax bracket (state and federal combined) and a capital gains rate of 28 percent. This means that investors in this fund were able to preserve 98 percent of their total returns. Compared to other equity funds, this fund's tax savings are considered to be excellent.

Expenses   ★★★★★
Smith Barney Aggressive Growth's expense ratio is 1.1 percent; it has averaged 1.2 percent annually over the past three calendar years. The average expense ratio for the 1,050 funds in this category is 1.6 percent. This fund's turnover rate over the past year has been 1 percent, while its peer group average has been 110 percent.

Summary
Smith Barney Aggressive Growth A tied for first as having the highest overall score. It is one of only two funds in its category that does a superb job during bear as well as bull markets. Additionally, it is the best tax minimizer, has the lowest turnover, and is one of only two funds in its category to have great performance in up as well as down markets. Risk-adjusted returns have been superb over the past one, three, and five years. The fund ranks in the top quintile when it comes to growth persistence: the ability to consistently outperform equity funds over the previous five years. This offering also excels when it comes to superior risk-adjusted return persistence. Investors would be wise to check out other offerings from the Smith Barney family of funds.

Profile
minimum initial investment . . . . . $1,000   *IRA accounts available* . . . . yes
subsequent minimum investment . . . $50   *IRA minimum investment* $250
available in all 50 states. . . . . yes   *date of inception* . . . . Oct. 1983
telephone exchanges. . . . . yes   *dividend/income paid* . . . . annually
number of funds in family 145   *largest sector weighting* . . . . health

State Street Research Aurora A

One Financial Center
Boston, MA 02111
(800) 882-0052
www.ssrfunds.com

total return	★★★★★
risk reduction	★★★★★
management	★★★★★
tax minimization	★★★★★
expense control	★★★★
symbol SSRAX	24 points
up-market performance	very good
down-market performance	poor
predictability of returns	very good

Total Return　　　★★★★★

Over the past five years (ending 12/31/00), State Street Research Aurora A has taken $10,000 and turned it into $35,630 ($15,520 over three years). This translates into an annualized return of 29 percent over the past five years and 16 percent over the past three years. Over the past five years, this fund has outperformed 99 percent of all mutual funds; within its general category, it has done better than 98 percent of its peers. Aggressive growth funds have averaged 14 percent annually over these same five years.

Risk/Volatility　　　★★★★★

Over the past five years, State Street Research has been safer than 85 percent of all aggressive growth funds. Over the past decade, the fund has had one negative year, while the S & P 500 has also had one (off 9 percent in 2000); the Russell 2000 fell three times (off 2 percent in 1994, 3 percent in 1998, and 3 percent in 2000). The fund has underperformed the S & P 500 once and the Russell 2000 three times in the past ten years.

	past 5 years		past 10 years	
worst year	-15%	1998	-15%	1998
best year	57%	1996	57%	1996

In the past, State Street Research has done better than 90 percent of its peer group in up markets but outperformed just 20 percent of its competition in down markets. Consistency, or predictability, of returns for State Street Research Aurora A can be described as very good. This fund's risk-related return is excellent.

Management　　　★★★★★

There are 295 stocks in this $625 million portfolio. The average aggressive growth fund today is $360 million in size. Close to 90 percent of the fund's holdings are in stocks. The stocks in this portfolio have an average price-earnings (p/e) ratio of

20 and a median market capitalization of $910 million. The portfolio's equity hold-ings can be categorized as small-cap and a blend of growth and value stocks.

Rudolph Kluiber has managed this fund for the past six years. At least two-thirds of the portfolio is always invested in small-cap value issues. However, man-agement does not necessarily shy away from technology or other growth industry groups, provided valuations and fundamentals are in check. There are eighty funds besides Aurora A within the State Street Research family. Overall, the fund family's risk-adjusted performance can be described as good.

Tax Minimization   ★★★★★
During the past five years, a $10,000 initial investment grew to $33,070 after taxes, assuming a 39.6 percent income tax bracket (state and federal combined) and a capital gains rate of 28 percent. This means that investors in this fund were able to preserve 90 percent of their total returns. Compared to other equity funds, this fund's tax savings are considered to be excellent.

Expenses   ★★★★
State Street Research Aurora's expense ratio is 1.5 percent; it has averaged 1.5 per-cent annually over the past three calendar years. The average expense ratio for the 1,050 funds in this category is 1.6 percent. This fund's turnover rate over the past year has been 60 percent, while its peer group average has been 110 percent.

Summary
State Street Research Aurora A ties for first as having the highest overall category score (24 out of 25 possible points). The fund also has the second-best five-year per-formance figures and is also ranked number two when it comes to risk reduction. Extremely high tax efficiency is another bonus for this winner. This offering also ranks in the top quintile when it comes to superior risk-adjusted return persistence.

Profile

minimum initial investment $2,500	*IRA accounts available* . . . . yes
subsequent minimum investment . . . $50	*IRA minimum investment* $2,000
available in all 50 states. . . . . yes	*date of inception* . . . . Feb. 1995
telephone exchanges. . . . . yes	*dividend/income paid* . . . . annually
number of funds in family 81	*largest sector weighting* . . . . . . services

Balanced Funds

The objective of balanced funds, also referred to as total return funds, is to provide both growth and income. Fund management purchases common stocks, bonds, and convertible securities. Portfolio composition is almost always exclusively U.S. securities. The weighting of stocks compared to bonds depends on the portfolio manager's perception of the stock market, interest rates, and risk levels. It is rare for less than 30 percent of the fund's holdings to be in stocks or bonds.

Balanced funds offer neither the best nor the worst of both worlds. These funds will often outperform the different categories of bond funds during bull markets but suffer greater percentage losses during stock market declines. On the other hand, when interest rates are on the rise, balanced funds will typically decline less on a total return basis (current yield plus or minus principal appreciation) than a bond fund. When rates are falling, balanced funds will also outperform bond funds if stocks are also doing well.

Over the past ten years, the average balanced fund had 72 percent of the return of growth funds (11.9 percent versus 16.6 percent) with 53 percent less risk. Balanced funds are the perfect choice for the investor who cannot decide between stocks and bonds. This hybrid security is a middle-of-the-road approach, ideal for someone who wants a fund manager to determine the portfolio's weighting of stocks, bonds, and convertibles.

The price-earnings ratio for stocks in a typical balanced fund is 30, roughly 7 percent lower than the S & P 500's p/e ratio. The average beta is 0.5, which

Balanced Funds

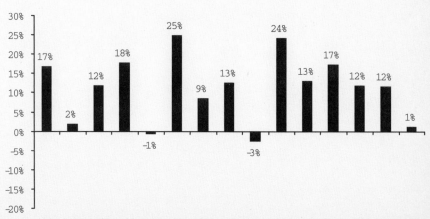

means that this group has only 50 percent of the market-related risk of the S & P 500. During the past three years, balanced funds have lagged the performance of the S & P 500 by over 4 percent annually. Over the past five years, this benchmark has outperformed balanced funds by an average of 7.6 percent per year. The figure falls to 5.5 percent annually for the past decade. Average turnover during the past three years has been 105 percent per annum. Balanced funds throw off an income stream of 2.6 percent annually. The typical annual expense ratio for this group is 1.3 percent.

Over 900 funds make up the entire balanced category (which includes asset allocation balanced, multi-asset global, and global); market capitalization is $285 billion. Three other categories—asset allocation (300 funds, total market capitalization of $85 billion), balanced (480 funds, total market capitalization of $185 billion), multi-asset global (100 funds, total market capitalization of $45 billion), and convertible (sixty funds, total market capitalization of $9 billion)—have been combined with balanced.

Alleghany/Montag & Caldwell Balanced Fund N
171 North Clark Street
Chicago, IL 60601
(800) 992-8151
www.alleghanyfunds.com

total return	★★★
risk reduction	★★★★★
management	★★★★
current income	★★
expense control	★★★★★
symbol MOBAX	19 points
up-market performance	fair
down-market performance	poor
predictability of returns	very good

Total Return   ★★★

Over the past five years (ending 12/31/00), Alleghany/Montag & Caldwell Balanced Fund N has taken $10,000 and turned it into $20,115 ($13,680 over three years). This translates into an annualized return of 15 percent over the past five years and 11 percent over the past three years. Over the past five years, this fund has outperformed 80 percent of all mutual funds; within its general category, it has done better than 92 percent of its peers. Balanced funds have averaged 11 percent annually over these same five years.

During the past five years, a $10,000 initial investment grew to $18,800 after taxes, assuming a 39.6 percent income tax bracket (state and federal combined) and a capital gains rate of 28 percent. This means that investors in this fund were able to preserve 87 percent of their total returns. Compared to other balanced and hybrid funds, this fund's tax savings are considered to be very good.

Risk/Volatility   ★★★★★

Over the past five years, Alleghany/Montag & Caldwell has been safer than 40 percent of all balanced funds. Over the past decade, the fund has had one negative year, while the S & P 500 has also had one (off 9 percent in 2000); the Lehman Brothers Aggregate Bond Index fell twice (off 3 percent in 1994 and 1 percent in 1999). The fund has underperformed the S & P 500 and the Lehman Brothers Aggregate Bond Index once in the past ten years.

	past 5 years		past 10 years	
worst year	-1%	2000	-1%	2000
best year	23%	1997	29%	1995

In the past, Alleghany/Montag & Caldwell has done better than 80 percent of its peer group in up markets but outperformed just 25 percent of its competition in down markets. Consistency, or predictability, of returns for Alleghany/Montag & Caldwell Balanced Fund N can be described as very good. This fund's risk-related return is very good.

Management   ★★★★

There are thirty-five stocks and forty fixed-income securities in this $165 million portfolio. The average balanced fund today is $340 million in size. Close to 65 percent of this fund's holdings are in stocks and 35 percent in bonds. The stocks in this portfolio have an average price-earnings (p/e) ratio of 39 and a median market capitalization of $85 billion. The average maturity of the bonds in this account is ten years; the weighted coupon rate averages 6.8 percent. The portfolio's equity holdings can be categorized as large-cap and growth-oriented issues. The portfolio's fixed-income holdings can be categorized as high-quality and medium-term.

Ronald E. Canakaris has managed this fund for the past seven years. He prefers growth over value equities. Canakaris has only experienced one bad year over the past six. Management always has somewhere between 50 percent and 70 percent in equities. The debt portion is largely in U.S. government securities and other investment-grade issues. There are fifteen funds besides Balanced Fund N within the Alleghany family. Overall, the fund family's risk-adjusted performance can be described as very good.

Current Income   ★★

Over the past year, Alleghany/Montag & Caldwell Balanced Fund N had a twelve-month yield of 1.9 percent. During this same twelve-month period, the typical balanced fund had a yield that averaged 2.6 percent.

Expenses   ★★★★★

Alleghany/Montag & Caldwell Balanced's expense ratio is 1.1 percent; it has averaged 1.1 percent annually over the past three calendar years. The average expense ratio for the 890 funds in this category is 1.4 percent. This fund's turnover rate over the past year has been 35 percent, while its peer group average has been 105 percent.

Summary

Alleghany/Montag & Caldwell Balanced Fund N excels when it comes to risk reduction and controlling expenses. The fund's turnover rate has been particularly low. Most important, management has outperformed over 92 percent of its large peer group. Investors would be smart to look into other offerings from the Alleghany/Montag & Caldwell group.

Profile

minimum initial investment $2,500	*IRA accounts available* . . . . yes
subsequent minimum investment . . . $50	*IRA minimum investment* $500
available in all 50 states. . . . . yes	*date of inception* . . . . Nov. 1994
telephone exchanges. . . . . yes	*dividend/income paid* . . . . quarterly
number of funds in family 16	*largest sector weighting* . . . . health

Calamos Convertible A
1111 East Warrenville Road
Naperville, IL 60563
(800) 823-7386
www.calamos.com

total return	★★★★
risk reduction	★★★★★
management	★★★★
current income	★★★
expense control	★★★★
symbol CCVIX	20 points
up-market performance	very good
down-market performance	very good
predictability of returns	very good

Total Return   ★★★★
Over the past five years (ending 12/31/00), Calamos Convertible A has taken $10,000 and turned it into $22,880 ($16,020 over three years and $48,070 over the past ten years). This translates into an annualized return of 18 percent over the past five years, 17 percent over the past three years, and 17 percent for the decade. Over the past five years, this fund has outperformed 90 percent of all mutual funds; within its general category, it has done better than 85 percent of its peers. Balanced funds have averaged 11 percent annually over these same five years.

During the past five years, a $10,000 initial investment grew to $20,045 after taxes, assuming a 39.6 percent income tax bracket (state and federal combined) and a capital gains rate of 28 percent. This means that investors in this fund were able to preserve 78 percent of their total returns. Compared to other balanced and hybrid funds, this fund's tax savings are considered to be good.

Risk/Volatility   ★★★★★
Over the past five years, Calamos has been safer than 85 percent of all balanced funds. Over the past decade, the fund has had one negative year, while the S & P 500 has also had one (off 9 percent in 2000); the Lehman Brothers Aggregate Bond Index fell twice (off 3 percent in 1994 and 1 percent in 1999). The fund has under-performed the S & P 500 once and the Lehman Brothers Aggregate Bond Index twice in the past ten years.

	past 5 years		past 10 years	
worst year	7%	2000	-7%	1994
best year	35%	1999	37%	1991

In the past, Calamos has done better than 85 percent of its peer group in up markets and outperformed 55 percent of its competition in down markets. Consistency, or predictability, of returns for Calamos Convertible A can be described as very good. This fund's risk-related return is excellent.

Management   ★★★★
There are twenty stocks and eighty fixed-income securities in this $130 million portfolio. The average balanced fund today is $340 million in size. Close to 85 percent of this fund's holdings are in convertibles and 12 percent in stocks. The stocks in this portfolio have an average price-earnings (p/e) ratio of 21 and a median market capitalization of $14 billion. The average quality of the convertibles in this account is BBB; the weighted yield averages 4.9 percent. The portfolio's equity holdings can be categorized as large-cap and value-oriented issues. The portfolio's convertible holdings can be categorized as barely investment grade.

John P. Calamos and Nick P. Calamos have comanaged this fund for the past fifteen years. Management has at least two-thirds of its assets in convertibles rated BBB or better. There are eight funds besides Convertible A within the Calamos family. Overall, the fund family's risk-adjusted performance can be described as excellent.

Current Income   ★★★
Over the past year, Calamos Convertible A had a twelve-month yield of 2.3 percent. During this same twelve-month period, the typical balanced fund had a yield that averaged 2.6 percent.

Expenses   ★★★★
Calamos Convertible A's expense ratio is 1.4 percent; it has averaged 1.4 percent annually over the past three calendar years. The average expense ratio for the 890 funds in this category is also 1.4 percent. This fund's turnover rate over the past year has been 90 percent, while its peer group average has been 105 percent.

Summary
Calamos Convertible A is one of only four funds in the entire book that does a very good job when it comes to predictability of returns, up-market performance, and down-market returns. The fund ranks in the top quintile when it comes to growth persistence: the ability to consistently outperform equity funds over the previous five years. This offering also excels when it comes to superior risk-adjusted return persistence. The name Calamos is synonymous with convertibles and superior risk-adjusted returns. As previously mentioned, investors are strongly encouraged to look at other Calamos funds. This group of funds has not received the attention it deserves.

Profile
minimum initial investment $500	*IRA accounts available* .... yes
subsequent minimum investment ... $50	*IRA minimum investment* $1
available in all 50 states. .... yes	*date of inception.* .... June 1985
telephone exchanges. .... yes	*dividend/income paid* .... quarterly
number of funds in family 9	*largest sector weighting* ...... services

Calamos Convertible Growth & Income A
1111 East Warrenville Road
Naperville, IL 60563
(800) 823-7386
www.calamos.com

total return	★★★★★
risk reduction	★★★★
management	★★★★
current income	★★
expense control	★★★
symbol CVTRX	18 points
up-market performance	very good
down-market performance	very good
predictability of returns	good

Total Return   ★★★★★

Over the past five years (ending 12/31/00), Calamos Convertible Growth & Income A has taken $10,000 and turned it into $28,155 ($19,070 over three years and $61,920 over the past ten years). This translates into an annualized return of 23 percent over the past five years, 24 percent over the past three years, and 20 percent for the decade. Over the past five years, this fund has outperformed 97 percent of all mutual funds; within its general category, it has done better than 99 percent of its peers. Balanced funds have averaged 11 percent annually over these same five years.

During the past five years, a $10,000 initial investment grew to $24,705 after taxes, assuming a 39.6 percent income tax bracket (state and federal combined) and a capital gains rate of 28 percent. This means that investors in this fund were able to preserve 81 percent of their total returns. Compared to other balanced and hybrid funds, this fund's tax savings are considered to be good.

Risk/Volatility   ★★★★

Over the past five years, Calamos has been safer than 65 percent of all balanced funds. Over the past decade, the fund has had one negative year, while the S & P 500 has also had one (off 9 percent in 2000); the Lehman Brothers Aggregate Bond Index fell twice (off 3 percent in 1994 and 1 percent in 1999). The fund has underperformed the S & P 500 once and the Lehman Brothers Aggregate Bond Index twice in the past ten years.

	past 5 years		past 10 years	
worst year	7%	2000	-5%	1994
best year	53%	1999	53%	1999

In the past, Calamos has done better than 75 percent of its peer group in up markets and outperformed 70 percent of its competition in down markets. Consistency, or predictability, of returns for Calamos Convertible Growth & Income A can be described as good. This fund's risk-related return is excellent.

Management   ★★★★
There are ten stocks and seventy fixed-income securities in this $65 million port-folio. The average balanced fund today is $340 million in size. Close to 85 percent of this fund's holdings are in convertibles, 10 percent is in cash, and 5 percent is in stocks. The stocks in this portfolio have an average price-earnings (p/e) ratio of 42 and a median market capitalization of $42 billion. The average quality rating of the convertibles in this account is BBB; the weighted yield averages 3.1 percent. The portfolio's equity holdings can be categorized as large-cap and growth-oriented issues. The portfolio's convertible holdings can be categorized as barely invest-ment grade.

John P. Calamos and Nick P. Calamos have comanaged this fund for the past thirteen years. Management will always have at least two-thirds of the portfolio in convertibles rated C or better; it may also invest up to a fourth of its assets in for-eign securities. This fund represents the most flexible of the Calamos offerings. There are eight funds besides Convertible Growth & Income A within the Calamos family. Overall, the fund family's risk-adjusted performance can be described as excellent.

Current Income   ★★
Over the past year, Calamos Convertible Growth & Income A had a twelve-month yield of 2.1 percent. During this same twelve-month period, the typical balanced fund had a yield that averaged 2.6 percent.

Expenses   ★★★
The expense ratio is 1.7 percent; it has averaged 1.9 percent annually over the past three calendar years. The average expense ratio for the 890 funds in this category is 1.4 percent. This fund's turnover rate over the past year has been 110 percent, while its peer group average has been 105 percent.

Summary
Calamos Convertible Growth & Income A ranks number two within its group for five-year returns. Phrased another way, it has outperformed 99 percent of all bal-anced, convertible, and other hybrid funds. The fund ranks in the top quintile when it comes to growth persistence: the ability to consistently outperform equity funds over the previous five years. This offering also excels when it comes to superior risk-adjusted return persistence. Investors are strongly encouraged to look at other Calamos funds. This group of funds has not received the attention it deserves.

Profile

minimum initial investment $500	*IRA accounts available* . . . . yes
subsequent minimum investment . . . $50	*IRA minimum investment* $1
available in all 50 states. . . . . yes	*date of inception* . . . . Sept. 1988
telephone exchanges. . . . . yes	*dividend/income paid* . . . . quarterly
number of funds in family 9	*largest sector weighting* . . . technology

Flag Investors Value Builder A
1 South Street
Baltimore, MD 21202
(800) 767-3524
www.flaginvestors.com

total return	★★★
risk reduction	★★★★
management	★★★★
current income	★★
expense control	★★★★★
symbol FLVBX	18 points
up-market performance	good
down-market performance	poor
predictability of returns	very good

Total Return   ★★★
Over the past five years (ending 12/31/00), Flag Investors Value Builder A has taken $10,000 and turned it into $20,115 ($13,310 over three years). This translates into an annualized return of 15 percent over the past five years and 10 percent over the past three years. Over the past five years, this fund has outperformed 80 percent of all mutual funds; within its general category, it has done better than 95 percent of its peers. Balanced funds have averaged 11 percent annually over these same five years.

During the past five years, a $10,000 initial investment grew to $19,105 after taxes, assuming a 39.6 percent income tax bracket (state and federal combined) and a capital gains rate of 28 percent. This means that investors in this fund were able to preserve 90 percent of their total returns. Compared to other balanced and hybrid funds, this fund's tax savings are considered to be excellent.

Risk/Volatility   ★★★★
Over the past five years, Flag Investors has been safer than just 20 percent of all balanced funds. Over the past decade, the fund has had two negative years, while the S & P 500 has had one (off 9 percent in 2000); the Lehman Brothers Aggregate Bond Index fell twice (off 3 percent in 1994 and 1 percent in 1999). The fund has underperformed the S & P 500 once and the Lehman Brothers Aggregate Bond Index twice in the past ten years.

	past 5 years		past 10 years	
worst year	0%	2000	0%	2000
best year	25%	1996	33%	1995

In the past, Flag Investors has done better than 85 percent of its peer group in up markets but outperformed just 15 percent of its competition in down markets. Consistency, or predictability, of returns for Flag Investors Value Builder A can be described as very good. This fund's risk-related return is fair.

Management   ★★★★
There are fifty-five stocks and sixty-five fixed-income securities in this $570 million portfolio. The average balanced fund today is $340 million in size. Close to 75 percent of this fund's holdings are in stocks and 25 percent in bonds. The stocks in this portfolio have an average price-earnings (p/e) ratio of 30 and a median market capitalization of $17 billion. The average maturity of the bonds in this account is seven years; the weighted coupon rate averages 7.3 percent. The portfolio's equity holdings can be categorized as large-cap and a blend of growth and value stocks. The portfolio's fixed-income holdings can be categorized as medium quality.

Hobart C. Buppert has managed this fund for the past nine years. Management invests somewhere between 40 percent and 75 percent of the portfolio in what it believes to be undervalued stocks; fixed-income always represents at least a quarter of the holdings, 90 percent or more of which must be invested in bonds rated BBB or better. Manager Buppert looks at things such as free cash flow, p/e ratios, and return on assets. There are forty-four funds besides Value Builder A within the Flag Investors family. Overall, the fund family's risk-adjusted performance can be described as good.

Current Income   ★★
Over the past year, Flag Investors Value Builder A had a twelve-month yield of 2.1 percent. During this same twelve-month period, the typical balanced fund had a yield that averaged 2.6 percent.

Expenses   ★★★★★
Flag Investors Value Builder's expense ratio is 1.1 percent; it has also averaged 1.1 percent annually over the past three calendar years. The average expense ratio for the 890 funds in this category is 1.4 percent. This fund's turnover rate over the past year has been 25 percent, while its peer group average has been 105 percent.

Summary
Flag Investors Value Builder A has annual returns that almost always place it in the top quartile. The fund has the lowest turnover of any balanced or convertible portfolio in the book and is the second-best tax minimizer in its group. This offering also excels when it comes to superior risk-adjusted return persistence. Its strongest suit is keeping overhead costs low, particularly when it comes to turnover (which can be a bigger, albeit hidden, cost than what is reflected in an expense ratio). When it comes to raw returns, this fund has outperformed 95 percent of its category and has done a particularly exceptional job when it comes to tax minimization.

Profile

minimum initial investment $2,000	*IRA accounts available* . . . . yes
subsequent minimum investment . . $100	*IRA minimum investment* $1,000
available in all 50 states . . . . yes	*date of inception* . . . . June 1992
telephone exchanges . . . . yes	*dividend/income paid* . . . . quarterly
number of funds in family 45	*largest sector weighting* . . . . . . services

Green Century Balanced
29 Temple Place, Suite 200
Boston, MA 02111
(800) 934-7336
www.greencentury.com

total return	★★★★★
risk reduction	★
management	★★★★
current income	★★★★
expense control	★
symbol GCBLX	15 points
up-market performance	excellent
down-market performance	poor
predictability of returns	fair

Total Return ★★★★★
Over the past five years (ending 12/31/00), Green Century Balanced has taken $10,000 and turned it into $27,030 ($18,160 over three years). This translates into an annualized return of 22 percent over the past three and five years. Over the past five years, this fund has outperformed 95 percent of all mutual funds; within its general category, it has done better than 90 percent of its peers. Balanced funds have averaged 11 percent annually over these same five years.

During the past five years, a $10,000 initial investment grew to $25,330 after taxes, assuming a 39.6 percent income tax bracket (state and federal combined) and a capital gains rate of 28 percent. This means that investors in this fund were able to preserve 90 percent of their total returns. Compared to other balanced and hybrid funds, this fund's tax savings are considered to be excellent.

Risk/Volatility ★
Over the past five years, Green Century has been safer than 85 percent of all balanced funds. Over the past decade, the fund has had three negative years, while the S & P 500 has had one (off 9 percent in 2000); the Lehman Brothers Aggregate Bond Index fell twice (off 3 percent in 1994 and 1 percent in 1999). The fund has underperformed the S & P 500 once and the Lehman Brothers Aggregate Bond Index three times in the past ten years.

	past 5 years		past 10 years	
worst year	-10%	1998	-10%	1998
best year	76%	1999	76%	1999

In the past, Green Century has done better than 99 percent of its peer group in up markets but outperformed just 10 percent of its competition in down markets. Consistency, or predictability, of returns for Green Century Balanced can be described as fair. This fund's risk-related return is excellent.

Management   ★★★★
There are forty stocks and thirty fixed-income securities in this $75 million port-
folio. The average balanced fund today is $340 million in size. Close to 75 percent
of this fund's holdings are in stocks and 25 percent in bonds. The stocks in this portfolio have an average price-earnings (p/e) ratio of 38 and a median market capitalization of $70 million. The average maturity of the bonds in this account is six years;
the weighted coupon rate averages 6 percent. The portfolio's equity holdings can be
categorized as small-cap and growth-oriented issues. The portfolio's fixed-income
holdings can be categorized as intermediate-term, high-quality debt. In fact, most of
the bonds are either backed by the U.S. government or one of its agencies.

Jackson Robinson has managed this fund for the past six years. Management
seeks out firms that are environmentally friendly. It cannot invest in producers of
nuclear power or tobacco products. Equity criteria includes high returns on capital
and solid earnings growth. Although classified by some sources as a "small growth
fund," Robinson has over a fourth of the fund's holdings in bonds, mostly high
yield. There is one other fund besides Balanced within the Green Century family.
Overall, the fund family's risk-adjusted performance can be described as good to
very good.

Current Income   ★★★★
Over the past year, Green Century Balanced had a twelve-month yield of 0.3 percent. During this same twelve-month period, the typical balanced fund had a yield
that averaged 2.6 percent.

Expenses   ★
Green Century Balanced's expense ratio is 2.5 percent; it has also averaged 2.5 percent annually over the past three calendar years. The average expense ratio for the
890 funds in this category is 1.4 percent. This fund's turnover rate over the past
year has been 110 percent, while its peer group average has been 105 percent.

Summary
Green Century Balanced receives top marks for performance. The fund is rated
number one among its peers during bull markets, yet also ranks number two for
capital preservation (tax minimization)—a difficult achievement. Current income
is very good and management also receives solid kudos for doing better than 90
percent of the competition.

Profile
minimum initial investment $2,000	*IRA accounts available* . . . . yes
subsequent minimum investment . . $100	*IRA minimum investment* $500
available in all 50 states. . . . . yes	*date of inception.* . . . . Mar. 1992
telephone exchanges. . . . . yes	*dividend/income paid.* . . . . semiannually
number of funds in family 2	*largest sector weighting* . . . technology

Leuthold Core Investment
100 North Sixth Street, Suite 700A
Minneapolis, MN 55403
(800) 273-6886
www.leutholdfunds.com

total return	★★★★
risk reduction	★★★★★
management	★★★
current income	★★★★★
expense control	★★★
symbol LCORX	19 points
up-market performance	poor
down-market performance	excellent
predictability of returns	excellent

Total Return   ★★★★

Over the past five years (ending 12/31/00), Leuthold Core Investment has taken $10,000 and turned it into $19,255 ($14,815 over three years). This translates into an annualized return of 14 percent over the past three and five years. Over the past five years, this fund has outperformed 75 percent of all mutual funds; within its general category, it has done better than 85 percent of its peers. Balanced funds have averaged 11 percent annually over these same five years.

During the past five years, a $10,000 initial investment grew to $17,220 after taxes, assuming a 39.6 percent income tax bracket (state and federal combined) and a capital gains rate of 28 percent. This means that investors in this fund were able to preserve 78 percent of their total returns. Compared to other balanced and hybrid funds, this fund's tax savings are considered to be good.

Risk/Volatility   ★★★★★

Over the past five years, Leuthold has been safer than 96 percent of all balanced funds. Over the past decade, the fund has had no negative years, while the S & P 500 has had one (off 9 percent in 2000); the Lehman Brothers Aggregate Bond Index fell twice (off 3 percent in 1994 and 1 percent in 1999). The fund has under-performed the S & P 500 and the Lehman Brothers Aggregate Bond Index once in the past ten years.

	past 5 years		past 10 years	
worst year	9%	1996	9%	1996
best year	23%	2000	23%	2000

In the past, Leuthold has done better than 70 percent of its peer group in up markets and outperformed 99 percent of its competition in down markets. Consistency, or predictability, of returns for Leuthold Core Investment can be described as excellent. This fund's risk-related return is excellent.

Management   ★★★

There are ninety stocks and ten fixed-income securities in this $95 million portfolio. The average balanced fund today is $340 million in size. Close to 60 percent of this fund's holdings are in stocks and 30 percent in bonds. The stocks in this portfolio have an average price-earnings (p/e) ratio of 31 and a median market capitalization of $3.2 billion. The average maturity of the bonds in this account is twenty-five years; the weighted coupon rate averages 6.9 percent. The portfolio's equity holdings can be categorized as mid-cap and a blend of growth and value stocks. The portfolio's fixed-income holdings can be categorized as high quality and long term.

Steven C. Leuthold has managed this fund for the past six years. Management fills the portfolio by following specific guidelines: 30–70 percent in equities, 30–70 percent in bonds, and 0–20 percent in money market instruments. The centerpiece of management's investment strategy is its proprietary quantitative-modeling system. Leuthold's bold bets have paid off in the past. Core Investment is the only fund within the Leuthold family.

Current Income   ★★★★★

Over the past year, Leuthold Core Investment had a twelve-month yield of 4.3 percent. During this same twelve-month period, the typical balanced fund had a yield that averaged 2.6 percent.

Expenses   ★★★

Leuthold Core Investment's expense ratio is 1.3 percent; it has also averaged 1.3 percent annually over the past three calendar years. The average expense ratio for the 890 funds in this category is 1.4 percent. This fund's turnover rate over the past year has been 150 percent, while its peer group average has been 105 percent.

Summary

Risk reduction and current income are the two most standout features of Leuthold Core Investment. The fund has the most predictable returns of any balanced, convertible, or hybrid offering as well as the lowest risk level. It also ranks number one among its peers during bear markets. Returns have also been impressive. The fund's management has outperformed 85 percent of its competitors.

Profile

minimum initial investment $10,000	*IRA accounts available* . . . . yes
subsequent minimum investment . . $100	*IRA minimum investment* $1,000
available in all 50 states. . . . . yes	*date of inception* . . . . Nov. 1995
telephone exchanges. . . . . yes	*dividend/income paid* . . . . quarterly
number of funds in family 1	*largest sector weighting* . . . . health

Nations Convertible Securities Investor A

One Bank of America Plaza, 33rd Floor
Charlotte, NC 28255
(800) 321-7854
www.bankofamerica.com/nationsfunds

total return	★★★★
risk reduction	★★★★★
management	★★★★
current income	★★★
expense control	★★★★
symbol PACIX	20 points
up-market performance	very good
down-market performance	excellent
predictability of returns	very good

Total Return   ★★★★

Over the past five years (ending 12/31/00), Nations Convertible Securities Investor A has taken $10,000 and turned it into $22,880 ($15,610 over three years and $52,340 over the past ten years). This translates into an annualized return of 18 percent over the past five years, 16 percent over the past three years, and 18 percent for the decade. Over the past five years, this fund has outperformed 90 percent of all mutual funds; within its general category, it has done better than 80 percent of its peers. Balanced funds have averaged 11 percent annually over these same five years.

During the past five years, a $10,000 initial investment grew to $19,015 after taxes, assuming a 39.6 percent income tax bracket (state and federal combined) and a capital gains rate of 28 percent. This means that investors in this fund were able to preserve 70 percent of their total returns. Compared to other balanced and hybrid funds, this fund's tax savings are considered to be poor.

Risk/Volatility   ★★★★★

Over the past five years, Nations has been safer than 90 percent of all balanced funds. Over the past decade, the fund has had one negative year, while the S & P 500 has also had one (off 9 percent in 2000); the Lehman Brothers Aggregate Bond Index fell twice (off 3 percent in 1994 and 1 percent in 1999). The fund has underperformed the S & P 500 once and the Lehman Brothers Aggregate Bond Index twice in the past ten years.

	past 5 years		past 10 years	
worst year	7%	1998	-6%	1994
best year	27%	1999	38%	1991

In the past, Nations has done better than 85 percent of its peer group in up markets and outperformed 85 percent of its competition in down markets. Consistency, or predictability, of returns for Nations Convertible Securities Investor A can be described as very good. This fund's risk-related return is excellent.

Management ★★★★

There are sixty-five stocks and sixty fixed-income securities in this $350 million portfolio. The average balanced fund today is $340 million in size. Close to 85 percent of this fund's holdings are in convertibles and 15 percent in stocks. The stocks in this portfolio have an average price-earnings (p/e) ratio of 34 and a median market capitalization of $8 billion. The average credit quality rating of the convertibles in this account is BB; the weighted yield averages 3.7 percent. The portfolio's equity holdings can be categorized as mid-cap and growth-oriented issues. The portfolio's convertible holdings can be categorized as just below investment grade.

Ed Cassens has managed this fund for the past seven years. At least two-thirds of the portfolio is normally invested in convertibles. Management favors convertibles with modest conversion premiums, thereby reducing downside risk. There are 178 funds besides Convertible Securities Investor A within the Nations family. Overall, the fund family's risk-adjusted performance can be described as good.

Current Income ★★★

Over the past year, Nations Convertible Securities Investor A had a twelve-month yield of 2.4 percent. During this same twelve-month period, the typical balanced fund had a yield that averaged 2.6 percent.

Expenses ★★★★

Nations Convertible Securities Investor's expense ratio is 1.2 percent; it has also averaged 1.2 percent annually over the past three calendar years. The average expense ratio for the 890 funds in this category is 1.4 percent. This fund's turnover rate over the past year has been 65 percent, while its peer group average has been 105 percent.

Summary

For its peer group, Nations Convertible Securities Investor A has the second-lowest risk level and is the second-best performer in a down market. Speaking of performance, the fund has outperformed 80 percent of its category. On a year-by-year basis, the fund's performance has only been in the bottom half of its category once in the past dozen years. Few funds in any category have turned in such enviable consistency. The fund ranks in the top two quintiles when it comes to growth persistence: the ability to consistently outperform equity funds over the previous five years. This offering also excels when it comes to superior risk-adjusted return persistence.

Profile

minimum initial investment $1,000	*IRA accounts available* . . . . yes
subsequent minimum investment . . $100	*IRA minimum investment* $500
available in all 50 states. . . . . yes	*date of inception* . . . . Sept. 1987
telephone exchanges. . . . . yes	*dividend/income paid* . . . . quarterly
number of funds in family 179	*largest sector weighting*. . . . . . services

Oppenheimer Global Growth & Income A

P.O. Box 5270
Denver, CO 80217
(800) 525-7048
www.oppenheimerfunds.com

total return	★★★★★
risk reduction	★★★
management	★★★★
current income	★★
expense control	★★★★
symbol OPGIX	18 points
up-market performance	very good
down-market performance	poor
predictability of returns	good

Total Return   ★★★★★

Over the past five years (ending 12/31/00), Oppenheimer Global Growth & Income A has taken $10,000 and turned it into $29,320 ($20,005 over three years and $52,340 over the past ten years). This translates into an annualized return of 24 percent over the past five years, 26 percent over the past three years, and 18 percent for the decade. Over the past five years, this fund has outperformed 98 percent of all mutual funds; within its general category, it has done better than 99 percent of its peers. Balanced funds have averaged 11 percent annually over these same five years.

During the past five years, a $10,000 initial investment grew to $26,425 after taxes, assuming a 39.6 percent income tax bracket (state and federal combined) and a capital gains rate of 28 percent. This means that investors in this fund were able to preserve 85 percent of their total returns. Compared to other balanced and hybrid funds, this fund's tax savings are considered to be very good.

Risk/Volatility   ★★★

Over the past five years, Oppenheimer has only been safer than 30 percent of all balanced funds. Over the past decade, the fund has had three negative years, while the S & P 500 has had one (off 9 percent in 2000); the Lehman Brothers Aggregate Bond Index fell twice (off 3 percent in 1994 and 1 percent in 1999). The fund has underperformed the S & P 500 once and the Lehman Brothers Aggregate Bond Index three times in the past ten years.

	past 5 years		past 10 years	
worst year	-4%	2000	-6%	1992
best year	87%	1999	87%	1999

In the past, Oppenheimer has done better than 98 percent of its peer group in up markets and outperformed 55 percent of its competition in down markets. Consistency, or predictability, of returns for Oppenheimer Global Growth & Income A can be described as good. This fund's risk-related return is excellent.

Management   ★★★★
There are fifty stocks and twenty-five fixed-income securities in this $1.5 billion portfolio. The average balanced fund today is $340 million in size. Close to 80 percent of this fund's holdings are in stocks and 20 percent in bonds. The stocks in this portfolio have an average price-earnings (p/e) ratio of 30 and a median market capitalization of $5.8 billion. The average maturity of the bonds in this account is twenty-three years. The portfolio's equity holdings can be categorized as mid-cap and growth-oriented issues. The portfolio's fixed-income holdings can be categorized as very high quality and long term.

Frank V. Jennings has managed this fund for the past six years. Management frequently owns securities in at least three foreign countries; overseas equities can constitute more than 40 percent of the portfolio's holdings. Jennings also has the prerogative to invest up to a quarter of the fund in below–investment grade bonds. There are 166 funds besides Global Growth & Income A within the Oppenheimer family. Overall, the fund family's risk-adjusted performance can be described as good.

Current Income   ★★
Over the past year, Oppenheimer Global Growth & Income A had a twelve-month yield of 0.2 percent. During this same twelve-month period, the typical balanced fund had a yield that averaged 2.6 percent.

Expenses   ★★★★
Oppenheimer Global Growth & Income's expense ratio is 1.3 percent; it has also averaged 1.3 percent annually over the past three calendar years. The average expense ratio for the 890 funds in this category is 1.4 percent. This fund's turnover rate over the past year has been 95 percent, while its peer group average has been 105 percent.

Summary
Oppenheimer Global Growth & Income A has the best five-year returns of any fund in its category, which includes balanced, convertible, and hybrid portfolios. Manager Jennings is considered to be an aggressive investor, but such an approach has certainly paid off. As an additional bonus, shareholders of this fund were able to keep 85 percent of their gains, thanks to management's savvy tax strategies. The fund ranks in the top quintile when it comes to growth persistence: the ability to consistently outperform equity funds over the previous five years. When it comes to sheer performance, this is the number one rated fund among its peers.

Profile

minimum initial investment $1,000	*IRA accounts available* . . . . yes
subsequent minimum investment . . . $25	*IRA minimum investment* $250
available in all 50 states. . . . . yes	*date of inception* . . . . Oct. 1990
telephone exchanges. . . . . yes	*dividend/income paid* . . . . annually
number of funds in family 167	*largest sector weighting* . . . technology

PaineWebber Tactical Allocation C
499 Washington Boulevard, 14th Floor
Jersey City, NJ 07310
(800) 647-1568
www.painewebber.com

total return	★★★★
risk reduction	★★★★
management	★★★★★
current income	★
expense control	★★★
symbol KPAAX	17 points
up-market performance	excellent
down-market performance	excellent
predictability of returns	very good

Total Return ★★★★
Over the past five years (ending 12/31/00), PaineWebber Tactical Allocation C has taken $10,000 and turned it into $22,880 ($14,430 over three years). This translates into an annualized return of 18 percent over the past five years and 13 percent over the past three years. Over the past five years, this fund has outperformed 95 percent of all mutual funds; within its general category, it has done better than 80 percent of its peers. Balanced funds have averaged 11 percent annually over these same five years.

During the past five years, a $10,000 initial investment grew to $22,365 after taxes, assuming a 39.6 percent income tax bracket (state and federal combined) and a capital gains rate of 28 percent. This means that investors in this fund were able to preserve 96 percent of their total returns. Compared to other balanced and hybrid funds, this fund's tax savings are considered to be excellent.

Risk/Volatility ★★★★
Over the past five years, PaineWebber has been safer than 90 percent of all balanced funds. Over the past decade, the fund has had two negative years, while the S & P 500 has had one (off 9 percent in 2000); the Lehman Brothers Aggregate Bond Index fell twice (off 3 percent in 1994 and 1 percent in 1999). The fund has underperformed the S & P 500 and the Lehman Brothers Aggregate Bond Index once in the past ten years.

	past 5 years		past 10 years	
worst year	-3%	2000	-3%	2000
best year	31%	1997	34%	1995

In the past, PaineWebber has done better than 97 percent of its peer group in up markets but outperformed just 10 percent of its competition in down markets. Consistency, or predictability, of returns for PaineWebber Tactical Allocation C can be described as very good. This fund's risk-related return is excellent.

Management   ★★★★★
There are 465 stocks and no bonds in this $825 million portfolio. The average balanced fund today is $340 million in size. Close to 35 percent of this fund's holdings are in stocks and 65 percent in money market instruments. The stocks in this portfolio have an average price-earnings (p/e) ratio of 31 and a median market capitalization of $69 billion. The average maturity of the debt instruments in this account is thirty days. The portfolio's fixed-income holdings can be categorized as extremely high quality and short term.

T. Kirkham Barneby has managed this fund for the past six years. Barneby uses an atypical approach, keeping roughly a third to half the portfolio in stocks that somewhat mimic the S & P 500 and the balance in money market instruments (or bonds when expectations are more favorable). Barneby's mix of cash, bonds, and equities is based on a quantitative model that considers short-term interest rates and stock prices, as well as expected earnings growth of U.S. equities. There are 104 funds besides Tactical Allocation C within the PaineWebber family. Overall, the fund family's risk-adjusted performance can be described as good.

Current Income   ★
Over the past year, PaineWebber Tactical Allocation C had a twelve-month yield of 1.6 percent. During this same twelve-month period, the typical balanced fund had a yield that averaged 2.6 percent.

Expenses   ★★★
PaineWebber Tactical Allocation's expense ratio is 1.6 percent; it has also averaged 1.6 percent annually over the past three calendar years. The average expense ratio for the 890 funds in this category is 1.4 percent. This fund's turnover rate over the past year has been 120 percent, while its peer group average has been 105 percent.

Summary
PaineWebber Tactical Allocation C is the only fund in its category that does a superb job during bear as well as bull markets. It is the best tax-managed balanced fund. Within its peer group, the fund ranks as the second-best performer in up markets. Manager Barneby is clearly an asset allocation tactician and one of the few managers in his business who properly understands the use of cash equivalents as well as their risk-adjusted benefits. The fund ranks in the top two quintiles when it comes to growth persistence: the ability to consistently outperform equity funds over the previous five years. This offering excels when it comes to superior risk-adjusted return persistence.

Profile
minimum initial investment $1,000	*IRA accounts available* . . . . yes
subsequent minimum investment . . $100	*IRA minimum investment* $250
available in all 50 states. . . . . yes	*date of inception* . . . . July 1992
telephone exchanges. . . . . yes	*dividend/income paid* . . . . annually
number of funds in family 105	*largest sector weighting* . . . technology

Vanguard Asset Allocation
Vanguard Financial Center
P.O. Box 2600
Valley Forge, PA 19482
(800) 662-7447
www.vanguard.com

total return	★★★
risk reduction	★★★★★
management	★★★★
current income	★★★★★
expense control	★★★★★
symbol VAAPX	22 points
up-market performance	poor
down-market performance	good
predictability of returns	excellent

Total Return   ★★★
Over the past five years (ending 12/31/00), Vanguard Asset Allocation has taken
$10,000 and turned it into $20,115 ($13,680 over three years and $40,460 over the
past ten years). This translates into an annualized return of 15 percent over the past
five years, 11 percent over the past three years, and 15 percent for the decade. Over
the past five years, this fund has outperformed 85 percent of all mutual funds;
within its general category, it has done better than 95 percent of its peers. Balanced
funds have averaged 11 percent annually over these same five years.

During the past five years, a $10,000 initial investment grew to $17,990 after
taxes, assuming a 39.6 percent income tax bracket (state and federal combined) and
a capital gains rate of 28 percent. This means that investors in this fund were able
to preserve 79 percent of their total returns. Compared to other balanced and hybrid
funds, this fund's tax savings are considered to be good.

Risk/Volatility   ★★★★★
Over the past five years, Vanguard has been safer than 75 percent of all balanced
funds. Over the past decade, the fund has had one negative year, while the S & P
500 has also had one (off 9 percent in 2000); the Lehman Brothers Aggregate Bond
Index fell twice (off 3 percent in 1994 and 1 percent in 1999). The fund has underperformed the S & P 500 and the Lehman Brothers Aggregate Bond Index once in
the past ten years.

	past 5 years		past 10 years	
worst year	5%	2000	-2%	1994
best year	27%	1997	35%	1995

In the past, Vanguard has done better than 60 percent of its peer group in up
markets and outperformed 75 percent of its competition in down markets.
Consistency, or predictability, of returns for Vanguard Asset Allocation can be
described as excellent. This fund's risk-related return is very good.

Management   ★★★★

There are 500 stocks and thirty fixed-income securities in this $8.6 billion port-folio. The average balanced fund today is $340 million in size. Close to 35 percent of this fund's holdings are in stocks and 50 percent in bonds, another 15 percent is in cash. The stocks in this portfolio have an average price-earnings (p/e) ratio of 33 and a median market capitalization of $70 billion. The average maturity of the bonds in this account is twenty-one years; the weighted coupon rate averages 8.2 percent. The portfolio's equity holdings can be categorized as large-cap and a blend of growth and value stocks. The portfolio's fixed-income holdings can be categorized as very high quality and long term.

William L. Fouse and Thomas F. Loeb have managed this fund for the past thirteen years. There are 101 funds besides Asset Allocation within the Vanguard family. Overall, the fund family's risk-adjusted performance can be described as very good.

Current Income   ★★★★★

Over the past year, Vanguard Asset Allocation had a twelve-month yield of 4.3 percent. During this same twelve-month period, the typical balanced fund had a yield that averaged 2.6 percent.

Expenses   ★★★★★

Vanguard Asset Allocation's expense ratio is 0.4 percent; it has averaged 0.5 per-cent annually over the past three calendar years. The average expense ratio for the 890 funds in this category is 1.4 percent. This fund's turnover rate over the past year has been 25 percent, while its peer group average has been 105 percent.

Summary

Vanguard Asset Allocation has had very good risk-adjusted returns over the past three, five, and ten years. The fund has the highest overall score of any fund in its category, is the second most predictable, ranks number two when it comes to risk reduction, and has the lowest expense ratio of any fund in its category. This Vanguard offering has outperformed 95 percent of its category. This offering also excels when it comes to superior risk-adjusted return persistence. Investors would be wise to check out other offerings from Vanguard.

Profile

minimum initial investment $3,000	*IRA accounts available* . . . . yes
subsequent minimum investment . . $100	*IRA minimum investment* $1,000
available in all 50 states. . . . . yes	*date of inception* . . . . Nov. 1988
telephone exchanges. . . . . yes	*dividend/income paid*. . . . semiannually
number of funds in family 102	*largest sector weighting* . . . technology

Corporate Bond Funds

Traditionally, bond funds are held by investors who require high current income and low risk. Interest income is normally paid on a monthly basis. Corporate bond funds are made up primarily of bonds issued by domestic corporations; government securities often represent a moderate part of these funds. Portfolio composition is almost always exclusively U.S. issues.

Bonds are normally purchased because of their income stream; one's principal in a bond fund fluctuates. The major influence on bond prices, and therefore the value of the fund's shares, is interest rates. There is an inverse relationship between interest rates and bond values; whatever one does, the other does the opposite. If interest rates rise, the price per share of a bond fund will fall, and vice versa.

The amount of appreciation or loss of a corporate bond fund primarily depends on the average maturity of the bonds in the portfolio; the cumulative amount of interest rate movement and the typical yield of the bonds in the fund's portfolio are distant secondary concerns. *Short-term* bond funds, made up of debt instruments with an average maturity of five years or less, are subject to very little interest-rate risk or reward. *Medium-term* bond funds, with maturities averaging between six and ten years, are subject to one-third to one-half the risk level of long-term funds. A long-term corporate bond fund will average an 8 percent increase or decrease in share price for every cumulative 1 percent change in interest rates.

Often investors can tell what kind of corporate bond fund they are purchasing by its name. Unless the fund includes the term "short" in its title, chances are that it is a medium- or long-term bond fund. Investors would be wise to contact the fund or counsel with an investment advisor to learn more about the portfolio's average maturity; most bond funds will dramatically reduce their portfolio's average maturity during periods of interest-rate uncertainty.

The average weighted maturity for the bonds in these funds is just over eight years, the average coupon rate is 6.8 percent, and the average weighted price is $985 (meaning that the bonds are worth $15 less than face value, on average). A price, or value, of par ($1,000 per bond) means that the bonds in a portfolio are worth face value and are not currently being traded at a discount (a price less than $1,000 per bond) or at a premium (some figure above $1,000). The portfolio of the "average" corporate bond fund is made up of securities purchased at a $15-per-bond discount ($985 versus $1,000 for bonds bought at face value). A portfolio manager purchases bonds at a discount for one of two reasons: to decrease the portfolio's current income, or to increase the fund's volatility slightly (the lower the coupon rate, the more susceptible a bond is to the effects of interest-rate changes).

During the past five and ten years, corporate bond funds have underperformed the Lehman Brothers Aggregate Bond Index by a little less than 1 percent per year.

Over the past three years the gap widens to a little over 1 percent. Average turnover during the past three years has been 135 percent, a surprisingly high figure given the general belief that stocks are traded (turned over) much more frequently than bonds. (The typical growth fund has a turnover rate of 105 percent annually.) The average corporate bond fund throws off an annual income stream of 6 percent. The typical annual expense ratio for this group is just under 1 percent.

Over the past fifteen years (ending 12/31/00), individual corporate bonds have underperformed common stocks by 6.5 percent per year. From 1986 through 2000, long-term corporate bonds averaged 9.5 percent compounded per year, compared to 16.0 percent for common stocks and 11.6 percent for small stocks. A $10,000 investment in corporate bonds grew to $48,700 over the past fifteen years; a similar initial investment in common stocks grew to $102,700 and $61,600 for small stocks.

Over the past half century, corporate bonds have only outpaced inflation on a pre-tax basis. A dollar invested in corporate bonds at the beginning of 1951 grew to $20.03 by the end of 2000. This translates into an average compound return of 6.2 percent per year. During this same period, $1 inflated to $6.96; this translates into an average annual inflation rate of 4 percent. Over the past fifty years, the worst year for long-term corporate bonds, on a total return basis (yield plus or minus principal appreciation or loss), was 1969, when a loss of 8 percent was suffered. The best year so far has been 1982, when corporate bonds posted a gain of 43 percent.

Over 900 funds make up the corporate bonds category. Total market capitalization of this category is $255 billion. Over the past three and five years, corporate bond funds have had an average compound return of 5 percent per year. For the decade, corporate bond funds have averaged 7 percent per year and 8 percent per annum for the past fifteen years. All of these figures represent total returns. This

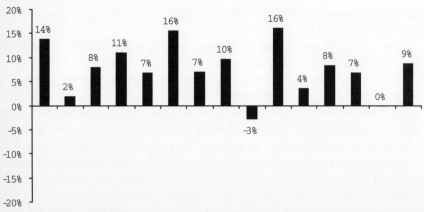

Corporate Bond Funds

means that bond appreciation (or depreciation) was added (or subtracted) from current yield.

The standard deviation for corporate bond funds has been 3 percent over the past three years. As you may recall, a low standard deviation means a greater predictability of returns (fewer surprises—for better or worse). If a fund, or fund category, such as corporate bonds, has an average annual return of 10 percent and a standard deviation of 3 percent, this means that returns for every two out of three years should be roughly 10 percent, plus or minus 3 percent (one standard deviation). If you want to increase certainty of returns, then you must look at two standard deviations. This means that returns, for about 95 percent of the time, would be 10 percent plus or minus 6 percent (or +4 percent to +16 percent). These funds have been less volatile than any equity fund and have shown similar return variances (volatility) as government bond funds.

Eaton Vance Prime Rate Reserves

255 State Street
Boston, MA 02109
(800) 225-6265
www.eatonvance.com

total return	★★★★
risk reduction	★★★★★
management	★★★★★
current income	★★★★★
expense control	★★★
symbol X3159	22 points
up-market performance	excellent
down-market performance	excellent
predictability of returns	excellent

Total Return   ★★★★

Over the past five years (ending 12/31/00), Eaton Vance Prime Rate Reserves has taken $10,000 and turned it into $13,385 ($11,910 over three years and $17,910 over the past ten years). This translates into an annualized return of 6 percent over the past three, five, and ten years. Over the past five years, this fund has outperformed 55 percent of all mutual funds; within its general category, it has done better than 90 percent of its peers. Corporate bond funds have averaged 5 percent annually over these same five years.

During the past five years, a $10,000 initial investment grew to $11,830 after taxes, assuming a 39.6 percent income tax bracket (state and federal combined) and a capital gains rate of 28 percent. This means that investors in this fund were able to preserve 54 percent of their total returns. Compared to other fixed-income funds, this fund's tax savings are considered to be very good.

Risk/Volatility   ★★★★★

Over the past five years, Eaton Vance has been safer than 90 percent of all corporate bond funds. Over the past decade, the fund has had no negative years, while the Lehman Brothers Aggregate Bond Index has had two (off 3 percent in 1994 and 1 percent in 1999); the Lehman Brothers Corporate Bond Index also fell twice (off 4 percent in 1994 and 2 percent in 1999). The fund has underperformed the Lehman Brothers Aggregate Bond Index twice and the Lehman Brothers Corporate Bond Index seven times in the past ten years.

	past 5 years		past 10 years	
worst year	4%	2000	4%	2000
best year	7%	1997	8%	1995

In the past, Eaton Vance has done better than 30 percent of its peer group in up markets and outperformed 70 percent of its competition in down markets. Consistency, or predictability, of returns for Eaton Vance Prime Rate Reserves can be described as excellent. This fund's risk-related return is very good.

Management   ★★★★★

There are 830 fixed-income securities in this $4 billion portfolio. The average corporate bond fund today is $280 million in size. Close to 100 percent of the fund's holdings are in bank loans. The average maturity of the loans in this account is three years. The portfolio's fixed-income holdings can be categorized as below investment grade.

Payson F. Swaffield and Scott H. Page have comanaged this fund for the past five years. Management only invests in investment-grade securities. The vast majority of debt instruments in the portfolio are always short term. The fund's comanagers believe in wide diversification; the top ten holdings make up just 10 percent of the entire portfolio. Although the fund is basically comprised of bank loans (which are frequently difficult to value on a daily basis), it should not be considered a substitute for a money market account. There are 148 funds besides Prime Rate Reserves within the Eaton Vance family. Overall, the fund family's risk-adjusted performance can be described as good.

Current Income   ★★★★★

Over the past year, Eaton Vance Prime Rate Reserves had a twelve-month yield of 8.1 percent. During this same twelve-month period, the typical corporate bond fund had a yield that averaged 6.1 percent.

Expenses   ★★★

Eaton Vance Prime Rate's expense ratio is 1.2 percent; it has also averaged 1.2 percent annually over the past three calendar years. The average expense ratio for the 900 funds in this category is 0.9 percent. This fund's turnover rate over the past year has been 60 percent, while its peer group average has been 135 percent.

Summary

Eaton Vance Prime Rate Reserves is the only fund in its category that does a superb job during bear as well as bull markets, as well as having the most predictable peer group results (and one of only four funds in the entire book that is classified as "excellent" in all three of these categories). As a corporate bond fund, it is the most predictable, second-best in an up market, and rated as the best when it comes to down-market performance. Risk-adjusted returns have been superb for the past three, five, and ten years. The fund has outperformed 90 percent of its peers and usually ends up in the top performance quartile on a year-by-year basis.

Profile

minimum initial investment $5,000	IRA accounts available . . . . yes
subsequent minimum investment . . . $50	IRA minimum investment $2,000
available in all 50 states. . . . . yes	date of inception . . . . Aug. 1989
telephone exchanges. . . . . yes	dividend/income paid. . . . . monthly
number of funds in family 149	average credit quality . . . . BB

FPA New Income

11400 West Olympic Boulevard, Suite 1200
Los Angeles, CA 90064
(800) 982-4372
www.fpa.com

total return	★★★★
risk reduction	★★★★
management	★★★★★
current income	★★★★★
expense control	★★★★★
symbol FPNIX	23 points
up-market performance	excellent
down-market performance	poor
predictability of returns	very good

Total Return   ★★★★

Over the past five years (ending 12/31/00), FPA New Income has taken $10,000 and turned it into $13,385 ($11,580 over three years and $23,675 over the past ten years). This translates into an annualized return of 6 percent over the past five years, 5 percent over the past three years, and 9 percent for the decade. Over the past five years, this fund has outperformed 55 percent of all mutual funds; within its general category, it has done better than 90 percent of its peers. Corporate bond funds have averaged 5 percent annually over these same five years.

During the past five years, a $10,000 initial investment grew to $11,830 after taxes, assuming a 39.6 percent income tax bracket (state and federal combined) and a capital gains rate of 28 percent. This means that investors in this fund were able to preserve 55 percent of their total returns. Compared to other fixed-income funds, this fund's tax savings are considered to be excellent.

Risk/Volatility   ★★★★

Over the past five years, FPA has been safer than 98 percent of all corporate bond funds. Over the past decade, the fund has had no negative years, while the Lehman Brothers Aggregate Bond Index has had two (off 3 percent in 1994 and 1 percent in 1999); the Lehman Brothers Corporate Bond Index also fell twice (off 4 percent in 1994 and 2 percent in 1999). The fund has underperformed the Lehman Brothers Aggregate Bond Index twice and the Lehman Brothers Corporate Bond Index four times in the past ten years.

	past 5 years		past 10 years	
worst year	3%	1999	1%	1994
best year	9%	2000	19%	1991

In the past, FPA has done better than 97 percent of its peer group in up markets but outperformed just 15 percent of its competition in down markets. Consistency, or predictability, of returns for FPA New Income can be described as very good. This fund's risk-related return is also very good.

Management ★★★★★

There are sixty-six fixed-income securities in this $490 million portfolio. The average corporate bond fund today is $280 million in size. Close to 90 percent of the fund's holdings are in bonds. The average maturity of the bonds in this account is ten years; the weighted coupon rate averages 5.5 percent. The portfolio's fixed-income holdings can be categorized as intermediate-term, high-quality debt.

Robert L. Rodriguez has managed this fund for the past seventeen years. Management invests at least 75 percent of its assets in debt instruments rated AA or higher. Although categorized as a "corporate" bond fund, this portfolio has U.S. government securities written all over it. Average maturity has varied widely over the years. Rodriguez is considered to be a contrarian among his colleagues. He also favors government-backed paper. There are three funds besides New Income within the FPA family. Overall, the fund family's risk-adjusted performance can be described as good.

Current Income ★★★★★

Over the past year, FPA New Income had a twelve-month yield of 7.4 percent. During this same twelve-month period, the typical corporate bond fund had a yield that averaged 6.1 percent.

Expenses ★★★★★

FPA New Income's expense ratio is 0.6 percent; it has also averaged 0.6 percent annually over the past three calendar years. The average expense ratio for the 900 funds in this category is 0.9 percent. This fund's turnover rate over the past year has been 20 percent, while its peer group average has been 135 percent.

Summary

FPA New Income ties for first as having the highest overall score of any fund in its category, as well as having the second-lowest turnover rate (why most bond funds have such a high turnover rate remains a mystery). This is also one of the highest scoring funds in the book, regardless of classification. This fund is appealing to any bond investor, particularly those looking for high current income with an eye toward management expense frugality. Tax savings are also considered to be excellent.

Profile

minimum initial investment $1,500	*IRA accounts available* . . . . yes
subsequent minimum investment . . $100	*IRA minimum investment* $100
available in all 50 states . . . . yes	*date of inception* . . . . Apr. 1969
telephone exchanges . . . . yes	*dividend/income paid* . . . . quarterly
number of funds in family 4	*average credit quality* . . . . AA

Fremont Bond
50 Beale Street, Suite 100
San Francisco, CA 94105
(800) 548-4539
www.fremontfunds.com

total return	★★★★★
risk reduction	★★★★
management	★★★★★
current income	★★★
expense control	★★★
symbol FBDFX	20 points
up-market performance	good
down-market performance	very good
predictability of returns	good

Total Return   ★★★★★
Over the past five years (ending 12/31/00), Fremont Bond has taken $10,000 and turned it into $14,030 ($12,250 over three years). This translates into an annualized return of 7 percent over the past five years and 7 percent over the past three years. Over the past five years, this fund has outperformed 55 percent of all mutual funds; within its general category, it has done better than 98 percent of its peers. Corporate bond funds have averaged 5 percent annually over these same five years.

During the past five years, a $10,000 initial investment grew to $12,300 after taxes, assuming a 39.6 percent income tax bracket (state and federal combined) and a capital gains rate of 28 percent. This means that investors in this fund were able to preserve 57 percent of their total returns. Compared to other fixed-income funds, this fund's tax savings are considered to be excellent.

Risk/Volatility   ★★★★
Over the past five years, Fremont has been safer than 55 percent of all corporate bond funds. Over the past decade, the fund has had two negative years, while the Lehman Brothers Aggregate Bond Index has also had two (off 3 percent in 1994 and 1 percent in 1999); the Lehman Brothers Corporate Bond Index also fell twice (off 4 percent in 1994 and 2 percent in 1999). The fund has underperformed the Lehman Brothers Aggregate Bond Index twice and the Lehman Brothers Corporate Bond Index three times in the past ten years.

	past 5 years		past 10 years	
worst year	-1%	1999	-4%	1994
best year	12%	2000	21%	1995

In the past, Fremont has done better than 95 percent of its peer group in up markets and outperformed 90 percent of its competition in down markets. Consistency, or predictability, of returns for Fremont Bond can be described as good. This fund's risk-related return is very good.

Management   ★★★★★
There are ninety-two fixed-income securities in this $255 million portfolio. The average corporate bond fund today is $280 million in size. Close to 92 percent of the fund's holdings are in bonds. The average maturity of the bonds in this account is nine years; the weighted coupon rate averages 6.7 percent. The portfolio's fixed-income holdings can be categorized as intermediate-term, high-quality debt.

William H. Gross has managed this fund for the past seven years. Even though this fund is considered to be "corporate," the majority of its assets are in U.S. agency–backed paper. Gross is considered to be one of, if not the best, bond fund managers in the country. He is also the best known and commands tremendous respect from analysts and commentators alike. Management is known for employing multiple strategies at any one time. There are nine funds besides Bond within the Fremont family. Overall, the fund family's risk-adjusted performance can be described as good.

Current Income   ★★★
Over the past year, Fremont Bond had a twelve-month yield of 6.3 percent. During this same twelve-month period, the typical corporate bond fund had a yield that averaged 6.1 percent.

Expenses   ★★★
Fremont Bond's expense ratio is 0.6 percent; it has also averaged 0.6 percent annually over the past three calendar years. The average expense ratio for the 900 funds in this category is 0.9 percent. This fund's turnover rate over the past year has been 290 percent, while its peer group average has been 135 percent.

Summary
Fremont Bond's annual returns have almost always been in the top quartile since the fund's inception. Management pursues multiple investment strategies whose diversification minimizes risk. Manager Bill Gross has been particularly adept at macroeconomics. Both returns and management are superb. Tax efficiency has also been exceptional. Risk-adjusted returns over the past three and five years have been very good.

Profile
minimum initial investment $2,000
subsequent minimum investment . . $100
available in all 50 states . . . . yes
telephone exchanges . . . . yes
number of funds in family 10

IRA accounts available . . . . yes
IRA minimum investment $1,000
date of inception . . . . Apr. 1993
dividend/income paid . . . . monthly
average credit quality . . . . AA

Lebenthal Taxable Municipal Bond
120 Broadway
New York, NY 10271
(800) 221-5822
www.lebenthal.com

total return	★★★★★
risk reduction	★★★
management	★★★★★
current income	★★★★
expense control	★★★★★
symbol X9118	22 points
up-market performance	poor
down-market performance	excellent
predictability of returns	fair

Total Return   ★★★★★
Over the past five years (ending 12/31/00), Lebenthal Taxable Municipal Bond has taken $10,000 and turned it into $14,030 ($11,910 over three years). This translates into an annualized return of 7 percent over the past five years and 6 percent over the past three years. Over the past five years, this fund has outperformed 55 percent of all mutual funds; within its general category, it has done better than 95 percent of its peers. Corporate bond funds have averaged 5 percent annually over these same five years.

During the past five years, a $10,000 initial investment grew to $12,340 after taxes, assuming a 39.6 percent income tax bracket (state and federal combined) and a capital gains rate of 28 percent. This means that investors in this fund were able to preserve 58 percent of their total returns. Compared to other fixed-income funds, this fund's tax savings are considered to be excellent.

Risk/Volatility   ★★★
Over the past five years, Lebenthal has been safer than 30 percent of all corporate bond funds. Over the past decade, the fund has had two negative years, while the Lehman Brothers Aggregate Bond Index has also had two (off 3 percent in 1994 and 1 percent in 1999); the Lehman Brothers Corporate Bond Index also fell twice (off 4 percent in 1994 and 2 percent in 1999). The fund has underperformed the Lehman Brothers Aggregate Bond Index twice and the Lehman Brothers Corporate Bond Index three times in the past ten years.

	past 5 years		past 10 years	
worst year	-7%	1999	-7%	1999
best year	16%	2000	22%	1995

In the past, Lebenthal has done better than 60 percent of its peer group in up markets and outperformed 99 percent of its competition in down markets. Consistency, or predictability, of returns for Lebenthal Taxable Municipal Bond can be described as fair. This fund's risk-related return is very good.

Management   ★★★★★

There are forty-five fixed-income securities in this $13 million portfolio. The average corporate bond fund today is $280 million in size. Close to 100 percent of the fund's holdings are in bonds. The average maturity of the bonds in this account is thirteen years; the weighted coupon rate averages 7.6 percent. The portfolio's fixed-income holdings can be categorized as long-term, high-quality debt.

James L. Gammon has managed this fund for the past seven years. There are three funds besides Taxable Municipal Bond within the Lebenthal family. Overall, the fund family's risk-adjusted performance can be described as very good to excellent.

Current Income   ★★★★

Over the past year, Lebenthal Taxable Municipal Bond had a twelve-month yield of 6.8 percent. During this same twelve-month period, the typical corporate bond fund had a yield that averaged 6.1 percent.

Expenses   ★★★★★

Lebenthal Taxable Municipal Bond's expense ratio is 0.8 percent; it has also averaged 0.8 percent annually over the past three calendar years. The average expense ratio for the 900 funds in this category is 0.9 percent. This fund's turnover rate over the past year has been 20 percent, while its peer group average has been 135 percent.

Summary

Lebenthal Taxable Municipal Bond is classified as a "corporate bond fund" because the vast majority of its holdings are in "tax-frees" issued by cities and states. Taxable munis represent a very small and narrow part of the bond market, and this offering should be considered a niche or diversification play by investors. Still, it is important to point out the numerous pluses of this fund when compared to its corporate debt peers: (1) it has the best five-year returns, (2) it ranks number one when it comes to tax minimization, (3) it has the lowest turnover, and (4) it is the best performer during down markets. Investors would also be wise to check out other offerings from Lebenthal.

Profile

minimum initial investment $2,500
subsequent minimum investment . . $250
available in all 50 states . . . . yes
telephone exchanges . . . . yes
number of funds in family 4

IRA accounts available . . . . yes
IRA minimum investment $1,000
date of inception . . . . Dec. 1993
dividend/income paid . . . . monthly
average credit quality . . . . AA

Stein Roe Intermediate Bond

P.O. Box 804058
Chicago, IL 60680
(800) 338-2550
www.steinroe.com

total return	★★★★
risk reduction	★★★★
management	★★★★
current income	★★★★
expense control	★★★
symbol SRBFX	19 points
up-market performance	excellent
down-market performance	excellent
predictability of returns	good

Total Return   ★★★★

Over the past five years (ending 12/31/00), Stein Roe Intermediate Bond has taken $10,000 and turned it into $13,385 ($11,910 over three years and $21,590 over the past ten years). This translates into an annualized return of 6 percent over the past five years, 6 percent over the past three years, and 8 percent for the decade. Over the past five years, this fund has outperformed 55 percent of all mutual funds; within its general category, it has done better than 90 percent of its peers. Corporate bond funds have averaged 5 percent annually over these same five years.

During the past five years, a $10,000 initial investment grew to $11,695 after taxes, assuming a 39.6 percent income tax bracket (state and federal combined) and a capital gains rate of 28 percent. This means that investors in this fund were able to preserve 55 percent of their total returns. Compared to other fixed-income funds, this fund's tax savings are considered to be excellent.

Risk/Volatility   ★★★★

Over the past five years, Stein Roe has been safer than 85 percent of all corporate bond funds. Over the past decade, the fund has had one negative year, while the Lehman Brothers Aggregate Bond Index has had two (off 3 percent in 1994 and 1 percent in 1999); the Lehman Brothers Corporate Bond Index also fell twice (off 4 percent in 1994 and 2 percent in 1999). The fund has underperformed the Lehman Brothers Aggregate Bond Index twice and the Lehman Brothers Corporate Bond Index six times in the past ten years.

	past 5 years		past 10 years	
worst year	1%	1999	-3%	1994
best year	11%	2000	17%	1995

In the past, Stein Roe has done better than 97 percent of its peer group in up markets and outperformed 98 percent of its competition in down markets. Consistency, or predictability, of returns for Stein Roe Intermediate Bond can be described as good. This fund's risk-related return is very good.

Management   ★★★★

There are 100 fixed-income securities in this $450 million portfolio. The average corporate bond fund today is $280 million in size. Close to 95 percent of the fund's holdings are in bonds. The average maturity of the bonds in this account is nine years; the weighted coupon rate averages 7.8 percent. The portfolio's fixed-income holdings can be categorized as intermediate-term, high-quality debt.

Michael T. Kennedy has managed this fund for the past thirteen years. Kennedy is considered to be a patient manager who keeps an eye toward the long-term when it comes to performance. He avoids interest-rate risks. His sector-rotation bets have usually paid off handsomely. There are sixteen funds besides Intermediate Bond within the Stein Roe family. Overall, the fund family's risk-adjusted performance can be described as good to very good.

Current Income   ★★★★

Over the past year, Stein Roe Intermediate Bond had a twelve-month yield of 7 percent. During this same twelve-month period, the typical corporate bond fund had a yield that averaged 6.1 percent.

Expenses   ★★★

Stein Roe Intermediate Bond's expense ratio is 0.7 percent; it has also averaged 0.7 percent annually over the past three calendar years. The average expense ratio for the 900 funds in this category is 0.9 percent. This fund's turnover rate over the past year has been 350 percent, while its peer group average has been 135 percent.

Summary

Stein Roe Intermediate Bond is one of only two funds in its category that does a superb job during bear as well as bull markets. For corporate bond funds, it is the second-best performer in up markets and the third-best during bear periods. This is also one of the few top-rated corporate bond funds that actually has the vast majority of its assets in corporate issues. (Note: a large number of "corporate" funds are heavily weighted in government and government agency issues.) The fund's risk-adjusted returns have consistently been very good over the past three, five, and ten years. Bull and bear market performance has been great.

Profile

minimum initial investment $2,500	*IRA accounts available* . . . . yes
subsequent minimum investment . . $100	*IRA minimum investment* $500
available in all 50 states. . . . . yes	*date of inception*. . . . . Dec. 1978
telephone exchanges. . . . . yes	*dividend/income paid*. . . . . monthly
number of funds in family 17	*average credit quality* . . . . A

Strong Advantage Fund-Investor Class
P.O. Box 2936
Milwaukee, WI 53201
(800) 368-1030
www.strongfunds.com

total return	★★★★
risk reduction	★★★★★
management	★★★★★
current income	★★★★
expense control	★★★
symbol STADX	21 points
up-market performance	very good
down-market performance	very good
predictability of returns	excellent

Total Return   ★★★★

Over the past five years (ending 12/31/00), Strong Advantage Fund-Investor Class has taken $10,000 and turned it into $13,385 ($11,910 over three years and $19,675 over the past ten years). This translates into an annualized return of 6 percent over the past three and five years, and 7 percent for the decade. Over the past five years, this fund has outperformed 55 percent of all mutual funds; within its general category, it has done better than 80 percent of its peers. Corporate bond funds have averaged 5 percent annually over these same five years.

During the past five years, a $10,000 initial investment grew to $11,965 after taxes, assuming a 39.6 percent income tax bracket (state and federal combined) and a capital gains rate of 28 percent. This means that investors in this fund were able to preserve 58 percent of their total returns. Compared to other fixed-income funds, this fund's tax savings are considered to be excellent.

Risk/Volatility   ★★★★★

Over the past five years, Strong has been safer than 60 percent of all corporate bond funds. Over the past decade, the fund has had no negative years, while the Lehman Brothers Aggregate Bond Index has had two (off 3 percent in 1994 and 1 percent in 1999); the Lehman Brothers Corporate Bond Index also fell twice (off 4 percent in 1994 and 2 percent in 1999). The fund has underperformed the Lehman Brothers Aggregate Bond Index twice and the Lehman Brothers Corporate Bond Index seven times in the past ten years.

	past 5 years		past 10 years	
worst year	5%	1998	4%	1994
best year	7%	2000	11%	1991

In the past, Strong has done better than 95 percent of its peer group in up markets but outperformed just 15 percent of its competition in down markets. Consistency, or predictability, of returns for Strong Advantage Fund-Investor Class can be described as excellent. This fund's risk-related return is very good.

Management ★★★★★
There are 260 fixed-income securities in this $2.1 billion portfolio. The average corporate bond fund today is $280 million in size. Close to 95 percent of the fund's holdings are in bonds. The average maturity of the bonds in this account is 0.8 years; the weighted coupon rate averages 7.2 percent. The portfolio's fixed-income holdings can be categorized as short-term, medium-quality debt.

Jeffrey A. Koch and Thomas A. Sontag have comanaged this fund for the past seven years. Management is extremely conservative when it comes to interest-rate risk but becomes much more adventurous when it comes to quality of ratings (although only a modest portion is in securities rated BB or lower). Koch and Sontag tend to invest more heavily than their peers in BB and BBB-rated paper. There are forty-five funds besides Advantage Fund-Investor Class within the Strong family. Overall, the fund family's risk-adjusted performance can be described as good.

Current Income ★★★★
Over the past year, Strong Advantage Fund-Investor Class had a twelve-month yield of 6.5 percent. During this same twelve-month period, the typical corporate bond fund had a yield that averaged 6.1 percent.

Expenses ★★★
Strong Advantage's expense ratio is 0.8 percent; it has also averaged 0.8 percent annually over the past three calendar years. The average expense ratio for the 900 funds in this category is 0.9 percent. This fund's turnover rate over the past year has been 45 percent, while its peer group average has been 135 percent.

Summary
Strong Advantage Fund-Investor Class has an amazing track record; its risk-adjusted returns have been exceptional over the past three, five, and ten years. The fund is the second-best predictable in its category. Its risk level is also lower than any other corporate bond portfolio in the book. Management has outperformed 80 percent of its peers. After-tax returns have also been tops on a comparative basis. When it comes to debt instrument management, this is as good as it gets. With such a short average maturity (less than a year), this fund could almost double as a money market account (but with a substantially higher yield).

Profile
minimum initial investment $2,500	IRA accounts available . . . . yes
subsequent minimum investment . . . $50	IRA minimum investment $250
available in all 50 states. . . . . yes	date of inception . . . . Nov. 1988
telephone exchanges. . . . . yes	dividend/income paid. . . . . monthly
number of funds in family 46	average credit quality . . . . A

Strong Corporate Bond Fund-Investor Class
P.O. Box 2936
Milwaukee, WI 53201
(800) 368-1030
www.strongfunds.com

total return	★★★★
risk reduction	★★★
management	★★★★★
current income	★★★★★
expense control	★★
symbol STCBX	19 points
up-market performance	very good
down-market performance	very good
predictability of returns	good

Total Return ★★★★
Over the past five years (ending 12/31/00), Strong Corporate Bond Fund-Investor Class has taken $10,000 and turned it into $13,385 ($11,580 over three years and $25,935 over the past ten years). This translates into an annualized return of 6 percent over the past five years, 5 percent over the past three years, and 10 percent for the decade. Over the past five years, this fund has outperformed 55 percent of all mutual funds; within its general category, it has done better than 95 percent of its peers. Corporate bond funds have averaged 5 percent annually over these same five years.

During the past five years, a $10,000 initial investment grew to $11,930 after taxes, assuming a 39.6 percent income tax bracket (state and federal combined) and a capital gains rate of 28 percent. This means that investors in this fund were able to preserve 57 percent of their total returns. Compared to other fixed-income funds, this fund's tax savings are considered to be excellent.

Risk/Volatility ★★★
Over the past five years, Strong has been safer than 80 percent of all corporate bond funds. Over the past decade, the fund has had two negative years, while the Lehman Brothers Aggregate Bond Index has also had two (off 3 percent in 1994 and 1 percent in 1999); the Lehman Brothers Corporate Bond Index also fell twice (off 4 percent in 1994 and 2 percent in 1999). The fund has underperformed the Lehman Brothers Aggregate Bond Index twice and the Lehman Brothers Corporate Bond Index three times in the past ten years.

	past 5 years		past 10 years	
worst year	0%	1999	-1%	1994
best year	12%	1997	25%	1995

In the past, Strong has done better than 65 percent of its peer group in up markets but outperformed just 15 percent of its competition in down markets.

Consistency, or predictability, of returns for Strong Corporate Bond Fund-Investor Class can be described as good. This fund's risk-related return is very good.

Management   ★★★★★
There are 170 fixed-income securities in this $955 million portfolio. The average corporate bond fund today is $280 million in size. Close to 98 percent of the fund's holdings are in bonds. The average maturity of the bonds in this account is eleven years; the weighted coupon rate averages 7.7 percent. The portfolio's fixed-income holdings can be categorized as intermediate-term, medium-quality debt.

A team has managed this fund for the past six years. Management has been willing to take on more credit risk than their peers, but this concentration in BBB-rated bonds has certainly paid off over the long haul. There are forty-five funds besides Corporate Bond Fund-Investor Class within the Strong family. Overall, the fund family's risk-adjusted performance can be described as good.

Current Income   ★★★★★
Over the past year, Strong Corporate Bond Fund-Investor Class had a twelve-month yield of 7.2 percent. During this same twelve-month period, the typical corporate bond fund had a yield that averaged 6.1 percent.

Expenses   ★★
Strong Corporate Bond's expense ratio is 0.8 percent; it has also averaged 0.8 percent annually over the past three calendar years. The average expense ratio for the 900 funds in this category is 0.9 percent. This fund's turnover rate over the past year has been 400 percent, while its peer group average has been 135 percent.

Summary
Strong Corporate Bond Fund-Investor Class is more vulnerable than most of its peers during periods of economic downturn, but the fund's superb risk-adjusted return record for the past decade speaks for itself. This portfolio has outperformed 95 percent of its peers and tax minimization has been outstanding (for a corporate bond fund). The fund ranks in the top quintile when it comes to growth persistence: the ability to consistently outperform equity funds over the previous five years. This offering also provides very good risk-adjusted return persistence. The name Strong is a dominant and highly respected name in the bond fund industry.

Profile
minimum initial investment . . . . . $2,500   *IRA accounts available* . . . . yes
subsequent minimum investment . . . $50   *IRA minimum investment* $250
available in all 50 states. . . . . yes   *date of inception*. . . . . Dec. 1985
telephone exchanges. . . . . yes   *dividend/income paid*. . . . . monthly
number of funds in family 46   *average credit quality*. . . . . BBB

Vanguard Short-Term Corporate

Vanguard Financial Center
P.O. Box 2600
Valley Forge, PA 19482
(800) 662-7447
www.vanguard.com

total return	★★★★
risk reduction	★★★★★
management	★★★★★
current income	★★★★
expense control	★★★★★
symbol VFSTX	23 points
up-market performance	excellent
down-market performance	very good
predictability of returns	very good

Total Return   ★★★★

Over the past five years (ending 12/31/00), Vanguard Short-Term Corporate has taken $10,000 and turned it into $13,385 ($11,910 over three years and $19,675 over the past ten years). This translates into an annualized return of 6 percent over the past three and five years, and 7 percent for the decade. Over the past five years, this fund has outperformed 50 percent of all mutual funds; within its general category, it has done better than 85 percent of its peers. Corporate bond funds have averaged 5 percent annually over these same five years.

During the past five years, a $10,000 initial investment grew to $11,895 after taxes, assuming a 39.6 percent income tax bracket (state and federal combined) and a capital gains rate of 28 percent. This means that investors in this fund were able to preserve 56 percent of their total returns. Compared to other fixed-income funds, this fund's tax savings are considered to be excellent.

Risk/Volatility   ★★★★★

Over the past five years, Vanguard has been safer than 60 percent of all corporate bond funds. Over the past decade, the fund has had one negative year, while the Lehman Brothers Aggregate Bond Index has had two (off 3 percent in 1994 and 1 percent in 1999); the Lehman Brothers Corporate Bond Index also fell twice (off 4 percent in 1994 and 2 percent in 1999). The fund has underperformed the Lehman Brothers Aggregate Bond Index twice and the Lehman Brothers Corporate Bond Index seven times in the past ten years.

	past 5 years		past 10 years	
worst year	3%	1999	-1%	1994
best year	8%	2000	13%	1991

In the past, Vanguard has done better than 95 percent of its peer group in up markets but outperformed just 25 percent of its competition in down markets.

Consistency, or predictability, of returns for Vanguard Short-Term Corporate can be described as very good. This fund's risk-related return is also very good.

Management   ★★★★★
There are 340 fixed-income securities in this $7.3 billion portfolio. The average corporate bond fund today is $280 million in size. Close to 97 percent of the fund's holdings are in bonds. The average maturity of the bonds in this account is 2.5 years; the weighted coupon rate averages 7 percent. The portfolio's fixed-income holdings can be categorized as short-term, medium-quality debt.

Ian A. MacKinnon and Robert F. Auwaerter have co-managed this fund for the past eighteen years. At least four-fifths of the portfolio comes from securities within the Lehman Brothers 5–10 Year Government/Corporate Bond Index. Management has some flexibility when it comes to buying and selling since it can "cherry pick" what it believes to be the very bonds within the Lehman index. There are 101 funds besides Short-Term Corporate within the Vanguard family. Overall, the fund family's risk-adjusted performance can be described as very good.

Current Income   ★★★★
Over the past year, Vanguard Short-Term Corporate had a twelve-month yield of 6.7 percent. During this same twelve-month period, the typical corporate bond fund had a yield that averaged 6.1 percent.

Expenses   ★★★★★
Vanguard Short-Term Corporate's expense ratio is 0.3 percent; it has also averaged 0.3 percent annually over the past three calendar years. The average expense ratio for the 900 funds in this category is 0.9 percent. This fund's turnover rate over the past year has been 50 percent, while its peer group average has been 135 percent.

Summary
Vanguard Short-Term Corporate, like other Vanguard funds, gets a meaningful leg up on its competitors from the get-go just by having extremely low overhead costs. This particular fund ties for first as having the highest overall score of any fund in its category and the lowest expense ratio, and it is considered the best corporate bond fund performer during bull markets. With a near-perfect overall score of 23 (out of 25 possible points), this fund is simply outstanding. Investors would be wise to check out other offerings from Vanguard.

Profile

minimum initial investment $3,000	*IRA accounts available* . . . . yes
subsequent minimum investment . . $100	*IRA minimum investment* $1,000
available in all 50 states. . . . . yes	*date of inception* . . . . Oct. 1982
telephone exchanges. . . . . yes	*dividend/income paid.* . . . . monthly
number of funds in family 102	*average credit quality* . . . . A

Global Equity Funds

International, also known as "foreign," funds invest only in stocks of foreign companies, while global funds invest in both foreign and U.S. stocks. For the purposes of this book, the universe of global equity funds shown encompasses both foreign (international) and world (global) portfolios.

The economic outlook of foreign countries is the major factor in mutual fund management's decision as to which nations and industries are to be favored. A secondary concern is the future anticipated value of the U.S. dollar relative to foreign currencies. A strong or weak dollar can detract or add to an international fund's overall performance. A strong dollar will lower a foreign portfolio's return; a weak dollar will enhance international performance. Trying to gauge the direction of any currency is as difficult as trying to figure out what the U.S. stock market will do tomorrow, next week, or the following year.

Investors who do not wish to be subjected to currency swings may wish to use a fund family that practices currency hedging for their foreign holdings. Currency hedging means that management is buying a kind of insurance policy that pays off in the event of a strong U.S. dollar. Basically, the foreign or international fund that is being hurt by the dollar is making a killing in currency futures contracts. When done properly, the gains in the futures contracts, the insurance policy, offset some, most, or all security losses attributable to a strong dollar. Some people may feel that buying currency contracts is risky business for the fund; it is not.

Like automobile insurance, currency hedging only pays off if there is an accident; that is, if the U.S. dollar increases in value against the currencies represented by the portfolio's securities. If the dollar remains level or decreases in value, so much the better; the foreign securities increase in value and the currency contracts become virtually worthless. The price of these contracts becomes a cost of doing business; as with car insurance, the protection is simply renewed. In the case of a currency contract, the contract expires and a new one is purchased, covering another period of time.

It is wise to consider investing abroad, since different economies experience prosperity and recession at different times. During the 1980s, foreign stocks were the number one performing investment, averaging a compound return of over 22 percent per year, compared to 18 percent for U.S. stocks and 5 percent for residential real estate. But during the past ten years (ending 12/31/01), U.S. stocks have outperformed foreign stocks (17.5 percent versus 8.3 percent). Over the past fifteen years (ending December 31, 2000), U.S. stocks have had an average compound annual return of 16 percent versus 11.4 percent for foreign stocks. To give you a broader perspective, take a look at how U.S. securities have fared against their foreign counterparts over each of the past twenty-five years.

Why Global Stocks and Bonds Deserve a Place in Every Investor's Portfolio

The following table shows the total return for each investment category in each of the past twenty-nine years.

year	U.S. stocks	U.S. bonds	non–U.S. stocks	non–U.S. bonds
1972	+19.0	+ 7.3	+37.4	+ 4.4
1973	−14.6	+ 2.3	−14.2	+ 6.3
1974	−26.5	+ 0.2	−22.1	+ 5.3
1975	+37.2	+12.3	+37.0	+ 8.8
1976	+24.0	+15.6	+ 3.8	+10.5
1977	− 7.2	+ 3.0	+19.4	+38.9
1978	+ 6.5	+ 1.2	+34.3	+18.5
1979	+18.6	+ 2.3	+ 6.2	− 5.0
1980	+32.3	+ 3.1	+24.4	+13.7
1981	− 5.0	+ 7.3	− 1.0	− 4.6
1982	+21.5	+31.1	− 0.9	+11.9
1983	+22.6	+ 8.0	+24.6	+ 4.3
1984	+ 6.3	+15.0	+ 7.9	− 2.0
1985	+31.7	+21.3	+56.7	+37.2
1986	+18.6	+15.6	+67.9	+33.9
1987	+ 5.3	+ 2.3	+24.9	+36.1
1988	+16.6	+ 7.6	+28.6	+ 3.0
1989	+31.6	+14.2	+10.8	− 4.5
1990	− 3.1	+ 8.3	−14.9	+14.1
1991	+30.4	+16.1	+12.5	+17.9
1992	+ 7.7	+ 8.1	−12.2	+ 7.1
1993	+10.1	+18.2	+32.6	+15.1
1994	+ 1.3	− 7.8	+ 7.8	+ 6.7
1995	+37.4	+31.7	+11.2	+19.6
1996	+23.1	− 0.9	+6.1	+4.1
1997	+ 33.3	+ 16.0	+ 1.8	- 4.3
1998	+28.6	+13.1	+20.0	+17.8
1999	+21.0	− 9.0	+27.0	− 5.1
2000	− 9.1	+ 21.5	− 14.2	− 2.6
number of years this category achieved the best results	**10**	**5**	**9**	**5**

Increasing your investment returns and reducing portfolio risk are two compelling reasons for investing worldwide. Global investing allows you to maximize your returns by investing in some of the world's best managed and most profitable companies. Japan, for example, is the world's leading producer of sophisticated electronics goods; Germany of heavy machinery; the United States of biotechnology; and Southeast Asia of commodity-manufactured goods.

Diversification reduces investment risk: Recent studies have once again proved this most basic investment principle. A 1996 study showed that the least volatile investment portfolio over the past twenty-five years (1972–1996) would have been composed of 60 percent U.S. equities and 40 percent foreign equities. These results reflect the importance of balancing a portfolio between U.S. and foreign equities.

Japan, the most economically mature country in the Pacific Basin, has become the dominant force behind the development of the newly industrialized countries (NICs) of Hong Kong, Korea, Thailand, Singapore, Malaysia, and Taiwan. As demand for Japanese products has grown and costs in Japan have risen, the search for affordable production of goods has caused Japanese investment to flow into neighboring countries, fostering their development as economically independent and prosperous nations.

The NICs, with some of the cheapest labor forces and richest untapped natural resources in the world, have recently experienced an enormous influx of international investment capital and today represent the world's fastest growing source of low-cost manufacturing. The Pacific Region, which includes Japan, Hong Kong, Korea, Taiwan, Thailand, Singapore, Malaysia, and Australia, has experienced outstanding economic growth and today represents 25 percent of the world's stock market capital—nearly double what it was fifteen years ago.

The newly industrialized countries are favored locations for the manufacture and assembly of consumer electronics products. Displaced from high-cost countries such as the United States and Japan, electronics factories in these developing countries significantly benefit from reduced labor costs. Today, in fact, Korea is the world's third-largest manufacturer of semiconductors.

The Pacific Region yields yet another country with strong economic growth: China. Opportunities to benefit from the industrialization of China come from firms listed on the Hong Kong Stock Exchange, in such basic areas as electricity, construction materials, public transportation, and fundamental telecommunications. Indeed, these low-tech and essential industries, once growth industries in the United States, are now the foundation of a natural growth progression occurring in the NICs of Southeast Asia.

Companies such as China Light and Power (Hong Kong), Siam Cement (Thailand), and Hyundai (Korea) offer much the same profit potential today as their northern European counterparts did 100 years ago, their U.S. counterparts forty years ago, and their Japanese counterparts as recently as twenty years ago.

Investors have long been familiar with the names of many of Europe's major producers—Nestlé, Olivetti, Shell, Bayer, Volkswagen, and Perrier, to name just a few. Europe's impressive manufacturing capacity, diverse industrial base, quality labor pools, and many leading, multinational, blue-chip corporations can make it an environment for growth, accessible to you through foreign funds.

With economic deregulation and the elimination of internal trade barriers, many European companies are, for the first time in history, investing in and competing for exposure to the whole European market. Companies currently restricted to manufacturing and distributing within their national boundaries will soon be able to locate facilities anywhere in Europe, maximizing the efficient employment of labor, capital, and raw materials.

The global stock category is made up of 1,500 funds: 350 "World" ($210 billion), 760 "Foreign" ($275 billion), 170 "European" ($27 billion), and 220 "Pacific" ($23 billion). Total market capitalization of this entire category is $535 billion. These funds typically throw off a dividend of less than 1 percent and have an expense ratio of 1.8 percent. The price-earnings (p/e) ratio is 30, versus a p/e ratio of 32 for the typical stock in the S & P 500.

Over the past three years, global equity funds have had an average compound return of 9.5 percent per year. The annual return for the past five years has been 8.5 percent, 9.6 percent for the past ten years, and 11.6 percent for the past fifteen years. The standard deviation for global equity funds has been 25 percent over the past three years. This means that global equity funds have experienced about 12 percent less volatility than growth funds.

International, or foreign, funds should be part of everyone's portfolio. They provide superior returns and reduce overall portfolio risk. As with any other fund category, this one should not be looked at in a vacuum. The real beauty of foreign funds shines through when they are combined with other categories of U.S. equities. According to a Stanford University study, one's overall risk level is cut in half when a global portfolio of stocks is used instead of one based on U.S. issues alone. Moreover, as already demonstrated, returns are greater when we look for opportunities worldwide instead of just domestically.

Global Equity Funds

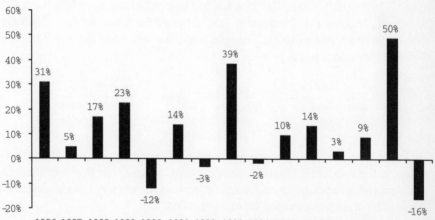

Artisan International

P.O. Box 8412
Boston, MA 02266
(800) 344-1770
www.artisanfunds.com

total return	★★★★
risk reduction	★★★★
management	★★★★★
tax minimization	★★★★
expense control	★★★★
symbol ARTIX	21 points
up-market performance	excellent
down-market performance	poor
predictability of returns	good

Total Return   ★★★★

Over the past five years (ending 12/31/00), Artisan International has taken $10,000 and turned it into $29,320 ($21,470 over three years). This translates into an annualized return of 24 percent over the past five years and 29 percent over the past three years. Over the past five years, this fund has outperformed 96 percent of all mutual funds; within its general category, it has done better than 96 percent of its peers. Global equity funds have averaged 8 percent annually over these same five years.

Risk/Volatility   ★★★★

Over the past five years, Artisan has been safer than 80 percent of all global equity funds. Over the past decade, the fund has had one negative year, while the S & P 500 has also had one (off 9 percent in 2000); the EAFE fell twice (off 12 percent in 1992 and 14 percent in 2000). The fund has underperformed the S & P 500 and the EAFE Index once in the past ten years.

	past 5 years		past 10 years	
worst year	-11%	2000	-11%	2000
best year	81%	1999	81%	1999

In the past, Artisan has done better than 97 percent of its peer group in up markets but outperformed just 10 percent of its competition in down markets. Consistency, or predictability, of returns for Artisan International can be described as good. This fund's risk-related return is excellent.

Management   ★★★★★

There are ninety-five stocks in this $3.3 billion portfolio. The average global equity fund today is $325 million in size. Close to 90 percent of the fund's holdings are in stocks. The stocks in this portfolio have an average price-earnings (p/e) ratio of 27 and a median market capitalization of $13 billion. The portfolio's equity holdings can be categorized as large-cap and a blend of growth and value stocks.

Mark L. Yockey has managed this fund for the past six years. Management invests at least two-thirds of the portfolio's assets in foreign equities. Yockey avoids entire marketplaces he believes are overvalued. He favors stocks of companies that are either market leaders or are increasing market share in what are considered strong industry groups. Approximately one-fifth of the fund is in United Kingdom stocks, with Japan representing about 10 percent of the holdings. There are three funds besides International within the Artisan family. Overall, the fund family's risk-adjusted performance can be described as very good.

Tax Minimization ★★★★

During the past five years, a $10,000 initial investment grew to $26,615 after taxes, assuming a 39.6 percent income tax bracket (state and federal combined) and a capital gains rate of 28 percent. This means that investors in this fund were able to preserve 86 percent of their total returns. Compared to other equity funds, this fund's tax savings are considered to be very good.

Expenses ★★★★

Artisan International's expense ratio is 1.3 percent; it has averaged 1.4 percent annually over the past three calendar years. The average expense ratio for the 1,500 funds in this category is 1.8 percent. This fund's turnover rate over the past year has been 95 percent, while its peer group average has been 90 percent.

Summary

Artisan International scores a very good or excellent in every single category; fund management is considered to be outstanding. Since the fund's inception, risk-adjusted returns have been great. U.S. equities represent only a very small part of the portfolio. Overall score is an impressive 21 (out of 25 possible points). Management excels during bull market periods. Tax minimization has also been quite good. Investors would be wise to check out other offerings from the Artisan family of funds.

Profile

minimum initial investment $1,000	*IRA accounts available* . . . . yes
subsequent minimum investment . . . $50	*IRA minimum investment* $1,000
available in all 50 states. . . . . yes	*date of inception*. . . . . Dec. 1995
telephone exchanges. . . . . yes	*dividend/income paid* . . . . annually
number of funds in family 4	*largest sector weighting*. . . . . . services

Citizens Global Equity-Standard Shares
230 Commerce Way, Suite 300
Portsmouth, NH 03801
(800) 223-7010
www.citizensfunds.com

total return	★★★★
risk reduction	★★★★
management	★★★★
tax minimization	★★★★★
expense control	★★★
symbol WAGEX	20 points
up-market performance	very good
down-market performance	very good
predictability of returns	very good

Total Return   ★★★★

Over the past five years (ending 12/31/00), Citizens Global Equity-Standard Shares has taken $10,000 and turned it into $24,885 ($18,610 over three years). This translates into an annualized return of 20 percent over the past five years and 23 percent over the past three years. Over the past five years, this fund has outperformed 95 percent of all mutual funds; within its general category, it has done better than 90 percent of its peers. Global equity funds have averaged 8 percent annually over these same five years.

Risk/Volatility   ★★★★

Over the past five years, Citizens has been safer than 50 percent of all global equity funds. Over the past decade, the fund has had one negative year, while the S & P 500 has had one (off 9 percent in 2000); the EAFE fell twice (off 12 percent in 1992 and 14 percent in 2000). The fund has underperformed the S & P 500 twice and has outperformed the EAFE Index every year for the past ten years.

	past 5 years		past 10 years	
worst year	-19%	2000	-19%	2000
best year	74%	1999	74%	1999

In the past, Citizens has done better than 85 percent of its peer group in up markets but outperformed just 40 percent of its competition in down markets. Consistency, or predictability, of returns for Citizens Global Equity-Standard Shares can be described as very good. This fund's risk-related return is excellent.

Management   ★★★★

There are seventy-five stocks in this $320 million portfolio. The average global equity fund today is $325 million in size. Close to 90 percent of the fund's holdings are in stocks. The stocks in this portfolio have an average price-earnings (p/e) ratio of 38 and a median market capitalization of $31 billion. The portfolio's equity holdings can be categorized as large-cap and growth-oriented issues.

Sevgi Ipek has managed this fund for the past six years. A little over a third of the portfolio is in domestic stocks, with the United Kingdom, Japan, and France running a distant second, third, and fourth place. Management is very concerned with a company's financial strength and will not consider a corporation involved with alcohol, tobacco, or weapons. Ipek is particularly fond of companies with improving market share in rapidly growing industries. There are seven funds besides Global Equity-Standard Shares within the Citizens family. Overall, the fund family's risk-adjusted performance can be described as very good.

Tax Minimization ★★★★★
During the past five years, a $10,000 initial investment grew to $24,440 after taxes, assuming a 39.6 percent income tax bracket (state and federal combined) and a capital gains rate of 28 percent. This means that investors in this fund were able to preserve 97 percent of their total returns. Compared to other equity funds, this fund's tax savings are considered to be excellent.

Expenses ★★★
Citizens Global Equity-Standard's expense ratio is 2 percent; it has averaged 2.1 percent annually over the past three calendar years. The average expense ratio for the 1,500 funds in this category is 1.8 percent. This fund's turnover rate over the past year has been 60 percent, while its peer group average has been 90 percent.

Summary
Citizens Global Equity-Standard is one of only four funds in the entire book that does a very good job when it comes to predictability of returns and up- and down-market performance. Risk-adjusted returns have been superior over the past three and five years. This fund is also the most tax-efficient in its entire category (foreign and global equity funds). The fund ranks in the top quintile when it comes to growth persistence: the ability to consistently outperform equity funds over the previous five years. Investors would be wise to check out other offerings from the Citizens family.

Profile
minimum initial investment $2,500	*IRA accounts available* . . . . yes
subsequent minimum investment . . . $50	*IRA minimum investment* $1,000
available in all 50 states. . . . . yes	*date of inception* . . . . Feb. 1994
telephone exchanges. . . . . yes	*dividend/income paid* . . . . annually
number of funds in family 8	*largest sector weighting* . . . technology

Julius Baer International Equity A

Exchange Place
P.O. Box 1376
Boston, MA 02104
(800) 435-4659
www.juliusbaer.com

total return	★★★★
risk reduction	★★★★
management	★★★★
tax minimization	★★★★★
expense control	★★★
symbol BJBIX	20 points
up-market performance	very good
down-market performance	poor
predictability of returns	very good

Total Return   ★★★★

Over the past five years (ending 12/31/00), Julius Baer International Equity A has taken $10,000 and turned it into $28,155 ($20,485 over three years). This translates into an annualized return of 23 percent over the past five years and 27 percent over the past three years. Over the past five years, this fund has outperformed 97 percent of all mutual funds; within its general category, it has done better than 97 percent of its peers. Global equity funds have averaged 8 percent annually over these same five years.

Risk/Volatility   ★★★★

Over the past five years, Julius Baer has been safer than 75 percent of all global equity funds. Over the past decade, the fund has had three negative years, while the S & P 500 has had one (off 9 percent in 2000); the EAFE fell twice (off 12 percent in 1992 and 14 percent in 2000). The fund has underperformed the S & P 500 and the EAFE Index once in the past ten years.

	past 5 years		past 10 years	
worst year	-8%	2000	-34%	1994
best year	77%	1999	77%	1999

In the past, Julius Baer has done better than 95 percent of its peer group in up markets but outperformed just 20 percent of its competition in down markets. Consistency, or predictability, of returns for Julius Baer International Equity A can be described as very good. This fund's risk-related return is excellent.

Management   ★★★★

There are 200 stocks in this $240 million portfolio. The average global equity fund today is $325 million in size. Close to 85 percent of the fund's holdings are in stocks. The stocks in this portfolio have an average price-earnings (p/e) ratio of 27 and a median market capitalization of $19 billion. The portfolio's equity holdings can be categorized as large-cap and a blend of growth and value stocks.

Rudolph-Riad Younes and Richard C. Pell have managed this fund for the past six years. Management does not invest in U.S. securities. The four largest country weightings are the United Kingdom, Germany, France, and Japan. Regional weighting is based on the mangers' expectations concerning a country's projected level of inflation, governmental impact on corporations, prospects for economic growth, and strength in currency. Younes and Pell use a quantitative approach that can vary from country to country. There is one other fund besides International Equity A within the Julius Baer Investment family. Overall, the fund family's risk-adjusted performance can be described as very good.

Tax Minimization   ★★★★★
During the past five years, a $10,000 initial investment grew to $27,430 after taxes, assuming a 39.6 percent income tax bracket (state and federal combined) and a capital gains rate of 28 percent. This means that investors in this fund were able to preserve 96 percent of their total returns. Compared to other equity funds, this fund's tax savings are considered to be excellent.

Expenses   ★★★
Julius Baer International's expense ratio is 2 percent; it has averaged 2 percent annually over the past three calendar years. The average expense ratio for the 1,500 funds in this category is 1.8 percent. This fund's turnover rate over the past year has been 70 percent, while its peer group average has been 90 percent.

Summary
Julius Baer International has turned in excellent risk-adjusted returns for the past three and five years. On a sheer performance basis, management has outshone 95 of its competitors. Returns on an after-tax basis have also been extremely impressive; the fund ranks number two within its category when it comes to tax efficiency. The fund rates in the top quintile when it comes to growth persistence: the ability to consistently outperform equity funds over the previous five years. This offering also excels when it comes to superior risk-adjusted return persistence. Investors would be wise to check out other offerings from the Julius Baer group.

Profile
minimum initial investment $2,500
subsequent minimum investment . $1,000
available in all 50 states. . . . . yes
telephone exchanges. . . . . yes
number of funds in family 2

IRA accounts available . . . . yes
IRA minimum investment $100
date of inception . . . . Oct. 1993
dividend/income paid . . . . annually
largest sector weighting . . . . financials

Merrill Lynch Global SmallCap D
Box 9011
Princeton, NJ 08543
(800) 995-6526
www.ml.com

total return	★★★★
risk reduction	★★★★
management	★★★★
tax minimization	★★★★★
expense control	★★
symbol MDGCX	19 points
up-market performance	excellent
down-market performance	very good
predictability of returns	good

Total Return   ★★★★
Over the past five years (ending 12/31/00), Merrill Lynch Global SmallCap D has taken $10,000 and turned it into $24,885 ($24,065 over three years). This translates into an annualized return of 20 percent over the past five years and 34 percent over the past three years. Over the past five years, this fund has outperformed 95 percent of all mutual funds; within its general category, it has done better than 90 percent of its peers. Global equity funds have averaged 8 percent annually over these same five years.

Risk/Volatility   ★★★★
Over the past five years, Merrill Lynch has been safer than 45 percent of all global equity funds. Over the past decade, the fund has had one negative year, while the S & P 500 has also had one (off 9 percent in 2000); the EAFE fell twice (off 12 percent in 1992 and 14 percent in 2000). The fund has underperformed the S & P 500 once and has outperformed the EAFE Index every year for the past ten years.

	past 5 years		past 10 years	
worst year	-9%	1997	-9%	1997
best year	107%	1999	107%	1999

In the past, Merrill Lynch has done better than 99 percent of its peer group in up markets but outperformed just 35 percent of its competition in down markets. Consistency, or predictability, of returns for Merrill Lynch Global SmallCap D can be described as good. This fund's risk-related return is excellent.

Management   ★★★★
There are 185 stocks in this $34 million portfolio. The average global equity fund today is $325 million in size. Close to 90 percent of the fund's holdings are in stocks. The stocks in this portfolio have an average price-earnings (p/e) ratio of 31 and a median market capitalization of $1.2 billion. The portfolio's equity holdings can be categorized as mid-cap and growth-oriented issues. The description of the

typical equity holding being "mid-cap" is somewhat misleading since roughly two-thirds of the fund's assets are in small-cap companies. Ken Chiang has managed this fund for the past seven years. With roughly half the portfolio in U.S. issues, Japan, Germany, and South Korea are distant second, third, and fourth when it comes to country exposure.

There are 260 funds besides Global SmallCap D within the Merrill Lynch family. Overall, the fund family's risk-adjusted performance is good.

Tax Minimization   ★★★★★
During the past five years, a $10,000 initial investment grew to $23,845 after taxes, assuming a 39.6 percent income tax bracket (state and federal combined) and a capital gains rate of 28 percent. This means that investors in this fund were able to preserve 93 percent of their total returns. Compared to other equity funds, this fund's tax savings are considered to be excellent.

Expenses   ★★
Merrill Lynch Global SmallCap's expense ratio is 1.6 percent; it has averaged 2 percent annually over the past three calendar years. The average expense ratio for the 1,500 funds in this category is 1.8 percent. This fund's turnover rate over the past year has been 215 percent, while its peer group average has been 90 percent.

Summary
Merrill Lynch Global SmallCap D has outperformed 95 percent of all mutual funds and 90 percent of all global and foreign stock funds. Within its category, it is rated as the number one performer during a bull market. Tax minimization has also been outstanding. It has outperformed the EAFE index for each of the past ten years and has only underperformed the S & P 500 once during the same period. Management takes a fundamental approach toward the portfolio. Equity changes can sometimes take place rather quickly.

Profile
minimum initial investment $1,000
subsequent minimum investment . . . $50
available in all 50 states. . . . . yes
telephone exchanges. . . . . yes
number of funds in family 261

IRA accounts available . . . . yes
IRA minimum investment $100
date of inception . . . . Aug. 1994
dividend/income paid . . . . annually
largest sector weighting . . . . financials

New Perspective
333 South Hope Street
Los Angeles, CA 90071
(800) 421-4120
www.americanfunds.com

total return	★★★
risk reduction	★★★★★
management	★★★★★
tax minimization	★★★★
expense control	★★★★★
symbol ANWPX	22 points
up-market performance	good
down-market performance	excellent
predictability of returns	excellent

Total Return   ★★★

Over the past five years (ending 12/31/00), New Perspective has taken $10,000 and turned it into $22,880 ($16,850 over three years and $44,115 over the past ten years). This translates into an annualized return of 18 percent over the past five years, 19 percent over the past three years, and 16 percent for the decade. Over the past five years, this fund has outperformed 90 percent of all mutual funds; within its general category, it has done better than 85 percent of its peers. Global equity funds have averaged 8 percent annually over these same five years.

Risk/Volatility   ★★★★★

Over the past five years, New Perspective has been safer than 90 percent of all global equity funds. Over the past decade, the fund has had one negative year, while the S & P 500 has also had one (off 9 percent in 2000); the EAFE fell twice (off 12 percent in 1992 and 14 percent in 2000). The fund has underperformed the S & P 500 once and has outperformed the EAFE Index every year for the past ten years.

	past 5 years		past 10 years	
worst year	-7%	2000	-7%	2000
best year	40%	1999	40%	1999

In the past, New Perspective has done better than 75 percent of its peer group in up markets and outperformed 90 percent of its competition in down markets. Consistency, or predictability, of returns for New Perspective can be described as excellent. This fund's risk-related return is excellent.

Management   ★★★★★

There are 260 stocks in this $31 billion portfolio. The average global equity fund today is $325 million in size. Close to 85 percent of the fund's holdings are in stocks, the balance is in money market instruments. The stocks in this portfolio have an average price-earnings (p/e) ratio of 32 and a median market capitalization of $27 billion. The portfolio's equity holdings can be categorized as large-cap and growth-oriented issues.

A team has managed this fund for the past nineteen years. This is a global fund, with the United States representing close to a third of the entire portfolio, followed by Japan (10 percent), the United Kingdom (8 percent), and France (4 percent). Management looks for changes in international-trade patterns as well as alterations in political relationships. The multimanager approach to running this fund has been extremely beneficial. There are twenty-nine funds besides New Perspective within the American Funds family. Overall, the fund family's risk-adjusted performance can be described as very good.

Tax Minimization ★★★★
During the past five years, a $10,000 initial investment grew to $21,335 after taxes, assuming a 39.6 percent income tax bracket (state and federal combined) and a capital gains rate of 28 percent. This means that investors in this fund were able to preserve 88 percent of their total returns. Compared to other equity funds, this fund's tax savings are considered to be very good.

Expenses ★★★★★
New Perspective's expense ratio is 0.8 percent; it has also averaged 0.8 percent annually over the past three calendar years. The average expense ratio for the 1,500 funds in this category is 1.8 percent. This fund's turnover rate over the past year has been 25 percent, while its peer group average has been 90 percent.

Summary
New Perspective is just one of several members of the American Funds group to appear in this and all previous eleven editions of this book. Despite its low-key approach and almost avoidance of publicity, American Funds has been one of the largest and most popular fund families in the country. (Note: Few of the offerings include the word "American" in their title.) New Perspective ties for first as having the highest overall score of any fund in its category and is the second most consistent within its entire category (foreign and global stock funds). The fund also has the lowest expense ratio and the second-lowest turnover. It ranks number one among its peers for bear market returns. Investors would be wise to check out other offerings from the American Funds group.

Profile
minimum initial investment $250
subsequent minimum investment . . . $50
available in all 50 states. . . . . yes
telephone exchanges. . . . . yes
number of funds in family 30

IRA accounts available . . . . yes
IRA minimum investment $250
date of inception. . . . . Mar. 1973
dividend/income paid. . . . semiannually
largest sector weighting . . . technology

Oppenheimer Global A
P.O. Box 5270
Denver, CO 80217
(800) 525-7048
www.oppenheimerfunds.com

total return	★★★★
risk reduction	★★★★
management	★★★★
tax minimization	★★★
expense control	★★★★
symbol OPPAX	19 points
up-market performance	excellent
down-market performance	excellent
predictability of returns	very good

Total Return   ★★★★
Over the past five years (ending 12/31/00), Oppenheimer Global A has taken $10,000 and turned it into $27,030 ($18,609 over three years and $48,068 over the past ten years). This translates into an annualized return of 22 percent over the past five years, 23 percent over the past three years, and 17 percent for the decade. Over the past five years, this fund has outperformed 96 percent of all mutual funds; within its general category, it has done better than 93 percent of its peers. Global equity funds have averaged 8 percent annually over these same five years.

Risk/Volatility   ★★★★
Over the past five years, Oppenheimer Global A has been safer than 75 percent of all global equity funds. Over the past decade, the fund has had two negative years, while the S & P 500 has had one (off 9 percent in 2000); the EAFE fell twice (off 12 percent in 1992 and 14 percent in 2000). The fund has underperformed the S & P 500 once and has outperformed the EAFE Index every year for the past ten years.

	past 5 years		past 10 years	
worst year	4%	2000	-14%	1992
best year	58%	1999	58%	1999

In the past, Oppenheimer Global A has done better than 96 percent of its peer group in up markets but outperformed just 38 percent of its competition in down markets. Consistency, or predictability, of returns for Oppenheimer Global A can be described as very good. This fund's risk-related return is excellent.

Management   ★★★★
There are 115 stocks in this $6.2 billion portfolio. The average global equity fund today is $325 million in size. Close to 90 percent of the fund's holdings are in stocks. The stocks in this portfolio have an average price-earnings (p/e) ratio of 31 and a median market capitalization of $12 billion. The portfolio's equity holdings can be categorized as large-cap and growth-oriented issues.

William L. Wilby has managed this fund for the past nine years. Country exposure is as follows: over a third in U.S. equities, roughly 15 percent in U.K. stocks, 10 percent in France, and 9 percent in Germany. Wilby has become more value-conscious in recent quarters. There are 166 funds besides Global A within the Oppenheimer family. Overall, the fund family's risk-adjusted performance can be described as good.

Tax Minimization   ★★★
During the past five years, a $10,000 initial investment grew to $24,135 after taxes, assuming a 39.6 percent income tax bracket (state and federal combined) and a capital gains rate of 28 percent. This means that investors in this fund were able to preserve 83 percent of their total returns. Compared to other equity funds, this fund's tax savings are considered to be good.

Expenses   ★★★★
Oppenheimer Global's expense ratio is 1.2 percent; it has also averaged 1.2 percent annually over the past three calendar years. The average expense ratio for the 1,500 funds in this category is 1.8 percent. This fund's turnover rate over the past year has been 65 percent, while its peer group average has been 90 percent.

Summary
Oppenheimer Global A is the only fund in its category that does a superb job during bear as well as bull markets. When it comes to raw numbers, the fund has outperformed 93 percent of its peer group and done better than the EAFE index for each of the past ten years. Risk-adjusted returns have been excellent for the past three, five, and ten years. This Oppenheimer offering gets solid marks across the board. It should not disappoint world equity investors in any respect.

Profile
minimum initial investment . . . . . $1,000   *IRA accounts available* . . . . yes
subsequent minimum investment . . . $25   *IRA minimum investment* $250
available in all 50 states. . . . . yes   *date of inception*. . . . . Dec. 1969
telephone exchanges. . . . . yes   *dividend/income paid* . . . . annually
number of funds in family 167   *largest sector weighting* . . . technology

Pilgrim International SmallCap A
40 North Central Avenue, Suite 1200
Phoenix, AZ 85004
(800) 334-3444
www.pilgrimfunds.com

total return	★★★★★
risk reduction	★★★
management	★★★★
tax minimization	★★★★★
expense control	★★
symbol NIGRX	19 points
up-market performance	excellent
down-market performance	fair
predictability of returns	good

Total Return   ★★★★★
Over the past five years (ending 12/31/00), Pilgrim International SmallCap A has taken $10,000 and turned it into $33,040 ($25,155 over three years). This translates into an annualized return of 27 percent over the past five years and 36 percent over the past three years. Over the past five years, this fund has outperformed 99 percent of all mutual funds; within its general category, it has done better than 99 percent of its peers. Global equity funds have averaged 8 percent annually over these same five years.

Risk/Volatility   ★★★
Over the past five years, Pilgrim has been safer than 30 percent of all global equity funds. Over the past decade, the fund has had one negative year, while the S & P 500 has also had one (off 9 percent in 2000); the EAFE fell twice (off 12 percent in 1992 and 14 percent in 2000). The fund has underperformed the S & P 500 once and the EAFE Index once in the past ten years.

	past 5 years		past 10 years	
worst year	-17%	2000	-17%	2000
best year	122%	1999	122%	1999

In the past, Pilgrim has done better than 97 percent of its peer group in up markets and outperformed 50 percent of its competition in down markets. Consistency, or predictability, of returns for Pilgrim International SmallCap A can be described as good. This fund's risk-related return is excellent.

Management   ★★★★
There are 135 stocks in this $230 million portfolio. The average global equity fund today is $325 million in size. Close to 92 percent of the fund's holdings are in stocks. The stocks in this portfolio have an average price-earnings (p/e) ratio of 36 and a median market capitalization of $2.2 billion. The portfolio's equity holdings can be categorized as mid-cap and growth-oriented issues.

A team has managed this fund for the past seven years. Management does not invest in U.S. equities. The four most heavily weighted countries in the portfolio are Japan, Germany, Switzerland, and Canada. A small amount of the fund is invested in emerging markets. Management has been successful at blending old with new economy stocks. There are ninety-seven funds besides International SmallCap A within the Pilgrim family. Overall, the fund family's risk-adjusted performance can be described as good.

Tax Minimization ★★★★★

During the past five years, a $10,000 initial investment grew to $31,200 after taxes, assuming a 39.6 percent income tax bracket (state and federal combined) and a capital gains rate of 28 percent. This means that investors in this fund were able to preserve 92 percent of their total returns. Compared to other equity funds, this fund's tax savings are considered to be excellent.

Expenses ★★

Pilgrim International SmallCap's expense ratio is 1.7 percent; it has averaged 1.9 percent annually over the past three calendar years. The average expense ratio for the 1,500 funds in this category is 1.8 percent. This fund's turnover rate over the past year has been 160 percent, while its peer group average has been 90 percent.

Summary

Pilgrim International SmallCap A ranks as the best three- and five-year performer in its category, foreign and global stock funds. Management has outperformed more than 99 percent of its competition. Risk-adjusted returns have been just as impressive over the past three and five years. Tax efficiency has also been exceptional. On a year-by-year basis, annual returns are usually in the top quartile of its peer group. The funds managers are to be congratulated for being able to successfully integrate more conservative positions with high-growth prospects.

Profile

minimum initial investment $1,000	*IRA accounts available* . . . . yes
subsequent minimum investment . . $100	*IRA minimum investment* $250
available in all 50 states. . . . . yes	*date of inception* . . . . Aug. 1994
telephone exchanges. . . . . yes	*dividend/income paid* . . . . annually
number of funds in family 98	*largest sector weighting* . . . technology

Tweedy, Browne Global Value

52 Vanderbilt Avenue
New York, NY 10017
(800) 432-4789
www.tweedy.com

total return	★★★
risk reduction	★★★★★
management	★★★★★
tax minimization	★★★★
expense control	★★★★★
symbol TBGVX	22 points
up-market performance	fair
down-market performance	fair
predictability of returns	excellent

Total Return   ★★★

Over the past five years (ending 12/31/00), Tweedy, Browne Global Value has taken $10,000 and turned it into $22,880 ($15,610 over three years). This translates into an annualized return of 18 percent over the past five years and 16 percent over the past three years. Over the past five years, this fund has outperformed 95 percent of all mutual funds; within its general category, it has done better than 96 percent of its peers. Global equity funds have averaged 8 percent annually over these same five years.

Risk/Volatility   ★★★★★

Over the past five years, Tweedy, Browne has been safer than 99 percent of all global equity funds. Over the past decade, the fund has had no negative years, while the S & P 500 has had one (off 9 percent in 2000); the EAFE fell twice (off 12 percent in 1992 and 14 percent in 2000). The fund has underperformed the S & P 500 once and the EAFE Index once in the past ten years.

	past 5 years		past 10 years	
worst year	11%	1998	4%	1994
best year	25%	1999	25%	1999

In the past, Tweedy, Browne has done better than 85 percent of its peer group in up markets and outperformed 55 percent of its competition in down markets. Consistency, or predictability, of returns for Tweedy, Browne Global Value can be described as excellent. This fund's risk-related return is excellent.

Management   ★★★★★

There are 209 stocks in this $3.5 billion portfolio. The average global equity fund today is $325 million in size. Close to 85 percent of the fund's holdings are in stocks. The stocks in this portfolio have an average price-earnings (p/e) ratio of 22 and a median market capitalization of $2.5 billion. The portfolio's equity holdings can be categorized as mid-cap and value-oriented issues.

A team has managed this fund for the past eight years. The four most heavily weighted countries in the portfolio are Japan, the United States, the United Kingdom, and Switzerland. Management prefers to invest only in companies that have at least three years of operations. The managers look for stocks they believe are undervalued compared to the company's earning power or assets. There is one other fund besides Global Value within the Tweedy, Browne family. Overall, the fund family's risk-adjusted performance can be described as excellent.

Tax Minimization ★★★★
During the past five years, a $10,000 initial investment grew to $21,150 after taxes, assuming a 39.6 percent income tax bracket (state and federal combined) and a capital gains rate of 28 percent. This means that investors in this fund were able to preserve 89 percent of their total returns. Compared to other equity funds, this fund's tax savings are considered to be very good.

Expenses ★★★★★
Tweedy, Browne Global Value's expense ratio is 1.4 percent; it has also averaged 1.4 percent annually over the past three calendar years. The average expense ratio for the 1,500 funds in this category is 1.8 percent. This fund's turnover rate over the past year has been 16 percent, while its peer group average has been 90 percent.

Summary
Tweedy, Browne Global Value ties for first as having the highest overall score of any fund in its category. It is also the most predictable, has the lowest risk, and has the lowest turnover of any global or foreign equity fund in the book. The fund has outperformed 96 percent of its peers and tax efficiency has been very good. Risk-adjusted returns have been superior for the past three and five years. Historically, the fund has had high returns with low risk. Investors are strongly encouraged to look at other Tweedy, Browne offerings.

Profile

minimum initial investment $2,500	*IRA accounts available* . . . . yes
subsequent minimum investment . . $250	*IRA minimum investment* $500
available in all 50 states. . . . . yes	*date of inception*. . . . . June 1993
telephone exchanges. . . . . yes	*dividend/income paid* . . . . annually
number of funds in family 2	*largest sector weighting* . . . . financials

W&R International Growth C

6300 Lamar Avenue
P.O. Box 29217
Shawnee Mission, KS 66201
(800) 366-5465
www.waddell.com

total return	★★★★
risk reduction	★★★
management	★★★★
tax minimization	★★★★★
expense control	★★
symbol WRICX	18 points
up-market performance	very good
down-market performance	good
predictability of returns	good

Total Return   ★★★★

Over the past five years (ending 12/31/00), W&R International Growth C has taken $10,000 and turned it into $25,935 ($18,610 over three years). This translates into an annualized return of 21 percent over the past five years and 23 percent over the past three years. Over the past five years, this fund has outperformed 95 percent of all mutual funds; within its general category, it has done better than 97 percent of its peers. Global equity funds have averaged 8 percent annually over these same five years.

Risk/Volatility   ★★★

Over the past five years, W&R has only been safer than 20 percent of all global equity funds. Over the past decade, the fund has had one negative year, while the S & P 500 has also had one (off 9 percent in 2000); the EAFE fell twice (off 12 percent in 1992 and 14 percent in 2000). The fund has underperformed the S & P 500 once and the EAFE Index once in the past ten years.

	past 5 years		past 10 years	
worst year	-24%	2000	-24%	2000
best year	89%	1999	89%	1999

In the past, W&R has done better than 852 percent of its peer group in up markets but outperformed just 10 percent of its competition in down markets. Consistency, or predictability, of returns for W&R International Growth C can be described as good. This fund's risk-related return is excellent.

Management   ★★★★

There are eighty-five stocks in this $155 million portfolio. The average global equity fund today is $325 million in size. Close to 90 percent of the fund's holdings are in stocks. The stocks in this portfolio have an average price-earnings (p/e) ratio of 35 and a median market capitalization of $7 billion. The portfolio's equity holdings can be categorized as large-cap and growth-oriented issues.

Thomas A. Mengel has managed this fund for the past five years. Management seeks out fast growers with dominant market share as well as turn-around candidates. The four most heavily weighted countries in the portfolio are Japan, United Kingdom, France, and Germany. The fund does not invest in U.S. stocks. There are sixteen funds besides International Growth within the W&R family. Overall, the fund family's risk-adjusted performance can be described as good.

Tax Minimization   ★★★★★
During the past five years, a $10,000 initial investment grew to $24,345 after taxes, assuming a 39.6 percent income tax bracket (state and federal combined) and a capital gains rate of 28 percent. This means that investors in this fund were able to preserve 90 percent of their total returns. Compared to other equity funds, this fund's tax savings are considered to be excellent.

Expenses   ★★
W&R International Growth's expense ratio is 2.4 percent; it has also averaged 2.4 percent annually over the past three calendar years. The average expense ratio for the 1,500 funds in this category is 1.8 percent. This fund's turnover rate over the past year has been 125 percent, while its peer group average has been 90 percent.

Summary
W&R International Growth C has had exceptional risk-adjusted returns for the past three and five years. The fund has outperformed 97 percent of its peer group and tax efficiency has been great. This Waddell & Reed offering scores solid results across the board. The fund ranks in the top quintile when it comes to growth persistence: the ability to consistently outperform equity funds over the previous five years.

Profile
minimum initial investment . . . . . $1,000   *IRA accounts available* . . . . yes
subsequent minimum investment . . . . $1   *IRA minimum investment* $50
available in all 50 states. . . . . yes   *date of inception* . . . . Sept. 1992
telephone exchanges. . . . . yes   *dividend/income paid* . . . . annually
number of funds in family 17   *largest sector weighting* . . . . . . services

William Blair International Growth N

222 West Adams Street, 34th Floor
Chicago, IL 60606
(800) 742-7272
www.wmblair.com

total return	★★★
risk reduction	★★★★
management	★★★★
tax minimization	★★★★
expense control	★★★★
symbol WBIGX	19 points
up-market performance	excellent
down-market performance	fair
predictability of returns	very good

Total Return   ★★★

Over the past five years (ending 12/31/00), William Blair International Growth N has taken $10,000 and turned it into $23,865 ($20,005 over three years). This translates into an annualized return of 19 percent over the past five years and 26 percent over the past three years. Over the past five years, this fund has outperformed 95 percent of all mutual funds; within its general category, it has also done better than 95 percent of its peers. Global equity funds have averaged 8 percent annually over these same five years.

Risk/Volatility   ★★★★

Over the past five years, William Blair has been safer than 70 percent of all global equity funds. Over the past decade, the fund has had two negative years, while the S & P 500 has had one (off 9 percent in 2000); the EAFE fell twice (off 12 percent in 1992 and 14 percent in 2000). The fund has underperformed the S & P 500 and the EAFE Index once in the past ten years.

	past 5 years		past 10 years	
worst year	-8%	2000	-8%	2000
best year	96%	1999	96%	1999

In the past, William Blair has done better than 99 percent of its peer group in up markets but outperformed just 45 percent of its competition in down markets. Consistency, or predictability, of returns for William Blair International Growth N can be described as very good. This fund's risk-related return is excellent.

Management   ★★★★

There are 125 stocks in this $115 million portfolio. The average global equity fund today is $325 million in size. Close to 96 percent of the fund's holdings are in stocks. The stocks in this portfolio have an average price-earnings (p/e) ratio of 34 and a median market capitalization of $4 billion. The portfolio's equity holdings can be categorized as mid-cap and growth-oriented issues.

W. George Greig has managed this fund for the past five years. The four most heavily weighted countries in the portfolio are United Kingdom, Japan, France, and Switzerland. The fund does not invest in U.S. securities. Grieg uses a bottom-up approach when selecting equities. Management looks for reasonably valued companies that are leaders in their field. There are forty-six funds besides International Growth within the William Blair family. Overall, the fund family's risk-adjusted performance can be described as good to very good.

Tax Minimization ★★★★

During the past five years, a $10,000 initial investment grew to $22,340 after taxes, assuming a 39.6 percent income tax bracket (state and federal combined) and a capital gains rate of 28 percent. This means that investors in this fund were able to preserve 89 percent of their total returns. Compared to other equity funds, this fund's tax savings are considered to be very good.

Expenses ★★★★

William Blair International Growth's expense ratio is 1.4 percent; it has also averaged 1.4 percent annually over the past three calendar years. The average expense ratio for the 1,500 funds in this category is 1.8 percent. This fund's turnover rate over the past year has been 120 percent, while its peer group average has been 90 percent.

Summary

William Blair International Growth N has outperformed 95 percent of all mutual funds and 95 percent of all foreign and global stock funds. Within its category, it is the second-best performer during bull markets. Risk-adjusted returns for the past three and five years have been outstanding. The fund receives good or very good marks across the board. The fund has only underperformed the S & P 500 and EAFE index once since its inception.

Profile

minimum initial investment $5,000	*IRA accounts available* . . . . yes
subsequent minimum investment . $1,000	*IRA minimum investment* $2,000
available in all 50 states. . . . . yes	*date of inception* . . . . Oct. 1992
telephone exchanges. . . . . yes	*dividend/income paid* . . . . annually
number of funds in family 47	*largest sector weighting* . . . . . . services

Government Bond Funds

These funds invest in direct and indirect U.S. government obligations. Government bond funds are made up of one or more of the following: T-bills, T-notes, T-bonds, GNMAs, and FNMAs. Treasury bills, notes, and bonds make up the entire marketable debt of the U.S. government. Such instruments are exempt from state income taxes.

Although GNMAs are considered an indirect obligation of the government, they are still backed by the full faith and credit of the United States. FNMAs are not issued by the government but are considered virtually identical in safety to GNMAs. FNMAs and GNMAs are both subject to state and local income taxes. All of the securities in a government bond fund are subject to federal income taxes.

The average maturity of securities found in government bond funds varies broadly depending on the type of fund as well as on management's perception of risk and the future direction of interest rates. A more thorough discussion of interest rates and the volatility of bond fund prices can be found in the introductory pages of the corporate bond section.

Over the past fifteen years (1986–2000), government bonds have returned an average compound return of 10.4 percent—versus 9.5 percent for corporate bonds. A $10,000 investment in U.S. government bonds grew to $54,300 over the past fifteen years; a similar initial investment in corporate bonds grew to $48,700. During this same period, government bond *funds* have underperformed corporate bond funds, returning 7.9 percent, compared to 7.5 percent.

Looking at a longer time frame (1951–2000), government bonds have only slightly outperformed inflation. A dollar invested in governments at the beginning of 1951 grew to $19.14 by the end of 2000. This translates into an average compound return of 6.4 percent per year. Adjusted for inflation, the figure falls to $3.61. Over the past fifty years, the worst year for government bonds was 1967, when a loss of 9 percent was suffered. The second worst year was 1999, when the bonds suffered a loss of just under 9 percent. The best year so far has been 1982, when government bonds posted a gain of 40 percent. All of these figures are based on total return (current yield plus or minus any appreciation or loss of principal). The second best year was 1995, when these debt instruments had a total return of just under 32 percent.

Over the past half century, there have been forty-six 5-year periods (1951–1955, 1952–1956, etc.). On a pre-tax basis, government bonds have outperformed inflation during twenty-six of the forty-six 5-year periods. The last 5-year period in which inflation outperformed long-term government bonds was 1979–1983 (8.4 percent versus 6.4 percent for bonds). Over the past fifty years, there have been forty-one 10-year periods (1950–1959, 1951–1960, etc.). On a pre-tax basis, government bonds have outperformed inflation during only twenty-two of the forty-one 10-year periods. The last 10-year period in which inflation outperformed long-term government bonds was 1975–1984 (7.3 percent versus 7.0 percent for bonds). Over the past half century, there have been thirty-one 20-year periods (1946–1965, 1947–1966, etc.). On a pre-tax basis, government bonds have outperformed inflation during only fifteen of these thirty-one periods. The last 20-year period in which inflation outperformed long-term government bonds was 1966–1985 (6.4 percent versus 6.0 percent for bonds).

Six hundred funds make up the government bonds category. Total market capitalization of this category is $120 billion.

Over the past three and five years (all periods ending December 31, 2000), government funds have had an average compound annual return of 5.5 percent. For the decade, these funds have averaged 7 percent a year; over the past fifteen years, 7.5 percent a year. The standard deviation for government bond funds has been 3 percent over the past three years. This means that these funds have been less volatile than any other category except money market funds.

Government bond funds are the perfect choice for the conservative investor who wants to avoid any possibility of defaults. These securities should be avoided by even conservative investors who are in a high tax bracket or who are unable to shelter such an investment in a retirement plan or annuity. Such investors should first look at the advantages of municipal bond funds.

The prospective investor should always remember that government and corporate bonds are generally not a good investment once inflation and taxes are factored in. The investor who appreciates the cumulative effects of even low levels of inflation should probably avoid government and corporate bonds except as part of a retirement plan.

Government Bond Funds

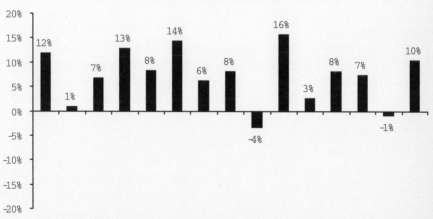

AIM Limited Maturity Treasury Fund-Retail Shares

11 Greenway Plaza, Suite 1919
Houston, TX 77046
(800) 959-4246
www.aimfunds.com

total return	★★
risk reduction	★★★★★
management	★★★★
current income	★★★
expense control	★★★
symbol SHTIX	17 points
up-market performance	very good
down-market performance	very good
predictability of returns	excellent

Total Return   ★★

Over the past five years (ending 12/31/00), AIM Limited Maturity Treasury Fund-Retail Shares has taken $10,000 and turned it into $12,765 ($11,580 over three years and $17,910 over the past ten years). This translates into an annualized return of 5 percent over the past three and five years, and 6 percent for the decade. Over the past five years, this fund has outperformed 40 percent of all mutual funds; within its general category, it has done better than 55 percent of its peers. Government bond funds have averaged 5 percent annually over these same five years.

During the past five years, a $10,000 initial investment grew to $11,630 after taxes, assuming a 39.6 percent income tax bracket (state and federal combined) and a capital gains rate of 28 percent. This means that investors in this fund were able to preserve 59 percent of their total returns. Compared to other fixed-income funds, this fund's tax savings are considered to be very good.

Risk/Volatility   ★★★★★

Over the past five years, AIM has been safer than 90 percent of all government bond funds. Over the past decade, the fund has had no negative years, while the Lehman Brothers Aggregate Bond Index had two (off 3 percent in 1994 and 1 percent in 1999). The fund has outperformed the Lehman Brothers Aggregate Bond Index every year and underperformed the Lehman Brothers Government Bond Index twice in the past ten years.

	past 5 years		past 10 years	
worst year	3%	1999	1%	1994
best year	7%	2000	10%	1991

In the past, AIM has done better than 75 percent of its peer group in up markets but outperformed just 20 percent of its competition in down markets. Consistency, or predictability, of returns for AIM Limited Maturity Treasury Fund-Retail Shares can be described as excellent. This fund's risk-related return is very good.

Management   ★★★★

There are fifteen fixed-income securities in this $310 million portfolio. The average government bond fund today is $200 million in size. Close to 100 percent of the fund's holdings are in U.S. Treasury notes. The average maturity of the bonds in this account is 1.5 years; the weighted coupon rate averages 6.1 percent. The portfolio's fixed-income holdings can be categorized as very short-term, high-quality debt.

A team has managed this fund for the past five years. The fund may not invest in securities with maturities greater than three years. Lead manager Scott Johnson typically buys two-year Treasury notes at auction and then sells them a year later. There are 159 funds besides Limited Maturity Treasury within the AIM family. Overall, the fund family's risk-adjusted performance can be described as good.

Current Income   ★★★

Over the past year, AIM Limited Maturity Treasury Fund-Retail Shares had a twelve-month yield of 5.4 percent. During this same twelve-month period, the typical government bond fund had a yield that averaged 5.6 percent.

Expenses   ★★★

AIM Limited Maturity's expense ratio is 0.5 percent; it has also averaged 0.5 percent annually over the past three calendar years. The average expense ratio for the 575 funds in this category is 1.1 percent. This fund's turnover rate over the past year has been 120 percent, while its peer group average has been 160 percent.

Summary

AIM Limited Maturity Treasury Fund-Retail Shares is the only fund in its category that does a superb job during bear as well as bull markets. It has more predictable returns than any other government bond fund in the book. Risk-adjusted returns over the past three and five years have been very good. The risk level of the fund is low for two reasons: paper that is short-term and the backing of the U.S. government. The safety level of this fund is so good; it makes a good alternative for money market investors looking for a superior yield.

Profile

minimum initial investment $500	*IRA accounts available* .... yes
subsequent minimum investment ... $50	*IRA minimum investment* $250
available in all 50 states. .... yes	*date of inception.* .... Dec. 1987
telephone exchanges. .... yes	*dividend/income paid.* .... monthly
number of funds in family 160	*average credit quality* .... AAA

American Century Target Maturities Trust 2020

4500 Main Street, P.O. Box 419200
Kansas City, MO 64141
(800) 345-2021
www.americancentury.com

total return	★★★★★
risk reduction	★
management	★★★★★
current income	★★
expense control	★★★★★
symbol BTTTX	18 points
up-market performance	excellent
down-market performance	excellent
predictability of returns	poor

Total Return   ★★★★★

Over the past five years (ending 12/31/00), American Century Target Maturities Trust 2020 has taken $10,000 and turned it into $14,695 ($12,250 over three years and $31,060 over the past ten years). This translates into an annualized return of 8 percent over the past five years, 7 percent over the past three years, and 12 percent for the decade. Over the past five years, this fund has outperformed 60 percent of all mutual funds; within its general category, it has done better than 99 percent of its peers. Government bond funds have averaged 5 percent annually over these same five years.

During the past five years, a $10,000 initial investment grew to $12,725 after taxes, assuming a 39.6 percent income tax bracket (state and federal combined) and a capital gains rate of 28 percent. This means that investors in this fund were able to preserve 58 percent of their total returns. Compared to other fixed-income funds, this fund's tax savings are considered to be very good.

Risk/Volatility   ★

Over the past five years, American Century has only been safer than 10 percent of all government bond funds. Over the past decade, the fund has had three negative years, while the Lehman Brothers Aggregate Bond Index had two (off 3 percent in 1994 and 1 percent in 1999). The fund has underperformed the Lehman Brothers Aggregate Bond Index twice and the Lehman Brothers Government Bond Index three times in the past ten years.

	past 5 years		past 10 years	
worst year	-18%	1999	-18%	1999
best year	30%	1997	65%	1995

In the past, American Century has done better than 98 percent of its peer group in up markets and outperformed 96 percent of its competition in down markets. Consistency of returns for American Century Target Maturities Trust 2020 can be described as poor. This fund's risk-related return has varied from poor to excellent.

Management   ★★★★★

There are sixteen fixed-income securities in this $285 million portfolio. The average government bond fund today is $200 million in size. Close to 100 percent of the fund's holdings are in U.S. government bonds. The average maturity of the bonds in this account is twenty years; the weighted coupon rate is zero. The portfolio's fixed-income holdings can be categorized as long-term, very high-quality debt.

A team has managed this fund for the past eight years. The portfolio is comprised of zero-coupon bonds (hence the zero coupon rate). However, the portfolio does accrete (somewhat similar to accrue) interest daily at roughly a 5 percent annualized rate. This accretion means that investors are credited interest, but interest is not paid out as it is with traditional government securities or money market instruments. There are ninety-nine funds besides Target Maturities Trust 2020 within the American Century family. Overall, the fund family's risk-adjusted performance can be described as very good.

Current Income   ★★

Over the past year, American Century Target Maturities Trust 2020 had a twelve-month accreted yield of 4.9 percent. During this same twelve-month period, the typical government bond fund had a yield that averaged 5.6 percent.

Expenses   ★★★★★

American Century Target Maturities Trust's expense ratio is 0.6 percent; it has also averaged 0.6 percent annually over the past three calendar years. The average expense ratio for the 575 funds in this category is 1.1 percent. This fund's turnover rate over the past year has been 10 percent, while its peer group average has been 160 percent.

Summary

American Century Target Maturities Trust 2020 is the best three- and five-year performer in its category. It also has the second-lowest turnover rate of any government bond fund and is rated as number one during bull and bear markets. Since this is a portfolio of long-term zero-coupon bonds, investors should realize that this portfolio has roughly three times the volatility of a fund that owns "regular" (or interest-bearing) twenty-year government securities. The portfolio is definitely not suited for anyone seeking current income. The fund should only be owned by those who believe interest rates will either fall or remain level; when interest rates rise, all long-term zero-coupon portfolios can sustain anywhere from modest to substantial paper losses. Investors would be wise to check out other offerings from the American Century family of funds.

Profile

minimum initial investment $2,500	IRA accounts available . . . . yes
subsequent minimum investment . . . $50	IRA minimum investment $1,000
available in all 50 states. . . . . yes	date of inception. . . . . Dec. 1989
telephone exchanges. . . . . yes	dividend/income paid . . . . annually
number of funds in family 100	average credit quality . . . . AAA

Montgomery Short Duration Government Bond R

101 California Street
San Francisco, CA 94111
(800) 572-3863
www.montgomeryfunds.com

total return	★★★
risk reduction	★★★★★
management	★★★★
current income	★★★★
expense control	★★★
symbol MNSGX	19 points
up-market performance	good
down-market performance	good
predictability of returns	excellent

Total Return   ★★★

Over the past five years (ending 12/31/00), Montgomery Short Duration Government Bond R has taken $10,000 and turned it into $13,385 ($11,910 over three years). This translates into an annualized return of 6 percent over the past three and five years. Over the past five years, this fund has outperformed 50 percent of all mutual funds; within its general category, it has done better than 95 percent of its peers. Government bond funds have averaged 5 percent annually over these same five years.

During the past five years, a $10,000 initial investment grew to $12,030 after taxes, assuming a 39.6 percent income tax bracket (state and federal combined) and a capital gains rate of 28 percent. This means that investors in this fund were able to preserve 60 percent of their total returns. Compared to other fixed-income funds, this fund's tax savings are considered to be very good.

Risk/Volatility   ★★★★★

Over the past five years, Montgomery has been safer than 80 percent of all government bond funds. Over the past decade, the fund has had no negative years, while the Lehman Brothers Aggregate Bond Index had two (off 3 percent in 1994 and 1 percent in 1999). The fund has underperformed the Lehman Brothers Aggregate Bond Index and the Lehman Brothers Government Bond Index twice in the past ten years.

	past 5 years		past 10 years	
worst year	3%	1999	1%	1994
best year	8%	2000	12%	1995

In the past, Montgomery has done better than 90 percent of its peer group in up markets but outperformed just 35 percent of its competition in down markets. Consistency, or predictability, of returns for Montgomery Short Duration Government Bond R can be described as excellent. This fund's risk-related return is very good.

Management ★★★★

There are ninety fixed-income securities in this $200 million portfolio. The average government bond fund today is $200 million in size. Close to 95 percent of the fund's holdings are in bonds. The average maturity of the bonds in this account is three years; the weighted coupon rate averages 6.4 percent. The portfolio's fixed-income holdings can be categorized as extremely high quality and very short term.

William C. Stevens and Marie Chandoha have comanaged this fund for the past six years. Management has been quite successful investing in a wide range of quality instruments, such as Treasury bills and notes, FNMAs, agency-backed student loans, and commercial paper. The comanagers have been quite nimble when it comes to moving from sector to sector as relative debt values have changed. There are twenty-six funds besides Short Duration Government Bond R within the Montgomery family. Overall, the fund family's risk-adjusted performance can be described as fair.

Current Income ★★★★

Over the past year, Montgomery Short Duration Government Bond R had a twelve-month yield of 5.9 percent. During this same twelve-month period, the typical government bond fund had a yield that averaged 5.6 percent.

Expenses ★★★

Montgomery Short Duration Government Bond's expense ratio is 0.6 percent; it has averaged 0.5 percent annually over the past three calendar years. The average expense ratio for the 575 funds in this category is 1.1 percent. This fund's turnover rate over the past year has been 195 percent, while its peer group average has been 160 percent.

Summary

Montgomery Short Duration Government Bond R is the second most predictable bond fund in the book. It also has the second-lowest risk level of any government securities portfolio. Risk-adjusted returns over the past three and five years have been outstanding. The fund has finished in the top half (and usually in the top quartile) on a calendar-year basis every year since its inception roughly a decade ago. This portfolio is a great choice for someone for wants a very safe portfolio and comparatively high yield.

Profile

minimum initial investment $1,000
subsequent minimum investment . . $100
available in all 50 states . . . . yes
telephone exchanges . . . . yes
number of funds in family 27

IRA accounts available . . . . yes
IRA minimum investment $1,000
date of inception . . . . Dec. 1992
dividend/income paid . . . . monthly
average credit quality . . . . AAA

Pilgrim GNMA Income A
40 North Central Avenue, Suite 1200
Phoenix, AZ 85004
(800) 992-0180
www.pilgrimfunds.com

total return	★★★★
risk reduction	★★★★★
management	★★★★★
current income	★★★★★
expense control	★★★★
symbol LEXNX	23 points
up-market performance	very good
down-market performance	very good
predictability of returns	very good

Total Return   ★★★★

Over the past five years (ending 12/31/00), Pilgrim GNMA Income A has taken $10,000 and turned it into $14,030 ($11,910 over three years and $21,590 over the past ten years). This translates into an annualized return of 7 percent over the past five years, 6 percent over the past three years, and 8 percent for the decade. Over the past five years, this fund has outperformed 55 percent of all mutual funds; within its general category, it has done better than 99 percent of its peers. Government bond funds have averaged 5 percent annually over these same five years.

During the past five years, a $10,000 initial investment grew to $12,540 after taxes, assuming a 39.6 percent income tax bracket (state and federal combined) and a capital gains rate of 28 percent. This means that investors in this fund were able to preserve 63 percent of their total returns. Compared to other fixed-income funds, this fund's tax savings are considered to be excellent.

Risk/Volatility   ★★★★★

Over the past five years, Pilgrim GNMA Income A has been safer than 97 percent of all government bond funds. Over the past decade, the fund has had one negative year, while the Lehman Brothers Aggregate Bond Index had two (off 3 percent in 1994 and 1 percent in 1999). The fund has underperformed the Lehman Brothers Aggregate Bond Index twice and the Lehman Brothers Government Bond Index twice in the past ten years.

	past 5 years		past 10 years	
worst year	1%	1999	-2%	1994
best year	11%	2000	16%	1991

In the past, Pilgrim GNMA Income A has done better than 85 percent of its peer group in up markets and outperformed 55 percent of its competition in down markets. Consistency, or predictability, of returns for Pilgrim GNMA Income A can be described as very good. This fund's risk-related return is very good.

Management   ★★★★★
There are 195 fixed-income securities in this $365 million portfolio. The average government bond fund today is $200 million in size. Close to 100 percent of the fund's holdings are in U.S. government agency issues. The average maturity of the bonds in this account is fifteen years; the weighted coupon rate averages 7.4 percent. The portfolio's fixed-income holdings can be categorized as intermediate-term, high-quality debt.

Dennis P. Jamison and Roseann G. McCarthy have comanaged this fund for the past eleven years. Management's top priority is current income and safety. The comanagers use a value-oriented approach when selecting GNMAs and U.S. Treasuries. There is quite a bit of variance within the GNMA market (i.e., speed of refinancing and sales of homes within the pool), and these nuances are where Jamison and McCarthy have excelled. There are ninety-seven funds besides GNMA Income within the Pilgrim family. Overall, the fund family's risk-adjusted performance can be described as good.

Current Income   ★★★★★
Over the past year, Pilgrim GNMA Income A had a twelve-month yield of 6.2 percent. During this same twelve-month period, the typical government bond fund had a yield that averaged 5.6 percent.

Expenses   ★★★★
Pilgrim GNMA Income's expense ratio is 1 percent; it has also averaged 1 percent annually over the past three calendar years. The average expense ratio for the 575 funds in this category is 1.1 percent. This fund's turnover rate over the past year has been 25 percent, while its peer group average has been 160 percent.

Summary
Pilgrim GNMA Income A ties for first as having the highest overall score of any fund in its category (government bond). The fund is also the most tax efficient in its class and is one of only four funds in the entire book that does a very good job when it comes to predictability of returns, up-market performance, and down-market returns. Risk-adjusted returns over the past three, five, and ten years have been very good; a consistency that is not commonly found. The fund ranks in the top quintile when it comes to growth persistence: the ability to consistently out-perform equity funds over the previous five years. This offering also excels when it comes to superior risk-adjusted return persistence.

Profile

minimum initial investment $1,000	*IRA accounts available* . . . . yes
subsequent minimum investment . . . $50	*IRA minimum investment* $250
available in all 50 states. . . . . yes	*date of inception* . . . . Oct. 1973
telephone exchanges. . . . . yes	*dividend/income paid*. . . . . monthly
number of funds in family 98	*average credit quality* . . . . AAA

Vanguard GNMA
Vanguard Financial Center
P.O. Box 2600
Valley Forge, PA 19482
(800) 662-7447
www.vanguard.com

total return	★★★★
risk reduction	★★★★
management	★★★★★
current income	★★★★★
expense control	★★★★★
symbol VFIIX	23 points
up-market performance	excellent
down-market performance	poor
predictability of returns	very good

Total Return   ★★★★
Over the past five years (ending 12/31/00), Vanguard GNMA has taken $10,000 and turned it into $14,030 ($11,910 over three years and $21,590 over the past ten years). This translates into an annualized return of 7 percent over the past five years, 6 percent over the past three years, and 8 percent for the decade. Over the past five years, this fund has outperformed 55 percent of all mutual funds; within its general category, it has done better than 98 percent of its peers. Government bond funds have averaged 5 percent annually over these same five years.

During the past five years, a $10,000 initial investment grew to $12,340 after taxes, assuming a 39.6 percent income tax bracket (state and federal combined) and a capital gains rate of 28 percent. This means that investors in this fund were able to preserve 58 percent of their total returns. Compared to other fixed-income funds, this fund's tax savings are considered to be very good.

Risk/Volatility   ★★★★
Over the past five years, Vanguard has been safer than 85 percent of all government bond funds. Over the past decade, the fund has had one negative year, while the Lehman Brothers Aggregate Bond Index had two (off 3 percent in 1994 and 1 percent in 1999). The fund has underperformed the Lehman Brothers Aggregate Bond Index twice and the Lehman Brothers Government Bond Index twice in the past ten years.

	past 5 years		past 10 years	
worst year	1%	1999	-1%	1994
best year	11%	2000	17%	1995

In the past, Vanguard has done better than 98 percent of its peer group in up markets but outperformed just 15 percent of its competition in down markets. Consistency, or predictability, of returns for Vanguard GNMA can be described as very good. This fund's risk-related return is also very good.

Management   ★★★★★
There are over 21,000 fixed-income securities in this $14 billion portfolio. The average government bond fund today is $200 million in size. Close to 96 percent of the fund's holdings are in GNMAs. The average maturity of the bonds in this account is eight years; the weighted coupon rate averages 7.1 percent. The portfolio's fixed-income holdings can be categorized as intermediate-term, very high-quality debt.

Paul D. Kaplan has managed this fund for the past seven years. Management must invest at least 80 percent of the portfolio in GNMAs. The balance can be in repurchase agreements that are backed by U.S. government securities. There are 101 funds besides GNMA within the Vanguard family. Overall, the fund family's risk-adjusted performance can be described as very good.

Current Income   ★★★★★
Over the past year, Vanguard GNMA had a twelve-month yield of 6.7 percent. During this same twelve-month period, the typical government bond fund had a yield that averaged 5.6 percent.

Expenses   ★★★★★
Vanguard GNMA's expense ratio is 0.3 percent; it has also averaged 0.3 percent annually over the past three calendar years. The average expense ratio for the 575 funds in this category is 1.1 percent. This fund's turnover rate over the past year has been 5 percent, while its peer group average has been 160 percent.

Summary
Vanguard GNMA ties for first as having the highest overall score of any fund in its category. As one might suspect with a Vanguard offering, this fund has the lowest expenses and lowest turnover of any fund in its category. The fund has outperformed 98 percent of its peer group and is rated as the second-best up-market performer. The fund ranks in the top quintile when it comes to growth persistence: the ability to consistently outperform equity funds over the previous five years. This offering also excels when it comes to superior risk-adjusted return persistence. As previously mentioned, investors would be smart to check out other offerings from Vanguard.

Profile
minimum initial investment $3,000
subsequent minimum investment . . $100
available in all 50 states. . . . . yes
telephone exchanges. . . . . yes
number of funds in family 102

IRA accounts available . . . . yes
IRA minimum investment $1,000
date of inception. . . . . June 1980
dividend/income paid. . . . . monthly
average credit quality . . . . AAA

Growth Funds

These funds generally seek capital appreciation, with current income as a distant secondary concern. Growth funds typically invest in U.S. common stocks, while avoiding speculative issues and aggressive trading techniques. The goal of most of these funds is long-term growth. The approaches used to attain this appreciation can vary significantly among growth funds.

Over the past fifteen years, U.S. stocks have outperformed both corporate and government bonds. From 1985 through 1999, common stocks have averaged 18.5 percent compounded per year, compared to 9.4 percent for corporate bonds and 10.4 percent for government bonds. A $10,000 investment in stocks, as measured by the S & P 500, grew to over $102,670 over the past fifteen years; a similar initial investment in corporate bonds grew to $48,730.

Looking at a longer time frame, common stocks have also fared quite well. A dollar invested in stocks at the beginning of 1951 grew to $4,108 by the end of 2000. This translates into an average compound return of 12.8 percent per year. Over the past fifty years, the worst year for common stocks was 1974, when a loss of 26 percent was suffered. One year later, these same stocks posted a gain of 37 percent. The best year so far has been 1954, when growth stocks posted a gain of 53 percent.

Growth stocks have outperformed bonds in every single decade. If George Washington had invested $1 in common stocks with an average return of 12 percent, his investment would be worth over $455 billion today. If he had averaged 14 percent, his portfolio would be large enough to pay our national debt five times over!

Growth Funds

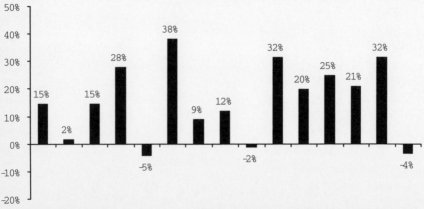

The following table covers 129 years and shows the odds of making money (a positive return) over each of several different time periods.

Standard & Poor's Composite 500 Stock Index
Various periods, 1871–1997 (dividends not included)

length of period	total number of periods	periods in which stock prices			percentage opportunity for profit (not including dividends)
		rose	declined	unchanged	
1 year	129	84	45	1	65
5 years	125	100	25	1	80
10 years	120	108	12	0	90
15 years	116	107	9	0	92
20 years	110	107	3	0	97
25 years	105	104	1	0	99
30 years	100	100	0	0	100

Twenty-five hundred funds make up the growth category. Total market capitalization is $1.4 trillion. The standard deviation is 27.6 percent; beta (stock market-related risk) is 1.0, the same as the overall market, as measured by the S & P 500. The typical portfolio is divided into: 90 percent U.S. stocks, 5 percent foreign stocks, and the balance in money market instruments. Turnover rate is 105 percent per year. The yield on growth funds averages about 0.3 percent annually. Fund expenses average 1.4 percent per year.

Volatility (standard deviation) in today's markets is unprecedented. As this chart shows, nearly half of the past year's 105 trading days (through May 31, 2000) saw changes of 1 percent. Nearly one-quarter saw changes greater than 2 percent. Finally, all but six days experienced at least a 1 percent change between the intraday low and high.

Percentage of Time S & P 500 Had 1–2% Daily Changes (1990–2000)

Year	S & P 500	% of trading days with changes of + or -			
		1%	2%	1% intraday	2% intraday
1990	-3.2%	29.6	5.1	60.1	14.7
1991	30.6%	23.3	3.6	50.2	7.1
1992	7.7%	11.0	0.0	28.0	0.8
1993	10.0%	6.7	0.4	14.6	1.6
1994	1.3%	10.7	0.8	27.0	1.6
1995	37.4%	5.2	0.0	17.9	1.2
1996	23.1%	15.0	1.2	39.4	4.4
1997	33.4%	32.0	5.9	70.8.	15.1
1998	28.6%	31.4	9.1	69.1	22.2
1999	21.1%	36.5	9.1	77.0	21.0
2000 *	-2.8%	48.1	22.1	94.2	44.2

* through May 31, 2000

Over the past three years, growth funds have had an average compound return of 14.0 percent per year; the annual return for the past five years has been 16.8 percent. For the past decade, growth funds have averaged 16.6 percent annually and 14.5 percent per year for the past fifteen years (all periods ending December 31, 2000).

Calamos Growth A
1111 East Warrenville Road
Naperville, IL 60563
(800) 823-7386
www.calamos.com

total return	★★★★★
risk reduction	★★★
management	★★★★
tax minimization	★★★
expense control	★
symbol CVGRX	16 points
up-market performance	excellent
down-market performance	poor
predictability of returns	poor

Total Return   ★★★★★
Over the past five years (ending 12/31/00), Calamos Growth A has taken $10,000 and turned it into $48,265 ($28,635 over three years and $85,945 over the past ten years). This translates into an annualized return of 37 percent over the past five years, 42 percent over the past three years, and 24 percent for the decade. Over the past five years, this fund has outperformed 99 percent of all mutual funds; within its general category, it has also done better than 99 percent of its peers. Growth funds have averaged 17 percent annually over these same five years.

Risk/Volatility   ★★★
Over the past five years, Calamos has been safer than 65 percent of all growth funds. Over the past decade, the fund has had one negative year, while the S & P 500 has also had one (off 9 percent in 2000). The fund has underperformed the S & P 500 once in the past ten years.

	past 5 years		past 10 years	
worst year	24%	1997	-6%	1994
best year	78%	1999	78%	1999

In the past, Calamos has done better than 99 percent of its peer group in up markets but outperformed just 20 percent of its competition in down markets. Consistency, or predictability, of returns for Calamos Growth A can be described as poor. This fund's risk-related return is excellent.

Management   ★★★★
There are seventy-five stocks in this $90 million portfolio. The average growth fund today is $550 million in size. Close to 100 percent of the fund's holdings are in stocks. The stocks in this portfolio have an average price-earnings (p/e) ratio of 32 and a median market capitalization of $1.8 billion. The portfolio's equity holdings can be categorized as mid-cap and growth-oriented issues.

John P. Calamos and John P. Calamos, Jr. have comanaged this fund for the past nine years. Management looks for companies with strong earnings-growth potential plus financial strength and stability. Although the fund has less than 6 percent of its assets in foreign equities, it has the flexibility in invest up to 25 percent in overseas stocks. The Calamoses often use a quick trading strategy and are frequently concentrated in just a handful of industry groups. There are eight funds besides Growth A within the Calamos family. Overall, the fund family's risk-adjusted performance can be described as excellent.

Tax Minimization   ★★★
During the past five years, a $10,000 initial investment grew to $41,760 after taxes, assuming a 39.6 percent income tax bracket (state and federal combined) and a capital gains rate of 28 percent. This means that investors in this fund were able to preserve 83 percent of their total returns. Compared to other equity funds, this fund's tax savings are considered to be good.

Expenses   ★
Calamos Growth's expense ratio is 2 percent; it has also averaged 2 percent annually over the past three calendar years. The average expense ratio for the 2,360 funds in this category is 1.4 percent. This fund's turnover rate over the past year has been 175 percent, while its peer group average has been 105 percent.

Summary
Calamos Growth A is the best three- and five-year performer in its category and has had the number one performance during bull markets. Risk-adjusted returns for the past three, five, and ten years have been superb. Performance has improved radically since 1995. The fund ranks in the top quintile when it comes to growth persistence: the ability to consistently outperform equity funds over the previous five years. This offering also excels when it comes to superior risk-adjusted return persistence. As previously mentioned, investors are strongly encouraged to look at other Calamos funds. This group of funds has not received the attention it deserves.

Profile
minimum initial investment $500
subsequent minimum investment . . . $50
available in all 50 states. . . . . yes
telephone exchanges. . . . . yes
number of funds in family 9

IRA accounts available . . . . yes
IRA minimum investment $1
date of inception . . . . Sept. 1990
dividend/income paid . . . . annually
largest sector weighting . . . technology

Franklin Growth & Income A

777 Mariners Island Boulevard
San Mateo, CA 94404
(800) 342-5236
www.franklin-templeton.com

total return	★★★
risk reduction	★★★★
management	★★★★
tax minimization	★★★★
expense control	★★★★
symbol FKREX	19 points
up-market performance	good
down-market performance	poor
predictability of returns	very good

Total Return   ★★★

Over the past five years (ending 12/31/00), Franklin Growth & Income A (formally known as Franklin Equity A) has taken $10,000 and turned it into $27,030 ($17,280 over three years and $52,340 over the past ten years). This translates into an annualized return of 22 percent over the past five years, 20 percent over the past three years, and 18 percent for the decade. Over the past five years, this fund has outperformed 96 percent of all mutual funds; within its general category, it has done better than 85 percent of its peers. Growth funds have averaged 17 percent annually over these same five years.

Risk/Volatility   ★★★★

Over the past five years, Franklin has been safer than 75 percent of all growth funds. Over the past decade, the fund has had one negative year, while the S & P 500 has also had one (off 9 percent in 2000). The fund has underperformed the S & P 500 once in the past ten years.

	past 5 years		past 10 years	
worst year	0%	2000	-1%	1994
best year	52%	1999	52%	1999

In the past, Franklin has done better than 95 percent of its peer group in up markets but outperformed just 15 percent of its competition in down markets. Consistency, or predictability, of returns for Franklin Growth & Income A can be described as very good. This fund's risk-related return is excellent.

Management   ★★★★

There are 110 stocks in this $1.1 billion portfolio. The average growth fund today is $550 million in size. Close to 90 percent of the fund's holdings are in stocks. The stocks in this portfolio have an average price-earnings (p/e) ratio of 39 and a median market capitalization of $30 billion. The portfolio's equity holdings can be categorized as large-cap and growth-oriented issues.

A team has managed this fund for the past five years. At least two-thirds of the portfolio must be in common stocks or convertibles. Management looks for companies that are expected to have strong future earnings growth and are fairly valued when compared to their peers. There are 165 funds besides Growth & Income A within the Franklin-Templeton family. Overall, the fund family's risk-adjusted performance can be described as very good.

Tax Minimization   ★★★★
During the past five years, a $10,000 initial investment grew to $25,160 after taxes, assuming a 39.6 percent income tax bracket (state and federal combined) and a capital gains rate of 28 percent. This means that investors in this fund were able to preserve 89 percent of their total returns. Compared to other equity funds, this fund's tax savings are considered to be very good.

Expenses   ★★★★
Franklin Growth & Income's expense ratio is 0.9 percent; it has also averaged 0.9 percent annually over the past three calendar years. The average expense ratio for the 2,360 funds in this category is 1.4 percent. This fund's turnover rate over the past year has been 45 percent, while its peer group average has been 105 percent.

Summary   ★★★★
Franklin Growth & Income A has had very good risk-adjusted returns over the past three and five years. It has outperformed 85 percent of all other growth funds and its after-tax returns are also quite good. The fund ranks in the top quintile when it comes to growth persistence: the ability to consistently outperform equity funds over the previous five years. This offering also excels when it comes to superior risk-adjusted return persistence. In fact, this growth fund scores very well in virtually every category measured. Investors would be wise to check out other offerings from the large Franklin-Templeton group of funds.

Profile

minimum initial investment $1,000	*IRA accounts available* . . . . yes
subsequent minimum investment . . . $50	*IRA minimum investment* $250
available in all 50 states. . . . . yes	*date of inception.* . . . . June 1933
telephone exchanges. . . . . yes	*dividend/income paid.* . . . . semiannually
number of funds in family 166	*largest sector weighting* . . . technology

Growth Fund of America

333 South Hope Street
Los Angeles, CA 90071
(800) 421-4120
www.americanfunds.com

total return	★★★
risk reduction	★★★★
management	★★★★
tax minimization	★★★★
expense control	★★★★★
symbol AGTHX	20 points
up-market performance	good
down-market performance	good
predictability of returns	excellent

Total Return   ★★★

Over the past five years (ending 12/31/00), Growth Fund of America (GFA) has taken $10,000 and turned it into $30,520 ($20,485 over three years and $67,275 over the past ten years). This translates into an annualized return of 25 percent over the past five years, 27 percent over the past three years, and 21 percent for the decade. Over the past five years, this fund has outperformed 98 percent of all mutual funds; within its general category, it has done better than 95 percent of its peers. Growth funds have averaged 17 percent annually over these same five years.

Risk/Volatility   ★★★★

Over the past five years, GFA has been safer than 95 percent of all growth funds. Over the past decade, the fund has had no negative years, while the S & P 500 has had one (off 9 percent in 2000). The fund has underperformed the S & P 500 once in the past ten years.

	past 5 years		past 10 years	
worst year	7%	2000	0%	1994
best year	46%	1999	46%	1999

In the past, GFA has done better than 95 percent of its peer group in up markets and outperformed 70 percent of its competition in down markets. Consistency, or predictability, of returns for Growth Fund of America can be described as excellent. This fund's risk-related return is excellent.

Management   ★★★★

There are 190 stocks in this $36 billion portfolio. The average growth fund today is $550 million in size. Close to 85 percent of the fund's holdings are in stocks. The stocks in this portfolio have an average price-earnings (p/e) ratio of 37 and a median market capitalization of $22 billion. The portfolio's equity holdings can be categorized as large-cap and a blend of growth and value stocks.

A team has managed this fund for the past fifteen years. Management invests in a wide range of companies, including turnarounds, unseasoned, growing, and profitable. Up to 15 percent of the portfolio can be in foreign securities. The management team has positioned roughly three-fourths of the portfolio in just two sectors (something unusual for any equity member of the American Funds group). There are twenty-nine funds besides Growth Fund of America within the American Funds family. Overall, the fund family's risk-adjusted performance can be described as very good.

Tax Minimization ★★★★
During the past five years, a $10,000 initial investment grew to $28,265 after taxes, assuming a 39.6 percent income tax bracket (state and federal combined) and a capital gains rate of 28 percent. This means that investors in this fund were able to preserve 89 percent of their total returns. Compared to other equity funds, this fund's tax savings are considered to be very good.

Expenses ★★★★★
Growth Fund of America's expense ratio is 0.7 percent; it has also averaged 0.7 percent annually over the past three calendar years. The average expense ratio for the 2,360 funds in this category is 1.4 percent. This fund's turnover rate over the past year has been 45 percent, while its peer group average has been 105 percent.

Summary
Growth Fund of America has had excellent risk-adjusted returns over the past three, five, and ten years. The fund has outperformed 95 percent of its peer group (roughly 2,400 funds) and has the lowest expense ratio of any growth portfolio in the book. The fund scores very well or excellent in every single category. The portfolio ranks in the top quintile when it comes to growth persistence: the ability to consistently outperform equity funds over the previous five years. This offering also excels when it comes to superior risk-adjusted return persistence. Investors would be smart to check out other offerings from the highly respected American Funds group.

Profile

minimum initial investment $1,000	*IRA accounts available* . . . . yes
subsequent minimum investment . . . $50	*IRA minimum investment* $250
available in all 50 states. . . . . yes	*date of inception* . . . . Jan. 1959
telephone exchanges. . . . . yes	*dividend/income paid* . . . . annually
number of funds in family 30	*largest sector weighting* . . . technology

Heritage Capital Appreciation A

880 Carillon Parkway
St. Petersburg, FL 33716
(800) 421-4184
www.heritagefunds.com

total return	★★★
risk reduction	★★★★
management	★★★★
tax minimization	★★★★
expense control	★★★★★
symbol HRCPX	20 points
up-market performance	fair
down-market performance	very good
predictability of returns	excellent

Total Return   ★★★

Over the past five years (ending 12/31/00), Heritage Capital Appreciation A has taken $10,000 and turned it into $29,320 ($17,280 over three years and $61,920 over the past ten years). This translates into an annualized return of 24 percent over the past five years, 20 percent over the past three years, and 20 percent for the decade. Over the past five years, this fund has outperformed 98 percent of all mutual funds; within its general category, it has done better than 99 percent of its peers. Growth funds have averaged 17 percent annually over these same five years.

Risk/Volatility   ★★★★

Over the past five years, Heritage has been safer than 80 percent of all growth funds. Over the past decade, the fund has had two negative years, while the S & P 500 has had one (off 9 percent in 2000). The fund has underperformed the S & P 500 once in the past ten years.

	past 5 years		past 10 years	
worst year	-9%	2000	-9%	2000
best year	43%	1997	43%	1997

In the past, Heritage has done better than 80 percent of its peer group in up markets and outperformed 80 percent of its competition in down markets. Consistency, or predictability, of returns for Heritage Capital Appreciation A can be described as excellent. This fund's risk-related return is excellent.

Management   ★★★★

There are fifty stocks in this $225 million portfolio. The average growth fund today is $550 million in size. Close to 96 percent of the fund's holdings are in stocks. The stocks in this portfolio have an average price-earnings (p/e) ratio of 35 and a median market capitalization of $24 billion. The portfolio's equity holdings can be categorized as large-cap and a blend of growth and value stocks.

Herbert E. Ehlers has managed this fund for the past sixteen years. The fund is heavily weighted in just a handful of industry groups. Ehlers uses a bottom-up investment approach while searching for strong growth companies that have a market capitalization greater than $10 billion. The companies selected often have long-product cycles, dominant market share, and high cash flow. There are thirty-three funds besides Capital Appreciation A within the Heritage family. Overall, the fund family's risk-adjusted performance can be described as good.

Tax Minimization   ★★★★
During the past five years, a $10,000 initial investment grew to $27,000 after taxes, assuming a 39.6 percent income tax bracket (state and federal combined) and a capital gains rate of 28 percent. This means that investors in this fund were able to preserve 88 percent of their total returns. Compared to other equity funds, this fund's tax savings are considered to be very good.

Expenses   ★★★★★
Heritage Capital Appreciation's expense ratio is 1.3 percent; it has also averaged 1.3 percent annually over the past three calendar years. The average expense ratio for the 2,360 funds in this category is 1.4 percent. This fund's turnover rate over the past year has been 40 percent, while its peer group average has been 105 percent.

Summary
Heritage Capital Appreciation A is the second most consistent growth fund in the book. Risk-adjusted returns over the past three, five, and ten years have been magnificent. The fund has outperformed 99 percent of its peers and scores very well or excellent in every single category rated. The fund ranks in the top quintile when it comes to growth persistence: the ability to consistently outperform equity funds over the previous five years. This offering also excels when it comes to superior risk-adjusted return persistence.

Profile
minimum initial investment $1,000	*IRA accounts available* . . . . yes
subsequent minimum investment $1	*IRA minimum investment* $1,000
available in all 50 states. . . . . yes	*date of inception.* . . . . Dec. 1985
telephone exchanges. . . . . yes	*dividend/income paid* . . . . annually
number of funds in family 34	*largest sector weighting* . . . . . . services

Janus Mercury
100 Fillmore Street, Suite 300
Denver, CO 80206
(800) 525-8983
www.janus.com

total return	★★★★
risk reduction	★★★★★
management	★★★★
tax minimization	★★★
expense control	★★★★
symbol JAMRX	20 points
up-market performance	good
down-market performance	excellent
predictability of returns	good

Total Return   ★★★★
Over the past five years (ending 12/31/00), Janus Mercury has taken $10,000 and turned it into $31,760 ($24,065 over three years). This translates into an annualized return of 26 percent over the past five years and 34 percent over the past three years. Over the past five years, this fund has outperformed 99 percent of all mutual funds; within its general category, it has done better than 96 percent of its peers. Growth funds have averaged 17 percent annually over these same five years.

Risk/Volatility   ★★★★★
Over the past five years, Janus has been safer than 40 percent of all growth funds. Over the past decade, the fund has had one negative year, while the S & P 500 has also had one (off 9 percent in 2000). The fund has underperformed the S & P 500 once in the past ten years.

	past 5 years		past 10 years	
worst year	-23%	2000	-23%	2000
best year	96%	1999	96%	1999

In the past, Janus has done better than 95 percent of its peer group in up markets and outperformed 95 percent of its competition in down markets. Consistency, or predictability, of returns for Janus Mercury can be described as good. This fund's risk-related return is excellent.

Management   ★★★★
There are eighty stocks in this $13.3 billion portfolio. The average growth fund today is $550 million in size. Close to 90 percent of the fund's holdings are in stocks. The stocks in this portfolio have an average price-earnings (p/e) ratio of 46 and a median market capitalization of $38 billion. The portfolio's equity holdings can be categorized as large-cap and growth-oriented issues.

Warren B. Lammert III has managed this fund for the past eight years. Because of its concentration, the fund is considered to be "nondiversified" and can invest in any stock around the world. Lammert is a bottom-up stock selector and looks for companies whose products are hard or impossible to emulate. Disappointments are quickly discarded while selected stocks are often heavily purchased. There are thirty-eight funds besides Mercury within the Janus family. Overall, the fund family's risk-adjusted performance can be described as good.

Tax Minimization   ★★★
During the past five years, a $10,000 initial investment grew to $28,280 after taxes, assuming a 39.6 percent income tax bracket (state and federal combined) and a capital gains rate of 28 percent. This means that investors in this fund were able to preserve 84 percent of their total returns. Compared to other equity funds, this fund's tax savings are considered to be good.

Expenses   ★★★★
Janus Mercury's expense ratio is 0.9 percent; it has also averaged 0.9 percent annually over the past three calendar years. The average expense ratio for the 2,360 funds in this category is 1.4 percent. This fund's turnover rate over the past year has been 85 percent, while its peer group average has been 105 percent.

Summary
Janus Mercury has excellent three- and five-year risk-adjusted returns. Out of all growth funds in the book, it has been the best performer during bear markets. The fund's expense ratio is on the low side and so is turnover on a comparative basis. Janus Mercury has outperformed 99 percent of all mutual funds and 96 percent of its peers. The fund's score ranges from good to excellent in every category measured.

Profile
minimum initial investment . . . . . $2,500   *IRA accounts available* . . . . yes
subsequent minimum investment . . $100   *IRA minimum investment* $500
available in all 50 states. . . . . yes   *date of inception*. . . . . May 1993
telephone exchanges. . . . . yes   *dividend/income paid* . . . . annually
number of funds in family 39   *largest sector weighting* . . . technology

Legg Mason Value Trust-Primary Class
111 South Calvert Street
P.O. Box 1476
Baltimore, MD 21203
(800) 577-8589
www.leggmason.com

total return	★★★★
risk reduction	★★★★
management	★★★★
tax minimization	★★★★★
expense control	★★★
symbol LMVTX	20 points
up-market performance	poor
down-market performance	poor
predictability of returns	very good

Total Return   ★★★★

Over the past five years (ending 12/31/00), Legg Mason Value Trust-Primary Class has taken $10,000 and turned it into $33,040 ($17,280 over three years and $79,260 over the past ten years). This translates into an annualized return of 27 percent over the past five years, 20 percent over the past three years, and 23 percent for the decade. Over the past five years, this fund has outperformed 99 percent of all mutual funds; within its general category, it has done better than 99 percent of its peers. Growth funds have averaged 17 percent annually over these same five years.

Risk/Volatility   ★★★★

Over the past five years, Legg Mason has only been safer than 25 percent of all growth funds. Over the past decade, the fund has had one negative year, while the S & P 500 has also had one (off 9 percent in 2000). The fund has underperformed the S & P 500 once in the past ten years.

	past 5 years		past 10 years	
worst year	-7%	2000	-7%	2000
best year	48%	1998	48%	1998

In the past, Legg Mason has done better than 80 percent of its peer group in up markets but outperformed just 25 percent of its competition in down markets. Consistency, or predictability, of returns for Legg Mason Value Trust-Primary Class can be described as very good. This fund's risk-related return is excellent.

Management   ★★★★

There are thirty-six stocks in this $10.7 billion portfolio. The average growth fund today is $550 million in size. Close to 99 percent of the fund's holdings are in stocks. The stocks in this portfolio have an average price-earnings (p/e) ratio of 23 and a median market capitalization of $22 billion. The portfolio's equity holdings can be categorized as large-cap and value-oriented issues.

William H. Miller III has managed this fund for the past nineteen years. Miller is concentrated in the financial and technical sectors. He uses a bottom-up, buy-and-hold approach to security selection. When possible, management looks for companies selling at a discount to their intrinsic value. There are twenty-six funds besides Value Trust-Primary Class within the Legg Mason family. Overall, the fund family's risk-adjusted performance can be described as good.

Tax Minimization   ★★★★★
During the past five years, a $10,000 initial investment grew to $31,660 after taxes, assuming a 39.6 percent income tax bracket (state and federal combined) and a capital gains rate of 28 percent. This means that investors in this fund were able to preserve 94 percent of their total returns. Compared to other equity funds, this fund's tax savings are considered to be excellent.

Expenses   ★★★
Legg Mason Value Trust's expense ratio is 1.7 percent; it has also averaged 1.7 percent annually over the past three calendar years. The average expense ratio for the 2,360 funds in this category is 1.4 percent. This fund's turnover rate over the past year has been 20 percent, while its peer group average has been 105 percent.

Summary
Legg Mason Value Trust-Primary Class is the second-best tax minimizer within its entire category (close to 2,400 funds) and is the second lowest when it comes to turnover. Not only has tax efficiency been outstanding, so have results: it has out-performed 99 percent of its peers and competitors alike. The fund ranks in the top quintile when it comes to growth persistence: the ability to consistently outperform equity funds over the previous five years. The fund's performance has been in the top quartile among its peers for seven of the past eight years.

Profile
minimum initial investment . . . . . $1,000   *IRA accounts available* . . . . yes
subsequent minimum investment . . $100   *IRA minimum investment* $1,000
available in all 50 states. . . . . yes   *date of inception* . . . . Apr. 1982
telephone exchanges. . . . . yes   *dividend/income paid* . . . . quarterly
number of funds in family 27   *largest sector weighting* . . . . financials

Meridian Value
60 East Sir Francis Drake Boulevard, #306
Larkspur, CA 94939
(800) 446-6662

total return	★★★★
risk reduction	★★★★★
management	★★★★★
tax minimization	★★★★★
expense control	★★
symbol MVALX	21 points
up-market performance	excellent
down-market performance	fair
predictability of returns	excellent

Total Return   ★★★★
Over the past five years (ending 12/31/00), Meridian Value has taken $10,000 and turned it into $35,725 ($22,485 over three years). This translates into an annualized return of 29 percent over the past five years and 31 percent over the past three years. Over the past five years, this fund has outperformed 99 percent of all mutual funds; within its general category, it has also done better than 99 percent of its peers. Growth funds have averaged 17 percent annually over these same five years.

Risk/Volatility   ★★★★★
Over the past five years, Meridian has been safer than 96 percent of all growth funds. Over the past decade, the fund has had no negative years, while the S & P 500 has had one (off 9 percent in 2000). The fund has underperformed the S & P 500 once in the past ten years.

	past 5 years		past 10 years	
worst year	19%	1998	19%	1998
best year	38%	1999	38%	1999

In the past, Meridian has done better than 98 percent of its peer group in up markets but outperformed just 40 percent of its competition in down markets. Consistency, or predictability, of returns for Meridian Value can be described as excellent. This fund's risk-related return is also excellent.

Management   ★★★★★
There are forty stocks in this $200 million portfolio. The average growth fund today is $550 million in size. Close to 100 percent of the fund's holdings are in stocks. The stocks in this portfolio have an average price-earnings (p/e) ratio of 28 and a median market capitalization of $2 billion. The portfolio's equity holdings can be categorized as mid-cap and a blend of growth and value stocks.

Kevin C. O'Boyle and Richard F. Aster Jr. have comanaged this fund for the past seven years. Management looks for companies with moderate valuations along with earnings growth. The comanagers look for a strong balance sheet and a large return on capital as well as low debt. There is one other fund besides Value within the Meridian family. Overall, the fund family's risk-adjusted performance can be described as very good to excellent.

Tax Minimization   ★★★★★
During the past five years, a $10,000 initial investment grew to $33,155 after taxes, assuming a 39.6 percent income tax bracket (state and federal combined) and a capital gains rate of 28 percent. This means that investors in this fund were able to preserve 90 percent of their total returns. Compared to other equity funds, this fund's tax savings are considered to be excellent.

Expenses   ★★
Meridian Value's expense ratio is 1.6 percent; it has averaged 1.8 percent annually over the past three calendar years. The average expense ratio for the 2,360 funds in this category is 1.4 percent. This fund's turnover rate over the past year has been 120 percent, while its peer group average has been 105 percent.

Summary
Meridian Value has had stellar risk-adjusted returns over the past three, five, and ten years. The fund has outperformed 99 percent of its peers, a difficult task when you consider that it is a value player and competes against close to 2,400 funds that are growth and/or value oriented. Meridan also has the lowest risk of any fund in its category. The fund ranks in the top quintile when it comes to growth persistence: the ability to consistently outperform equity funds over the previous five years. This offering also excels when it comes to superior risk-adjusted return persistence. Investors are strongly encouraged to look at other Meridian funds.

Profile
minimum initial investment $1,000	*IRA accounts available* . . . . yes
subsequent minimum investment . . . $50	*IRA minimum investment* $1,000
available in all 50 states. . . . . yes	*date of inception* . . . . Feb. 1994
telephone exchanges. . . . . yes	*dividend/income paid* . . . . annually
number of funds in family 2	*largest sector weighting* . . . technology

Thornburg Value A

119 East Marcy Street, Suite 202
Santa Fe, NM 87501
(800) 847-0200
www.thornburg.com

total return	★★★★
risk reduction	★★★★★
management	★★★★★
tax minimization	★★★★★
expense control	★★★
symbol TVAFX	22 points
up-market performance	excellent
down-market performance	good
predictability of returns	excellent

Total Return   ★★★★

Over the past five years (ending 12/31/00), Thornburg Value A has taken $10,000 and turned it into $31,760 ($17,280 over three years). This translates into an annualized return of 26 percent over the past five years and 20 percent over the past three years. Over the past five years, this fund has outperformed 99 percent of all mutual funds; within its general category, it has done better than 99 percent of its peers. Growth funds have averaged 17 percent annually over these same five years.

Risk/Volatility   ★★★★★

Over the past five years, Thornburg has been safer than 96 percent of all growth funds. Over the past decade, the fund has had no negative years, while the S & P 500 has had one (off 9 percent in 2000). The fund has underperformed the S & P 500 once in the past ten years.

	past 5 years		past 10 years	
worst year	4%	2000	4%	2000
best year	38%	1996	38%	1996

In the past, Thornburg has done better than 97 percent of its peer group in up markets but outperformed just 25 percent of its competition in down markets. Consistency, or predictability, of returns for Thornburg Value A can be described as excellent. This fund's risk-related return is also excellent.

Management   ★★★★★

There are fifty stocks in this $950 million portfolio. The average growth fund today is $550 million in size. Close to 96 percent of the fund's holdings are in stocks. The stocks in this portfolio have an average price-earnings (p/e) ratio of 30 and a median market capitalization of $27 billion. The portfolio's equity holdings can be categorized as large-cap and a blend of growth and value stocks.

William V. Fries has managed this fund for the past six years. Management invests 40 to 50 percent of the portfolio's assets in low price-to-earnings and price-to-book stocks. Fries also considers corporations that are consistent growers and represent emerging franchises and special situations. A target sell price is set by management once a stock is purchased. There are twenty-four funds besides Value A within the Thornburg family. Overall, the fund family's risk-adjusted performance can be described as good.

Tax Minimization   ★★★★★
During the past five years, a $10,000 initial investment grew to $30,455 after taxes, assuming a 39.6 percent income tax bracket (state and federal combined) and a capital gains rate of 28 percent. This means that investors in this fund were able to preserve 94 percent of their total returns. Compared to other equity funds, this fund's tax savings are considered to be excellent.

Expenses   ★★★
Thornburg Value's expense ratio is 1.4 percent; it has averaged 1.5 percent annually over the past three calendar years. The average expense ratio for the 2,360 funds in this category is 1.4 percent. This fund's turnover rate over the past year has been 60 percent, while its peer group average has been 105 percent.

Summary
Thornburg Value A ties for first as having the highest overall score of any fund in its category. It is the most predictable in its group, the second most tax efficient, and the second best performer during bull markets. It has outperformed 99 percent of its roughly 2,400 member peer group plus has exhibited excellent after-tax returns. The fund ranks in the top quintile when it comes to growth persistence: the ability to consistently outperform equity funds over the previous five years. This offering also excels when it comes to superior risk-adjusted return persistence.

Profile
minimum initial investment $5,000	*IRA accounts available* . . . . yes
subsequent minimum investment . . $100	*IRA minimum investment* $2,000
available in all 50 states. . . . . yes	*date of inception* . . . . Oct. 1995
telephone exchanges. . . . . yes	*dividend/income paid* . . . . quarterly
number of funds in family 25	*largest sector weighting* . . . . financials

White Oak Growth Stock

P.O. Box 419441
Kansas City, MO 64141
(888) 462-5386
www.oakassociates.com

total return	★★★★
risk reduction	★★★
management	★★★★★
tax minimization	★★★★★
expense control	★★★★★
symbol WOGSX	22 points
up-market performance	excellent
down-market performance	excellent
predictability of returns	good

Total Return   ★★★★

Over the past five years (ending 12/31/00), White Oak Growth Stock has taken $10,000 and turned it into $35,725 ($21,470 over three years). This translates into an annualized return of 29 percent over the past three and five years. Over the past five years, this fund has outperformed 99 percent of all mutual funds; within its general category, it has also done better than 99 percent of its peers. Growth funds have averaged 17 percent annually over these same five years.

Risk/Volatility   ★★★

Over the past five years, White Oak has only been safer than 30 percent of all growth funds. Over the past decade, the fund has had one negative year, while the S & P 500 has also had one (off 9 percent in 2000). The fund has underperformed the S & P 500 once in the past ten years.

	past 5 years		past 10 years	
worst year	4%	2000	0%	1993
best year	50%	1999	53%	1995

In the past, White Oak has done better than 97 percent of its peer group in up markets but outperformed just 10 percent of its competition in down markets. Consistency, or predictability, of returns for White Oak Growth Stock can be described as good. This fund's risk-related return is excellent.

Management   ★★★★★

There are twenty-five stocks in this $5.5 billion portfolio. The average growth fund today is $550 million in size. Close to 98 percent of the fund's holdings are in stocks. The stocks in this portfolio have an average price-earnings (p/e) ratio of 44 and a median market capitalization of $74 billion. The portfolio's equity holdings can be categorized as large-cap and growth-oriented issues.

James D. Oelschlager has managed this fund for the past nine years. Management invests in established mid- and large-cap companies. Portfolio changes are made slowly. Oelschlager sometimes invests in as little as three or four sectors. Current holdings are monitored based on their p/e multiple in relation to the companies' five-year growth rate. There are two funds besides Growth Stock within the Oak family. Overall, the fund family's risk-adjusted performance can be described as good.

Tax Minimization   ★★★★★
During the past five years, a $10,000 initial investment grew to $35,725 after taxes, assuming a 39.6 percent income tax bracket (state and federal combined) and a capital gains rate of 28 percent. This means that investors in this fund were able to preserve 100 percent of their total returns. Compared to other equity funds, this fund's tax savings are considered to be excellent.

Expenses   ★★★★★
White Oak Growth Stock's expense ratio is 1 percent; it has also averaged 1 percent annually over the past three calendar years. The average expense ratio for the 2,360 funds in this category is 1.4 percent. This fund's turnover rate over the past year has been 5 percent, while its peer group average has been 105 percent.

Summary
White Oak Growth Stock has had excellent three- and five-year risk-adjusted returns. The fund frequently finishes in the top quartile when it comes to annual returns. White Oak ties for first place as having the highest overall score of any fund in its category and is the only fund in its category that does a superb job during bear as well as bull markets. This fund is also more tax efficient than any of its peers in the book and has the lowest turnover rate. The fund ranks in the top quintile when it comes to growth persistence: the ability to consistently outperform equity funds over the previous five years.

Profile
minimum initial investment $2,000	*IRA accounts available* . . . . yes
subsequent minimum investment . . . $50	*IRA minimum investment* $2,000
available in all 50 states. . . . . yes	*date of inception* . . . . Aug. 1992
telephone exchanges. . . . . yes	*dividend/income paid* . . . . annually
number of funds in family 3	*largest sector weighting* . . . technology

Growth and Income Funds

These funds attempt to produce both capital appreciation and current income, with priority given to appreciation potential in the stocks purchased. Growth and income fund portfolios include seasoned, well-established firms that pay comparatively high cash dividends. But do not let this category's name mislead you. The average growth and "income" fund has an annual yield of just 0.9 percent, versus 0.3 percent for the typical growth fund. The goal of these funds is to provide long-term growth without excessive volatility in share price. Portfolio composition is almost always exclusively U.S. stocks, with an emphasis on financial, technology, industrial cyclical, services, health, and energy stocks.

Over the past fifty years (ending December 31, 2000), common stocks have outperformed inflation, on average, 70 percent of the time over 1-year periods, 83 percent of the time over 5-year periods, 83 percent of the time over 10-year periods, 94 percent of the time over 15-year periods, and 100 percent of the time over any given 20-year period of time. Over the same period, high-quality, long-term corporate bonds have outperformed inflation, on average, 60 percent of the time over 1-year periods, 65 percent of the time over 5-year periods, 61 percent of the time over 10-year periods, 67 percent of the time over 15-year periods, and 68 percent over any given 20-year period of time.

Twelve hundred funds make up the growth and income category. Total market capitalization of this category is $1 trillion. Another category, "equity-income" funds, has been combined with growth and income. Equity-income funds have had

Growth and Income Funds

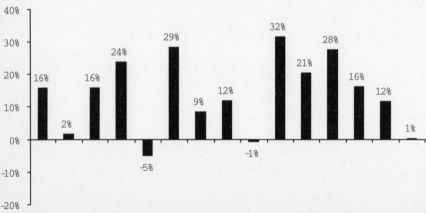

a standard deviation of 17.2 percent, an average annual dividend yield of 1.5 percent, a 70 percent turnover rate, and an average annual expense ratio of 1.4 percent. Over the past three years, equity-income funds have had an annualized return of 7.4 percent, 13.5 percent over the past five years, 14.5 percent for ten years, and 12.7 percent for the past fifteen years.

Over the past three and five years, growth and income funds have had an average compound return of 9.0 and 14.8 percent per year, respectively. These funds have averaged 14.9 percent annually over the past ten years and 13.0 percent annually for the past fifteen years. The standard deviation for growth and income funds has been 19.1 percent over the past three years (compared to 17.2 for equity-income and 27.6 percent for growth funds). This means that growth and income funds have been 45 percent more predictable than growth funds but have been about 11 percent less predictable than pure equity-income funds.

Alliance Growth & Income A

P.O. Box 1520
Secaucus, NJ 07096
(800) 227-4618
www.alliancecapital.com

total return	★★★
risk reduction	★★★★
management	★★★★
tax minimization	★★★
expense control	★★★★★
symbol CABDX	19 points
up-market performance	good
down-market performance	fair
predictability of returns	very good

Total Return ★★★

Over the past five years (ending 12/31/00), Alliance Growth & Income A has taken $10,000 and turned it into $24,885 ($15,210 over three years and $48,070 over the past ten years). This translates into an annualized return of 20 percent over the past five years, 15 percent over the past three years, and 17 percent for the decade. Over the past five years, this fund has outperformed 95 percent of all mutual funds; within its general category, it has also done better than 95 percent of its peers. Growth and income funds have averaged 15 percent annually over these same five years.

Risk/Volatility ★★★★

Over the past five years, Alliance has been safer than 55 percent of all growth and income funds. Over the past decade, the fund has had one negative year, while the S & P 500 has also had one (off 9 percent in 2000). The fund has underperformed the S & P 500 once in the past ten years.

	past 5 years		past 10 years	
worst year	11%	1999	-4%	1994
best year	29%	1997	38%	1995

In the past, Alliance has done better than 90 percent of its peer group in up markets but outperformed just 20 percent of its competition in down markets. Consistency, or predictability, of returns for Alliance Growth & Income A can be described as very good. This fund's risk-related return is excellent.

Management ★★★★

There are eighty-five stocks in this $2.1 billion portfolio. The average growth and income fund today is $850 million in size. Close to 95 percent of the fund's holdings are in stocks. The stocks in this portfolio have an average price-earnings (p/e) ratio of 23 and a median market capitalization of $23 billion. The portfolio's equity holdings can be categorized as large-cap and value-oriented issues.

Paul Rissman has managed this fund for the past seven years. Rissman is not required by prospectus to adhere to certain size companies, but he tends to favor large-cap issues. He feels equally comfortable with growth or value plays, provided there is future opportunity. There are 146 funds besides Growth & Income A within the Alliance family. Overall, the fund family's risk-adjusted performance can be described as good.

Tax Minimization ★★★
During the past five years, a $10,000 initial investment grew to $21,910 after taxes, assuming a 39.6 percent income tax bracket (state and federal combined) and a capital gains rate of 28 percent. This means that investors in this fund were able to preserve 80 percent of their total returns. Compared to other equity funds, this fund's tax savings are considered to be good.

Expenses ★★★★★
Alliance Growth & Income's expense ratio is 0.9 percent; it has also averaged 0.9 percent annually over the past three calendar years. The average expense ratio for the 1,300 funds in this category is 1.3 percent. This fund's turnover rate over the past year has been 45 percent, while its peer group average has been 70 percent.

Summary
Alliance Growth & Income A has had very good risk-adjusted returns over the past three and five years. The fund's annual performance figures have placed it in the top half or quartile for each of the past six years. Management has outperformed 95 percent of its growth and income peers. Although labeled as a "value" play, the fund has done quite well with growth as well as value equities. It has the lowest expense ratio of any portfolio in its group (1,300 competitors). The fund ranks in the top two quintiles when it comes to growth persistence: the ability to consistently outperform equity funds over the previous five years. This offering excels when it comes to superior risk-adjusted return persistence.

Profile

minimum initial investment $250	*IRA accounts available* . . . . yes
subsequent minimum investment . . . $50	*IRA minimum investment* $250
available in all 50 states. . . . . yes	*date of inception* . . . . July 1932
telephone exchanges. . . . . yes	*dividend/income paid* . . . . quarterly
number of funds in family 147	*largest sector weighting* . . . . financials

Ameristock
1301 East Ninth Street, 36th Floor
Cleveland, OH 44114
(800) 394-5064
www.ameristock.com

total return	★★★★
risk reduction	★★★★
management	★★★★
tax minimization	★★★★★
expense control	★★★★
symbol AMSTX	21 points
up-market performance	fair
down-market performance	very good
predictability of returns	excellent

Total Return   ★★★★
Over the past five years (ending 12/31/00), Ameristock has taken $10,000 and turned it into $28,155 ($16,430 over three years). This translates into an annualized return of 23 percent over the past five years and 18 percent over the past three years. Over the past five years, this fund has outperformed 97 percent of all mutual funds; within its general category, it has done better than 99 percent of its peers. Growth and income funds have averaged 15 percent annually over these same five years.

Risk/Volatility   ★★★★
Over the past five years, Ameristock has been safer than 85 percent of all growth and income funds. Over the past decade, the fund has had no negative years, while the S & P 500 has had one (off 9 percent in 2000). The fund has underperformed the S & P 500 once in the past ten years.

	past 5 years		past 10 years	
worst year	3%	1999	3%	1999
best year	33%	1997	33%	1997

In the past, Ameristock has done better than 85 percent of its peer group in up markets and outperformed 90 percent of its competition in down markets. Consistency, or predictability, of returns for Ameristock can be described as excellent. This fund's risk-related return is also excellent.

Management   ★★★★
There are fifty stocks in this $125 million portfolio. The average growth and income fund today is $850 million in size. Close to 98 percent of the fund's holdings are in stocks. The stocks in this portfolio have an average price-earnings (p/e) ratio of 22 and a median market capitalization of $63 billion. The portfolio's equity holdings can be categorized as large-cap and value-oriented issues.

Nicholas D. Gerber has managed this fund for the past six years. Gerber looks for large-cap stocks with large dividends. Management has relied on a relatively small research and analytical support staff that is quite amazing. Ameristock is the only fund within the Ameristock family.

Tax Minimization ★★★★★
During the past five years, a $10,000 initial investment grew to $27,430 after taxes, assuming a 39.6 percent income tax bracket (state and federal combined) and a capital gains rate of 28 percent. This means that investors in this fund were able to preserve 96 percent of their total returns. Compared to other equity funds, this fund's tax savings are considered to be excellent.

Expenses ★★★★
Ameristock's expense ratio is 1 percent; it has averaged 0.9 percent annually over the past three calendar years. The average expense ratio for the 1,300 funds in this category is 1.3 percent. This fund's turnover rate over the past year has been 30 percent, while its peer group average has been 70 percent.

Summary
Ameristock is the second most tax-efficient growth and income fund in the book. Risk-adjusted returns over the past five years have been outstanding and so has tax efficiency. The fund has outperformed over 99 percent of its 1,300-plus-member peer group of growth and income funds and has done so with below-average risk. Annual returns have been in the top quartile every year but one since the funds inception. I hope, the folks who run Ameristock will add other offerings to this one fund "family."

Profile
minimum initial investment $1,000
subsequent minimum investment . . $100
available in all 50 states. . . . . yes
telephone exchanges. . . . . yes
number of funds in family 1

IRA accounts available . . . . yes
IRA minimum investment $1,000
date of inception . . . . Aug. 1995
dividend/income paid . . . . semiannually
largest sector weighting . . . . financials

Burnham A

1325 Avenue of the Americas, 17th Floor
New York, NY 10019
(800) 874-3863
www.burnhamfunds.com

total return	★★★
risk reduction	★★★★
management	★★★★
tax minimization	★★★★★
expense control	★★★
symbol BURHX	19 points
up-market performance	very good
down-market performance	fair
predictability of returns	very good

Total Return   ★★★

Over the past five years (ending 12/31/00), Burnham A has taken $10,000 and turned it into $23,865 ($16,430 over three years and $40,460 over the past ten years). This translates into an annualized return of 19 percent over the past five years, 18 percent over the past three years, and 15 percent for the decade. Over the past five years, this fund has outperformed 95 percent of all mutual funds; within its general category, it has done better than 95 percent of its peers. Growth and income funds have averaged 15 percent annually over these same five years.

Risk/Volatility   ★★★★

Over the past five years, Burnham has been safer than 75 percent of all growth and income funds. Over the past decade, the fund has had one negative year, while the S & P 500 has also had one (off 9 percent in 2000). The fund has underperformed the S & P 500 once in the past ten years.

	past 5 years		past 10 years	
worst year	2%	2000	-2%	1994
best year	33%	1999	33%	1999

In the past, Burnham has done better than 95 percent of its peer group in up markets but outperformed just 20 percent of its competition in down markets. Consistency, or predictability, of returns for Burnham A can be described as very good. This fund's risk-related return is excellent.

Management   ★★★★

There are fifty-five stocks in this $200 million portfolio. The average growth and income fund today is $850 million in size. Close to 85 percent of the fund's holdings are in stocks. The stocks in this portfolio have an average price-earnings (p/e) ratio of 36 and a median market capitalization of $115 billion. The portfolio's equity holdings can be categorized as large-cap and growth-oriented issues.

Jon M. Burnham has managed this fund for the past six years. He considers management to be a long-term conservative investor. He uses a bottom-up approach, seeking large companies with strong balance sheets with earnings and revenue growth of 15 to 25 percent annually for at least the past three years. Burnham prefers well known issues and avoids out-of-favor issues. Stocks are sold if they drop more than 15 percent below their purchase price. There are four funds besides Burnham A within the Burnham family. Overall, the fund family's risk-adjusted performance can be described as very good to excellent.

Tax Minimization ★★★★★
During the past five years, a $10,000 initial investment grew to $22,620 after taxes, assuming a 39.6 percent income tax bracket (state and federal combined) and a capital gains rate of 28 percent. This means that investors in this fund were able to preserve 91 percent of their total returns. Compared to other equity funds, this fund's tax savings are considered to be excellent.

Expenses ★★★
Burnham's expense ratio is 1.3 percent; it has also averaged 1.3 percent annually over the past three calendar years. The average expense ratio for the 1,300 funds in this category is 1.3 percent. This fund's turnover rate over the past year has been 40 percent, while its peer group average has been 70 percent.

Summary
Burnham A ranks in the top quintile when it comes to growth persistence: the ability to consistently outperform equity funds over the previous five years. This offering also excels when it comes to superior risk-adjusted return persistence. This growth and income fund has outperformed 95 percent of its peers. Tax minimization has also been superb. Risk-adjusted returns during the past five years have been equally impressive. Burnham scores well in every respect. Investors should look into other offerings from Burnham.

Profile
minimum initial investment $1,000	*IRA accounts available* . . . . yes
subsequent minimum investment . . $250	*IRA minimum investment* $1,000
available in all 50 states. . . . . yes	*date of inception*. . . . . June 1975
telephone exchanges. . . . . yes	*dividend/income paid* . . . . quarterly
number of funds in family 5	*largest sector weighting* . . . technology

IPS Millennium
625 South Gay Street, Suite 630
Knoxville, TN 37902
(800) 249-6927
www.ipsfunds.com

total return	★★★★★
risk reduction	★★
management	★★★★
tax minimization	★★★★★
expense control	★★★
symbol IPSMX	19 points
up-market performance	excellent
down-market performance	excellent
predictability of returns	poor

Total Return   ★★★★★

Over the past five years (ending 12/31/00), IPS Millennium has taken $10,000 and turned it into $35,725 ($23,530 over three years). This translates into an annualized return of 29 percent over the past five years and 33 percent over the past three years. Over the past five years, this fund has outperformed 99 percent of all mutual funds; within its general category, it has done better than 97 percent of its peers. Growth and income funds have averaged 15 percent annually over these same five years.

Risk/Volatility   ★★

Over the past five years, IPS has only been safer than 15 percent of all growth and income funds. Over the past decade, the fund has had one negative year, while the S & P 500 has also had one (off 9 percent in 2000). The fund has underperformed the S & P 500 once in the past ten years.

	past 5 years		past 10 years	
worst year	-23%	2000	-23%	2000
best year	119%	1999	119%	1999

In the past, IPS has done better than 99 percent of its peer group in up markets and outperformed 95 percent of its competition in down markets. Consistency, or predictability, of returns for IPS Millennium can be described as poor. This fund's risk-related return is excellent.

Management   ★★★★

There are ninety-five stocks in this $425 million portfolio. The average growth and income fund today is $850 million in size. Close to 100 percent of the fund's holdings are in stocks. The stocks in this portfolio have an average price-earnings (p/e) ratio of 43 and a median market capitalization of $15 billion. The portfolio's equity holdings can be categorized as large-cap and growth-oriented issues.

Robert Loest has managed this fund for the past six years. Management looks for companies that are undervalued based on their financial fundamentals plus characteristics that should make them more resistant to economic downturns. There is one other fund besides Millennium within the IPS family. Overall, the fund family's risk-adjusted performance can be described as excellent.

Tax Minimization   ★★★★★
During the past five years, a $10,000 initial investment grew to $35,725 after taxes, assuming a 39.6 percent income tax bracket (state and federal combined) and a capital gains rate of 28 percent. This means that investors in this fund were able to preserve 100 percent of their total returns. Compared to other equity funds, this fund's tax savings are considered to be excellent.

Expenses   ★★★
IPS Millennium's expense ratio is 1.4 percent; it has also averaged 1.4 percent annually over the past three calendar years. The average expense ratio for the 1,300 funds in this category is 1.3 percent. This fund's turnover rate over the past year has been 50 percent, while its peer group average has been 70 percent.

Summary
IPS Millennium has the best three- and five-year performance figures of any growth and income fund in the book. It is also the most tax efficient and has been the best performer in up as well as down markets. This fund is only one of two funds in its category that does a superb job during bear as well as bull markets. Risk-adjusted returns over the past three and five years have been excellent. Investors would be smart to check out other offerings from the IPS group of funds.

Profile
minimum initial investment $2,500	*IRA accounts available* . . . . yes
subsequent minimum investment . . $100	*IRA minimum investment* $1,000
available in all 50 states. . . . . yes	*date of inception* . . . . Jan. 1995
telephone exchanges. . . . . yes	*dividend/income paid*. . . . semiannually
number of funds in family 2	*largest sector weighting* . . . technology

Oppenheimer Quest Balanced Value A

P.O. Box 5270
Denver, CO 80217
(800) 525-7048
www.oppenheimerfunds.com

total return	★★★
risk reduction	★★★★★
management	★★★★
tax minimization	★★★
expense control	★★★
symbol QVGIX	18 points
up-market performance	excellent
down-market performance	excellent
predictability of returns	excellent

Total Return   ★★★

Over the past five years (ending 12/31/00), Oppenheimer Quest Balanced Value A has taken $10,000 and turned it into $23,865 ($15,210 over three years). This translates into an annualized return of 19 percent over the past five years and 15 percent over the past three years. Over the past five years, this fund has outperformed 95 percent of all mutual funds; within its general category, it has done better than 99 percent of its peers. Growth and income funds have averaged 15 percent annually over these same five years.

Risk/Volatility   ★★★★★

Over the past five years, Oppenheimer has been safer than 55 percent of all growth and income funds. Over the past decade, the fund has had no negative years, while the S & P 500 has had one (off 9 percent in 2000). The fund has underperformed the S & P 500 once in the past ten years.

	past 5 years		past 10 years	
worst year	8%	2000	1%	1994
best year	31%	1997	31%	1997

In the past, Oppenheimer has done better than 96 percent of its peer group in up markets and outperformed 85 percent of its competition in down markets. Consistency, or predictability, of returns for Oppenheimer Quest Balanced Value A can be described as excellent. This fund's risk-related return is excellent.

Management   ★★★★

There are fifty-five stocks in this $1.1 billion portfolio. The average growth and income fund today is $850 million in size. Close to 23 percent of the fund's holdings are in stocks. The stocks in this portfolio have an average price-earnings (p/e) ratio of 23 and a median market capitalization of $31 billion. The portfolio's equity holdings can be categorized as large-cap and value-oriented issues.

Colin Glinsman has managed this fund for the past nine years. Glinsman has the majority of the equity portion of the fund in four industry groups. Management has close to 45 percent of the portfolio in bonds, the majority of which is in U.S. government paper. There are 166 funds besides Quest Balanced Value A within the Oppenheimer family. Overall, the fund family's risk-adjusted performance can be described as good.

Tax Minimization   ★★★
During the past five years, a $10,000 initial investment grew to $21,230 after taxes, assuming a 39.6 percent income tax bracket (state and federal combined) and a capital gains rate of 28 percent. This means that investors in this fund were able to preserve 81 percent of their total returns. Compared to other equity funds, this fund's tax savings are considered to be good.

Expenses   ★★★
Oppenheimer Quest Balanced Value's expense ratio is 1.5 percent; it has also averaged 1.5 percent annually over the past three calendar years. The average expense ratio for the 1,300 funds in this category is 1.3 percent. This fund's turnover rate over the past year has been 55 percent, while its peer group average has been 70 percent.

Summary
Oppenheimer Quest Balanced Value A is the only fund in its category that does a superb job during bear and bull markets, as well as having the most predictable results (and one of only four funds in the entire book that is classified as "excellent" in all three of these categories). Risk-adjusted returns over the past five years have been excellent. It is the second-best performer during bull markets and has done better than any of its group in the book during bear markets. Over the past seven calendar years, the fund has finished in the top-performance quartile six times.

Profile
minimum initial investment $1,000	*IRA accounts available* . . . . yes
subsequent minimum investment . . . $25	*IRA minimum investment* $250
available in all 50 states. . . . . yes	*date of inception* . . . . Nov. 1991
telephone exchanges. . . . . yes	*dividend/income paid* . . . . quarterly
number of funds in family 167	*largest sector weighting* . . . . financials

Pioneer A

60 State Street
Boston, MA 02109
(800) 225-6292
www.pioneerfunds.com

total return	★★★
risk reduction	★★★★
management	★★★★
tax minimization	★★★★
expense control	★★★★★
symbol PIODX	20 points
up-market performance	fair
down-market performance	good
predictability of returns	excellent

Total Return   ★★★

Over the past five years (ending 12/31/00), Pioneer A has taken $10,000 and turned it into $24,885 ($14,815 over three years and $48,070 over the past ten years). This translates into an annualized return of 20 percent over the past five years, 14 percent over the past three years, and 17 percent for the decade. Over the past five years, this fund has outperformed 95 percent of all mutual funds; within its general category, it has done better than 98 percent of its peers. Growth and income funds have averaged 15 percent annually over these same five years.

Risk/Volatility   ★★★★

Over the past five years, Pioneer has been safer than 90 percent of all growth and income funds. Over the past decade, the fund has had one negative year, while the S & P 500 has also had one (off 9 percent in 2000). The fund has underperformed the S & P 500 once in the past ten years.

	past 5 years		past 10 years	
worst year	0%	2000	-1%	1994
best year	38%	1997	38%	1997

In the past, Pioneer has done better than 80 percent of its peer group in up markets and outperformed 75 percent of its competition in down markets. Consistency, or predictability, of returns for Pioneer A can be described as excellent. This fund's risk-related return is also excellent.

Management   ★★★★

There are 145 stocks in this $6.6 billion portfolio. The average growth and income fund today is $850 million in size. Close to 100 percent of the fund's holdings are in stocks. The stocks in this portfolio have an average price-earnings (p/e) ratio of 27 and a median market capitalization of $37 billion. The portfolio's equity holdings can be categorized as large-cap and a blend of growth and value stocks.

John A. Carey has managed this fund for the past fifteen years. Carey has a value approach, seeking stocks that are trading below their fair market value. He favors companies with strong balance sheets and cash flows, and a healthy dose of insider ownership. Management is also attracted to corporations in either leadership or product transition. There are seventy funds besides Pioneer A within the Pioneer family. Overall, the fund family's risk-adjusted performance can be described as good.

Tax Minimization ★★★★
During the past five years, a $10,000 initial investment grew to $23,100 after taxes, assuming a 39.6 percent income tax bracket (state and federal combined) and a capital gains rate of 28 percent. This means that investors in this fund were able to preserve 88 percent of their total returns. Compared to other equity funds, this fund's tax savings are considered to be very good.

Expenses ★★★★★
Pioneer's expense ratio is 1.1 percent; it has also averaged 1.1 percent annually over the past three calendar years. The average expense ratio for the 1,300 funds in this category is 1.3 percent. This fund's turnover rate over the past year has been 10 percent, while its peer group average has been 70 percent.

Summary
Pioneer A scores good to excellent in every single category. It has lower turnover than any other growth and income fund in the book. The fund has outperformed 98 percent of its peer group, yet it has comparatively very high predictability when it comes to returns. Risk-adjusted returns over the past five years have been outstanding. The fund ranks in the top two quintiles when it comes to growth persistence: the ability to consistently outperform equity funds over the previous five years. This offering excels when it comes to superior risk-adjusted return persistence.

Profile
minimum initial investment $50
subsequent minimum investment . . . $50
available in all 50 states. . . . . yes
telephone exchanges. . . . . yes
number of funds in family 71

IRA accounts available . . . . yes
IRA minimum investment $50
date of inception . . . . Feb. 1928
dividend/income paid . . . . quarterly
largest sector weighting . . . . . . services

Selected American
2949 East Elvira Road, Suite 101
Tucson, AZ 85706
(800) 243-1575
www.selectedfunds.com

total return	★★★★
risk reduction	★★★★
management	★★★★★
tax minimization	★★★★★
expense control	★★★★★
symbol SLASX	23 points
up-market performance	very good
down-market performance	poor
predictability of returns	very good

Total Return   ★★★★
Over the past five years (ending 12/31/00), Selected American has taken $10,000 and turned it into $27,030 ($15,210 over three years and $61,920 over the past ten years). This translates into an annualized return of 22 percent over the past five years, 15 percent over the past three years, and 20 percent for the decade. Over the past five years, this fund has outperformed 96 percent of all mutual funds; within its general category, it has done better than 99 percent of its peers. Growth and income funds have averaged 15 percent annually over these same five years.

Risk/Volatility   ★★★★
Over the past five years, Selected has been safer than 75 percent of all growth and income funds. Over the past decade, the fund has had one negative year, while the S & P 500 has also had one (off 9 percent in 2000). The fund has underperformed the S & P 500 once in the past ten years.

	past 5 years		past 10 years	
worst year	9%	2000	-3%	1994
best year	38%	1997	47%	1991

In the past, Selected has done better than 95 percent of its peer group in up markets but outperformed just 15 percent of its competition in down markets. Consistency, or predictability, of returns for Selected American can be described as very good. This fund's risk-related return is excellent.

Management   ★★★★★
There are sixty-five stocks in this $4.8 billion portfolio. The average growth and income fund today is $850 million in size. Close to 85 percent of the fund's holdings are in stocks. The stocks in this portfolio have an average price-earnings (p/e) ratio of 25 and a median market capitalization of $63 billion. The portfolio's equity holdings can be categorized as large-cap and value-oriented issues.

Christopher C. Davis and Kenneth C. Feinberg have comanaged this fund for the past five years. Management uses a top-down and bottom-up approach to security selection. First, they look for companies that will benefit from long-term macroeconomic trends, such as shifting demographics. Next, they hone in on a candidate's financials. Stocks are sold once their price exceeds the comanagers, valuation. There are two funds besides American within the Selected family. Overall, the fund family's risk-adjusted performance can be described as very good.

Tax Minimization ★★★★★
During the past five years, a $10,000 initial investment grew to $25,500 after taxes, assuming a 39.6 percent income tax bracket (state and federal combined) and a capital gains rate of 28 percent. This means that investors in this fund were able to preserve 91 percent of their total returns. Compared to other equity funds, this fund's tax savings are considered to be excellent.

Expenses ★★★★★
Selected American's expense ratio is 0.9 percent; it has also averaged 0.9 percent annually over the past three calendar years. The average expense ratio for the 1,300 funds in this category is 1.3 percent. This fund's turnover rate over the past year has been 20 percent, while its peer group average has been 70 percent.

Summary
Selected American has the highest overall score of any fund in its category. It is the number one choice for the growth and income investor. It has outperformed over 99 percent of its peers and its tax efficiency has also been outstanding. The fund has the lowest expenses and the second-lowest turnover of its 1,300 competitors. The fund ranks in the top quintile when it comes to growth persistence: the ability to consistently outperform equity funds over the previous five years. This offering also excels when it comes to superior risk-adjusted return persistence. Investors would be wise to check out other offerings from Selected.

Profile
minimum initial investment $1,000
subsequent minimum investment . . . $25
available in all 50 states. . . . . yes
telephone exchanges. . . . . yes
number of funds in family 3

IRA accounts available . . . . yes
IRA minimum investment $250
date of inception . . . . Feb. 1933
dividend/income paid . . . . quarterly
largest sector weighting . . . . financials

Van Kampen Growth & Income A

One Parkview Plaza
Oakbrook Terrace, IL 60181
(800) 421-5666
www.vankampen.com

total return	★★★
risk reduction	★★★★★
management	★★★★
tax minimization	★★★
expense control	★★★★
symbol ACGIX	19 points
up-market performance	good
down-market performance	good
predictability of returns	excellent

Total Return   ★★★

Over the past five years (ending 12/31/00), Van Kampen Growth & Income A has taken $10,000 and turned it into $22,880 ($16,020 over three years and $52,3408 over the past ten years). This translates into an annualized return of 18 percent over the past five years, 17 percent over the past three years, and 18 percent for the decade. Over the past five years, this fund has outperformed 95 percent of all mutual funds; within its general category, it has also done better than 95 percent of its peers. Growth and income funds have averaged 15 percent annually over these same five years.

Risk/Volatility   ★★★★★

Over the past five years, Van Kampen has been safer than 96 percent of all growth and income funds. Over the past decade, the fund has had one negative year, while the S & P 500 has also had one (off 9 percent in 2000). The fund has underperformed the S & P 500 once in the past ten years.

	past 5 years		past 10 years	
worst year	13%	1999	-2%	1994
best year	24%	1997	36%	1995

In the past, Van Kampen has done better than 90 percent of its peer group in up markets and outperformed 55 percent of its competition in down markets. Consistency, or predictability, of returns for Van Kampen Growth & Income A can be described as excellent. This fund's risk-related return is also excellent.

Management   ★★★★

There are 105 stocks in this $1.4 billion portfolio. The average growth and income fund today is $850 million in size. Close to 90 percent of the fund's holdings are in stocks. The stocks in this portfolio have an average price-earnings (p/e) ratio of 29 and a median market capitalization of $26 billion. The portfolio's equity holdings can be categorized as large-cap and value-oriented issues.

A team has managed this fund for the past six years. The managers—James Gilligan, Scott Carroll, and James Roeder—are required to maintain a certain level of representation in twelve different industry groups designed by the parent company. Management uses a bottom-up approach, looking out for companies where there is some kind of catalyst for positive change. There are 137 funds besides Growth & Income within the Van Kampen family. Overall, the fund family's risk-adjusted performance can be described as good to very good.

Tax Minimization   ★★★
During the past five years, a $10,000 initial investment grew to $20,435 after taxes, assuming a 39.6 percent income tax bracket (state and federal combined) and a capital gains rate of 28 percent. This means that investors in this fund were able to preserve 81 percent of their total returns. Compared to other equity funds, this fund's tax savings are considered to be good.

Expenses   ★★★★
Van Kampen Growth & Income's expense ratio is 0.9 percent; it has also averaged 0.9 percent annually over the past three calendar years. The average expense ratio for the 1,300 funds in this category is 1.3 percent. This fund's turnover rate over the past year has been 90 percent, while its peer group average has been 70 percent.

Summary
Van Kampen Growth & Income A has had very good risk-adjusted returns for the past three, five, and ten years. It has outperformed 95 percent of all other mutual funds plus 95 percent of its entire category. Within its group, it is the second most predictable when it comes to returns and has the lowest risk level and the lowest expense ratio. The fund ranks in the top two quintiles when it comes to growth persistence: the ability to consistently outperform equity funds over the previous five years. This offering excels when it comes to superior risk-adjusted return persistence.

Profile
minimum initial investment . . . . . $1,000   *IRA accounts available* . . . . yes
subsequent minimum investment . . . $25   *IRA minimum investment* $500
available in all 50 states. . . . . yes   *date of inception* . . . . Aug. 1946
telephone exchanges. . . . . yes   *dividend/income paid* . . . . quarterly
number of funds in family 138   *largest sector weighting* . . . . financials

Victory Diversified Stock A

P.O. Box 8527
Boston, MA 02266
(800) 539-3863
www.victoryfunds.com

total return	★★★
risk reduction	★★★★
management	★★★★
tax minimization	★★
expense control	★★★★
symbol SRVEX	17 points
up-market performance	poor
down-market performance	very good
predictability of returns	very good

Total Return ★★★

Over the past five years (ending 12/31/00), Victory Diversified Stock A has taken $10,000 and turned it into $23,865 ($15,210 over three years and $52,340 over the past ten years). This translates into an annualized return of 19 percent over the past five years, 15 percent over the past three years, and 18 percent for the decade. Over the past five years, this fund has outperformed 95 percent of all mutual funds; within its general category, it has also done better than 95 percent of its peers. Growth and income funds have averaged 15 percent annually over these same five years.

Risk/Volatility ★★★★

Over the past five years, Victory has been safer than 35 percent of all growth and income funds. Over the past decade, the fund has had no negative years, while the S & P 500 has also had one (off 9 percent in 2000). The fund has underperformed the S & P 500 once in the past ten years.

	past 5 years		past 10 years	
worst year	1%	2000	1%	2000
best year	28%	1997	35%	1995

In the past, Victory has done better than 60 percent of its peer group in up markets and outperformed 95 percent of its competition in down markets. Consistency, or predictability, of returns for Victory Diversified Stock A can be described as very good. This fund's risk-related return is excellent.

Management ★★★★

There are seventy stocks in this $1 billion portfolio. The average growth and income fund today is $850 million in size. Close to 100 percent of the fund's holdings are in stocks. The stocks in this portfolio have an average price-earnings (p/e) ratio of 28 and a median market capitalization of $26 billion. The portfolio's equity holdings can be categorized as large-cap and value-oriented issues.

Lawrence G. Babin has managed this fund for the past twelve years. Management tries to maintain a portfolio that will withstand negative changing market conditions by including growth as well as value plays. Sector weightings are largely determined by a proprietary top-down approach, but Babin tries to keep these percentages in line with similar weightings found in the S & P 500. Stocks are sold once their value is in the bottom half of the stock universe and their representative sector weighting has also been downgraded. There are twenty-five funds besides Diversified Stock A within the Victory family. Overall, the fund family's risk-adjusted performance can be described as excellent.

Tax Minimization   ★★
During the past five years, a $10,000 initial investment grew to $20,680 after taxes, assuming a 39.6 percent income tax bracket (state and federal combined) and a capital gains rate of 28 percent. This means that investors in this fund were able to preserve 77 percent of their total returns. Compared to other equity funds, this fund's tax savings are considered to be fair.

Expenses   ★★★★
Victory Diversified Stock's expense ratio is 1.1 percent; it has also averaged 1.1 percent annually over the past three calendar years. The average expense ratio for the 1,300 funds in this category is 1.3 percent. This fund's turnover rate over the past year has been 80 percent, while its peer group average has been 70 percent.

Summary
Victory Diversified Stock A has outperformed 95 percent of all mutual funds as well as 95 percent of all growth and income funds. Risk-adjusted returns over the past three, five, and ten years have been very good. This fund is recommended for tax-sheltered (deferred) accounts since its tax efficiency is only considered to be fair. The fund ranks in the top two quintiles when it comes to growth persistence: the ability to consistently outperform equity funds over the previous five years. This offering excels when it comes to superior risk-adjusted return persistence. Investors are strongly advised to check out other funds from the Victory group.

Profile
minimum initial investment $500
subsequent minimum investment . . . $25
available in all 50 states. . . . . yes
telephone exchanges. . . . . yes
number of funds in family 26

IRA accounts available . . . . yes
IRA minimum investment $100
date of inception . . . . Oct. 1989
dividend/income paid . . . . quarterly
largest sector weighting . . . technology

Health Care

Sector funds, such as health care, technology, and utilities, allow investors the opportunity to invest in a particular area of the market without exposing their portfolios to the same risk as investing in just a few individual stocks. This sector includes pharmaceuticals, medical products, medical services, and biotechnology.

People spend money on health care even in a slowing economy, and the segment of the population that spends the most on health care has grown every year since 1929. According to Pharmaceutical Research and Manufacturers of America, those sixty-five years old and over spend nearly four times more on health care than those younger than sixty-five. In the United States, there are 35 million people sixty-five or older; the number is expected to increase to 40 million by 2010, 46 million by 2015, and 54 million by 2020.

These companies that make up this broad sector offer attractive revenue and earnings visibility that is generally immune to economic cycles. At the same time, the sector is benefiting from an overwhelming demographic shift.

Across the United States, Europe, and Asia, the sizable Baby Boom generation is aging and demanding more treatments to improve their lifestyles. This trend could drive tremendous industry demand growth over the next several decades. At the same time, groundbreaking discoveries in the biotechnology area are creating a multitude of exciting products to meet the demands of this aging population.

Biotechnology companies are developing advancements for medical, agricultural, and industrial application. A number of biotechnology companies have shown progressive leadership, but few have successfully marketed drugs or generated earnings. As a result, stocks in this area can be very volatile and highly sensitive to adverse news. For the 1999 calendar year, there were only seventeen profitable biotech companies; for the year 2000, that number increased to approximately twenty-two and is expected to further increase to thirty-five companies for 2001. It is for this reason that those health care mutual funds that have exposure to this "sub-sector" and are concerned with risk have only modest exposure to biotechnology. Research companies in areas such as genomics represent the ultimate in risk and reward potential.

Over the past couple of years, mutual fund managers have been more selective, focusing on profitable biotechs that have products in the pipeline or currently on the market. In response to this, biotechs have forged alliances with drug firms to expand their product portfolio and enhance profitability.

The medical supplies sub-sector remains strong. Increased demand for defibrillators, pacemakers, and cancer treatments such as radioactive seed implants, coupled with new-product approvals at the federal level, has kept this area's growth vigorous.

On the positive side, it is expected that the Bush administration will encourage and embrace market-driven policies. On the negative side, looming patent expirations and rising competition from generic drug companies continue to plague brand-dependent firms. The rising costs of brand-name drugs have prompted HMOs and PPOs to provide incentives for members to use less-expensive generic drugs. In response, brand-dependent firms have beefed up their research and development efforts by merging with other large drug firms.

The track record for the health care sector has been impressive. For the period 6/30/90 through 6/30/00, the S & P 500 had an average annualized return of 17.8 percent versus 23.5 percent for the S & P Health Care Sector Composite. The long-term growth prospects for health care are attractive and is largely based on three factors: people are living longer, products are coming to market faster, and the industry is benefiting from technological advances.

According to Data Resources, roughly 26 percent of the U.S. population is over fifty. By the year 2006, that number is expected to be 30 percent and close to 35 percent by the year 2015. Product approval cycles are shorter. According to the FDA, the mean number of approved products from 1989-1993 was twenty-five, with a mean approval time of twenty-nine months. Over the 1994-1998 period, the mean number increased to thirty-four and approval time dropped to seventeen months. Technological advances can also enhance profit potential.

Pharmaceutical sales are on the rise worldwide. As an example, sales in the United States increased by 11.5 percent in 1998, followed by a 15 percent gain in 1999. In Europe, there was a 4 percent increase in 1998 and a 7 percent increase in 1999. In Japan, "increases" went from a negative 5 percent in 1998 to a positive 2 percent in 1999.

There are fewer than 100 funds that make up this category; total market capitalization for this group is roughly $55 billion. Over the past three years, the average turnover rate has been an amazingly high 305 percent. The p/e ratio for health care funds is 45. Dividend yield is close to zero. Over the past three years, these funds have averaged a 27 percent annualized gain per year with a standard deviation of just under 38. For the past five and ten years, average annualized returns have been 21 percent; for the past fifteen years, annual returns have averaged over 20 percent. The category has underperformed the S & P 500 in six of the past ten years; yet for the entire ten-year period, average annual returns have been higher by 3 percent.

Health Care Funds

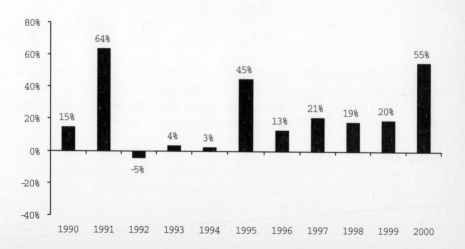

Eaton Vance Worldwide Health A

255 State Street
Boston, MA 02109
(800) 225-6265
www.eatonvance.com

total return	★★★★★
risk reduction	★★★★
management	★★★★
tax minimization	★★★★★
expense control	★★
symbol ETHSX	20 points
up-market performance	excellent
down-market performance	excellent
predictability of returns	good

Total Return   ★★★★★

Over the past five years (ending 12/31/00), Eaton Vance Worldwide Health A has taken $10,000 and turned it into $35,725 ($28,035 over three years and $100,860 over the past ten years). This translates into an annualized return of 29 percent over the past five years, 41 percent over the past three years, and 26 percent for the decade. Over the past five years, this fund has outperformed 99 percent of all mutual funds; within its general category, it has also done better than 99 percent of its peers. Health funds have averaged 21 percent annually over these same five years.

Risk/Volatility   ★★★★

Over the past five years, Eaton Vance has been safer than 60 percent of all health funds. Over the past decade, the fund has had one negative year, while the S & P 500 has also had one (off 9 percent in 2000); the Wilshire 5000 fell one time (off 11 percent in 2000). The fund has underperformed the S & P 500 once and the Wilshire 5000 twice in the past ten years.

	past 5 years		past 10 years	
worst year	11%	1997	-6%	1994
best year	82%	2000	82%	2000

In the past, Eaton Vance has done better than 80 percent of its peer group in up markets and outperformed 85 percent of its competition in down markets. Consistency, or predictability, of returns for Eaton Vance Worldwide Health A can be described as good. This fund's risk-related return is excellent.

Management   ★★★★

There are sixty stocks in this $530 million portfolio. The average health fund today is $610 million in size. Close to 97 percent of the fund's holdings are in stocks. The stocks in this portfolio have an average price-earnings (p/e) ratio of 47 and a median market capitalization of $10 billion. The portfolio's equity holdings can be categorized as mid-cap and growth-oriented issues.

Samuel D. Isaly has managed this fund for the past twelve years. Management invests in U.S. and foreign biotech and pharmaceuticals. The domestic portion of the portfolio can range from 30 to 70 percent. Price-to-cash flow is a favorite measurement used by management. Isaly sells a stock when he finds something better or when the current holding appears to be fully valued. There are 148 funds besides Worldwide Health A within the Eaton Vance family. Overall, the fund family's risk-adjusted performance can be described as good.

Tax Minimization   ★★★★★
During the past five years, a $10,000 initial investment grew to $34,695 after taxes, assuming a 39.6 percent income tax bracket (state and federal combined) and a capital gains rate of 28 percent. This means that investors in this fund were able to preserve 96 percent of their total returns. Compared to other equity funds, this fund's tax savings are considered to be excellent.

Expenses   ★★
Eaton Vance Worldwide Health's expense ratio is 1.8 percent; it has also averaged 1.8 percent annually over the past three calendar years. The average expense ratio for the eighty-five funds in this category is 1.7 percent. This fund's turnover rate over the past year has been 30 percent, while its peer group average has been 300 percent.

Summary
Eaton Vance Worldwide Health A rates number one within its category as having the best three-year returns. It is also the most tax efficient, the best up-market performer, and is one of only two funds in its category that does a superb job during bear as well as bull markets. This offering also excels when it comes to superior risk-adjusted return persistence. Risk-adjusted returns have been excellent over the past three, five, and ten years. This fund has outperformed over 99 percent of all other mutual funds.

Profile

minimum initial investment $1,000	*IRA accounts available* . . . . yes
subsequent minimum investment . . . $50	*IRA minimum investment* $50
available in all 50 states . . . . yes	*date of inception* . . . . July 1985
telephone exchanges . . . . yes	*dividend/income paid* . . . . annually
number of funds in family 149	*largest sector weighting* . . . . health

Vanguard Health Care

Vanguard Financial Center
P.O. Box 2600
Valley Forge, PA 19482
(800) 662-7447
www.vanguard.com

total return	★★★★★
risk reduction	★★★★★
management	★★★★★
tax minimization	★★★★★
expense control	★★★★★
symbol VGHCX	25 points
up-market performance	excellent
down-market performance	excellent
predictability of returns	excellent

Total Return   ★★★★★

Over the past five years (ending 12/31/00), Vanguard Health Care has taken $10,000 and turned it into $37,130 ($24,065 over three years and $93,135 over the past ten years). This translates into an annualized return of 30 percent over the past five years, 34 percent over the past three years, and 25 percent for the decade. Over the past five years, this fund has outperformed 99 percent of all mutual funds; within its general category, it has done better than 95 percent of its peers. Health funds have averaged 21 percent annually over these same five years.

Risk/Volatility   ★★★★★

Over the past five years, Vanguard has been safer than 99 percent of all health funds. Over the past decade, the fund has had one negative year, while the S & P 500 has also had one (off 9 percent in 2000); the Wilshire 5000 fell one time (off 11 percent in 2000). The fund has underperformed the S & P 500 once and the Wilshire 5000 twice in the past ten years.

	past 5 years		past 10 years	
worst year	7%	1999	-2%	1992
best year	61%	2000	61%	2000

In the past, Vanguard has done better than 70 percent of its peer group in up markets and outperformed 85 percent of its competition in down markets. Consistency, or predictability, of returns for Vanguard Health Care can be described as excellent. This fund's risk-related return is excellent.

Management   ★★★★★

There are 140 stocks in this $17.5 billion portfolio. The average health fund today is $615 million in size. Close to 92 percent of the fund's holdings are in stocks. The stocks in this portfolio have an average price-earnings (p/e) ratio of 42 and a median market capitalization of $19 billion. The portfolio's equity holdings can be categorized as large-cap and growth-oriented issues.

Edward P. Owens has managed this fund for the past seventeen years. Owens uses a bottom-up investment approach. To ensure diversification, management divides the portfolio into four sectors: international health services, medical products, large-cap pharmaceuticals, and speciality pharmaceuticals. Close to a fifth of the portfolio is in foreign issues. There are 101 funds besides Health Care within the Vanguard family. Overall, the fund family's risk-adjusted performance can be described as very good.

Tax Minimization ★★★★★
During the past five years, a $10,000 initial investment grew to $35,230 after taxes, assuming a 39.6 percent income tax bracket (state and federal combined) and a capital gains rate of 28 percent. This means that investors in this fund were able to preserve 93 percent of their total returns. Compared to other equity funds, this fund's tax savings are considered to be excellent.

Expenses ★★★★★
Vanguard Health Care's expense ratio is 0.4 percent; it has also averaged 0.4 percent annually over the past three calendar years. The average expense ratio for the eighty-five funds in this category is 1.7 percent. This fund's turnover rate over the past year has been 25 percent, while its peer group average has been 300 percent.

Summary
Vanguard Health Care has the highest overall score of any fund in its category and is the only fund in the book with a perfect score, 25 out of 25 possible points. It is also the only fund in its category that does a superb job during bear as well as bull markets, as well as having the most predictable results (and one of only four funds in the entire book that is classified as "excellent" in all three of these categories). It has the best five-year return figures, is the most predictable, has the lowest risk, lowest expense ratio, and smallest turnover rate, and is rated as the best down-market performer within its 85-member category. The fund ranks in the top quintile when it comes to growth persistence: the ability to consistently outperform equity funds over the previous five years. This offering also excels when it comes to superior risk-adjusted return persistence. As previously stated throughout this book, investors would be wise to look into other offerings from Vanguard.

Profile

minimum initial investment $25,000	*IRA accounts available* . . . . yes
subsequent minimum investment . . $100	*IRA minimum investment* $25,000
available in all 50 states. . . . . yes	*date of inception.* . . . . May 1984
telephone exchanges. . . . . yes	*dividend/income paid* . . . . annually
number of funds in family 102	*largest sector weighting* . . . . health

High-Yield Bond Funds

Sometimes referred to as "junk bond" funds, high-yield bond funds invest in corporate bonds rated lower than BBB or BAA. The world of bonds is divided into two general categories: investment grade and high-yield. Investment grade, sometimes referred to as "bank quality," means that the bond issue has been rated AAA, AA, A, or BAA (or BBB if the rating service is Standard and Poor's instead of Moody's). Certain institutions and fiduciaries are forbidden to invest their clients' monies in anything less than investment grade. Everything less than bank quality is considered junk.

Yet the world of bonds is not black and white. There are several categories of high-yield bonds. Junk bond funds contain issues that range from BB to C; a rating less than C means that the bond is in default, and payment of interest and/or principal is in arrears. High-yield bond funds perform best during good economic times. Such issues should be avoided by traditional investors during recessionary periods, since the underlying corporations may have difficulty making interest and principal payments when business slows down. However, these bonds, like common stocks, can perform very well during the second half of a recession.

Although junk bonds may exhibit greater volatility than their investment-grade peers, they are safer when it comes to interest-rate risk. Since junk issues have higher-yielding coupons and often shorter maturities than quality corporate bond funds, they fluctuate less in value when interest rates change. Thus, during expansionary periods in the economy when interest rates are rising, high-yield funds will generally drop less in value than high-quality corporate or government bond funds. Conversely, when interest rates are falling, government and corporate bonds will appreciate more in value than junk funds. High-yield bonds resemble equities at least as much as they do traditional bonds when it comes to economic cycles and certain important technical factors. Studies show that only 19 percent of the average junk fund's total return is explained by the up or down movement of the Lehman Brothers Government/Corporate Bond Index. To give an idea of how low this number is, 94 percent of a typical high-quality corporate bond fund's performance is explainable by movement in the same index. Indeed, even international bond funds have a higher correlation coefficient than junk, with 25 percent of their performance explained by the Lehman index.

The following table covers the five-year period ending December 31, 2000, and compares the total return of four well known bond indexes: Credit Suisse High Yield Index (bonds rated BBB or lower), the Lehman Aggregate Bond Index (securities from the Lehman Government/Corporate, Mortgage-Backed Securities, and Asset-Backed Indexes), the Lehman Government Bond Index (all publicly traded domestic debt of the U.S. government), and the Lehman Brothers Municipal Bond Index.

index	1 year	3 years	5 years	10 years
high-yield	-4.9%	-0.4%	4.6%	11.2%
aggregate	11.6%	6.4%	6.5%	8.0%
government	13.2%	6.7%	6.5%	7.9%
municipal	11.7%	5.2%	5.8%	7.3%

The high end of the junk bond market, those debentures rated BA and BB, have been able to withstand the general beating the junk bond market incurred during the late 1980s and early 1990s. Moderate and conservative investors who want high-yield bonds as part of their portfolio should focus on funds that have a high percentage of their assets in higher-rated bonds, BB or better.

According to Salomon Brothers, the people who are responsible for the Lehman Brothers corporate and government bond indexes used in this book, junk bond defaults averaged only 0.8 percent from 1980 to 1984. This rate almost tripled from 1985 to 1989 as defaults averaged 2.2 percent per year. Then, in 1990, defaults surged to 4.6 percent. Analysis based on historical data did not predict this huge increase in defaults. Bear in mind that BB-rated junk bonds can be expected to perform closer to high-quality bonds than will lower-rated junk. During 1990, for example, BB-rated bonds declined only slightly in price and actually delivered positive returns, whereas bonds rated CCC declined over 30 percent. During the mid-1990s, the default risk for the entire category had fallen to about 1.5 percent per year (well under 1 percent in the case of high-yield bond funds). From the mid-1990s through the first quarter of 2000, default rates increased to over 3.0 percent per year.

Over the past three and five years, high-yield corporate bond funds have had an average compound total return of -2.3 percent and 3.3 percent, respectively. The annual return for the past ten years has been 9.9 percent, and 7.6 percent for the past fifteen years (all figures as of December 31, 2000). The standard deviation for high-yield bond funds has been 7.9 percent over the past three years. This means that these funds have been less volatile than any equity fund category but have

High-Yield Bond Funds

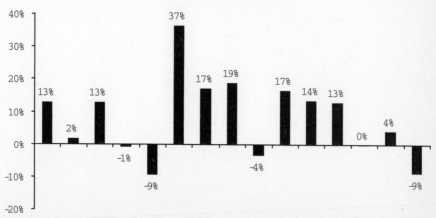

experienced over twice the return variances of other types of domestic bond funds. Turnover has averaged 85 percent. Three hundred and fifty funds make up the high-yield category. Total market capitalization of this category is $90 billion.

The majority of investors believe that the track record of high-yield bonds has been mixed, particularly in recent years. There was a crash in this market in 1990, but the overall track record has been quite good. These bond funds were up 13.4 percent in 1987, the year of the stock market crash. As the junk bond scare started in 1989, the fund category was still able to show a 12.8 percent return for the calendar year. The following year the group showed a negative return of 9.5 percent.

The 1990 loss was caused by regulatory agencies putting pressure on the insurance industry, formerly the largest owner of this investment category. This, together with the demise of Drexel Burnham, the largest issuer of junk bonds, caused high-yield bonds to suffer their biggest loss in recent memory. And yet the very next year, 1991, high-yield bond funds did better than ever before, up over 36.7 percent. The following two years were also quite good—up 17.5 percent in 1992 and up 19.0 percent in 1993. The following year, 1994, these funds fell 3.6 percent, followed by a gain of 13.9 percent in 1996, 13 percent in 1997, a loss of 0.4 percent in 1998, a gain of 4.1 percent in 1999, and a loss of 8.9 percent in 2000.

Fidelity Capital & Income
82 Devonshire Street
Boston, MA 02109
(800) 544-8888
www.fidelity.com

total return	★★★★
risk reduction	★★★
management	★★★★
current income	★★★
expense control	★★★★★
symbol FAGIX	19 points
up-market performance	excellent
down-market performance	poor
predictability of returns	good

Total Return ★★★★
Over the past five years (ending 12/31/00), Fidelity Capital & Income has taken $10,000 and turned it into $14,030 ($10,615 over three years and $31,060 over the past ten years). This translates into an annualized return of 7 percent over the past five years, 2 percent over the past three years, and 12 percent for the decade. Over the past five years, this fund has outperformed 50 percent of all mutual funds; within its general category, it has done better than 95 percent of its peers. High-yield bond funds have averaged 3 percent annually over these same five years.

During the past five years, a $10,000 initial investment grew to $11,615 after taxes, assuming a 39.6 percent income tax bracket (state and federal combined) and a capital gains rate of 28 percent. This means that investors in this fund were able to preserve 40 percent of their total returns. Compared to other fixed-income funds, this fund's tax savings are considered to be very good.

Risk/Volatility ★★★
Over the past five years, Fidelity has been safer than 45 percent of all high-yield bond funds. Over the past decade, the fund has had two negative years, while the Lehman Brothers Aggregate Bond Index has also had two (off 3 percent in 1994 and 1 percent in 1999); the Credit Suisse High-Yield Bond Index fell twice (off 1 percent in 1994 and 5 percent in 2000). The fund has underperformed the Lehman Brothers Aggregate Bond Index and the Credit Suisse High-Yield Bond Index twice in the past ten years.

	past 5 years		past 10 years	
worst year	-9%	2000	-9%	2000
best year	15%	1997	30%	1991

In the past, Fidelity has done better than 95 percent of its peer group in up markets but outperformed just 30 percent of its competition in down markets. Consistency, or predictability, of returns for Fidelity Capital & Income can be described as good. This fund's risk-related return is excellent.

Management   ★★★★

There are 295 fixed-income securities in this $2.7 billion portfolio. The average high-yield bond fund today is $250 million in size. Close to 80 percent of the fund's holdings are in bonds. The average maturity of the bonds in this account is less than five years; the weighted coupon rate averages 7.6 percent. The portfolio's fixed-income holdings can be categorized as being below BBB-rated.

David Glancy has managed this fund for the past five years. Management is able to have some modest stock exposure in order to beef up the fund's total return prospects. Glancy looks for possible corporate restructurings while avoiding firms that are capital intensive or economically sensitive. The modest stock portion frequently includes issues that the fund already owns on the bond side. There are 148 funds besides Capital & Income within the Fidelity family. Overall, the fund family's risk-adjusted performance can be described as good to very good.

Current Income   ★★★

Over the past year, Fidelity Capital & Income had a twelve-month yield of 9.7 percent. During this same twelve-month period, the typical high-yield bond fund had a yield that averaged 11.6 percent.

Expenses   ★★★★★

Fidelity Capital & Income's expense ratio is 0.8 percent; it has also averaged 0.8 percent annually over the past three calendar years. The average expense ratio for the 350 funds in this category is 1.3 percent. This fund's turnover rate over the past year has been 85 percent, while its peer group average has also been 85 percent.

Summary

Fidelity Capital & Income has had excellent risk-adjusted returns over the past ten years. It has outperformed 95 percent of all other high-yield corporate bond funds. It has the lowest expense ratio and second-lowest turnover rate. The fund ranks in the top quintile when it comes to growth persistence: the ability to consistently outperform equity funds over the previous five years.

Profile

minimum initial investment $2,500	*IRA accounts available* . . . . yes
subsequent minimum investment . . $250	*IRA minimum investment* $500
available in all 50 states. . . . . yes	*date of inception* . . . . Nov. 1977
telephone exchanges. . . . . yes	*dividend/income paid.* . . . . monthly
number of funds in family 149	*average credit quality* . . . . B

Janus High-Yield

100 Fillmore Street, Suite 300
Denver, CO 80206
(800) 525-8983
www.janus.com

total return	★★★★★
risk reduction	★★★★
management	★★★★★
current income	★★★
expense control	★★★
symbol JAHYX	20 points
up-market performance	excellent
down-market performance	good
predictability of returns	excellent

Total Return ★★★★★

Over the past five years (ending 12/31/00), Janus High-Yield has taken $10,000 and turned it into $15,390 ($10,930 over three years). This translates into an annualized return of 9 percent over the past five years and 3 percent over the past three years. Over the past five years, this fund has outperformed 20 percent of all mutual funds; within its general category, it has done better than 95 percent of its peers. High-yield bond funds have averaged 3 percent annually over these same five years.

During the past five years, a $10,000 initial investment grew to $12,160 after taxes, assuming a 39.6 percent income tax bracket (state and federal combined) and a capital gains rate of 28 percent. This means that investors in this fund were able to preserve 40 percent of their total returns. Compared to other fixed-income funds, this fund's tax savings are considered to be very good.

Risk/Volatility ★★★★

Over the past five years, Janus has been safer than 90 percent of all high-yield bond funds. Over the past decade, the fund has had no negative years, while the Lehman Brothers Aggregate Bond Index has had two (off 3 percent in 1994 and 1 percent in 1999); the Credit Suisse High-Yield Bond Index fell twice (off 1 percent in 1994 and 5 percent in 2000). The fund has underperformed the Lehman Brothers Aggregate Bond Index once and the Credit Suisse High-Yield Bond Index once in the past ten years.

	past 5 years		past 10 years	
worst year	1%	1998	1%	1998
best year	24%	1996	24%	1996

In the past, Janus has done better than 95 percent of its peer group in up markets and outperformed 65 percent of its competition in down markets. Consistency, or predictability, of returns for Janus High-Yield can be described as excellent. This fund's risk-related return is very good.

Management   ★★★★★

There are sixty fixed-income securities in this $300 million portfolio. The average high-yield bond fund today is $250 million in size. Close to 85 percent of the fund's holdings are in bonds and the balance is in cash equivalents. The average maturity of the bonds in this account is four years; the weighted coupon rate averages 9.8 percent. The portfolio's fixed-income holdings can be categorized as short-term, low-quality debt.

Sandy Rufenacht has managed this fund for the past five years. Management has wide discretion as to how it invests; the fund may own foreign securities, preferred stocks, convertibles, and government paper. It is required to have at least two-thirds of its assets in debt instruments rated below investment grade. Rufenacht has enjoyed a high level of success by simply avoiding the losers. There are thirty-eight funds besides High-Yield within the Janus family. Overall, the fund family's risk-adjusted performance can be described as good.

Current Income   ★★★

Over the past year, Janus High-Yield had a twelve-month yield of 8.8 percent. During this same twelve-month period, the typical high-yield bond fund had a yield that averaged 11.6 percent.

Expenses   ★★★

Janus High-Yield's expense ratio is 1 percent; it has also averaged 1 percent annually over the past three calendar years. The average expense ratio for the 350 funds in this category is 1.3 percent. This fund's turnover rate over the past year has been 310 percent, while its peer group average has been 85 percent.

Summary

Janus High-Yield is its category's best three- and five-year performer. The fund also boasts the lowest risk level and is the second-best when it comes to bull market returns. Roughly 60 percent of the fund is in bonds rated single B. The fund's overall score, 20 out of a possible 25, is quite impressive. This Janus offering receives good-to-excellent marks in every measured category. Tax efficiency for a bond portfolio is also considered to be quite good.

Profile

minimum initial investment $2,500	*IRA accounts available* . . . . yes
subsequent minimum investment . . $100	*IRA minimum investment* $500
available in all 50 states. . . . . yes	*date of inception.* . . . . Dec. 1995
telephone exchanges. . . . . yes	*dividend/income paid.* . . . . monthly
number of funds in family 39	*average credit quality* . . . . BB

Lord Abbett Bond-Debenture A

90 Hudson Street
Jersey City, NJ 07302
(800) 201-6984
www.lordabbett.com

total return	★★★
risk reduction	★★★★★
management	★★★★★
current income	★★★
expense control	★★★★★
symbol LBNDX	21 points
up-market performance	excellent
down-market performance	excellent
predictability of returns	excellent

Total Return   ★★★

Over the past five years (ending 12/31/00), Lord Abbett Bond-Debenture A has taken $10,000 and turned it into $13,385 ($10,930 over three years and $28,395 over the past ten years). This translates into an annualized return of 6 percent over the past five years, 3 percent over the past three years, and 11 percent for the decade. Over the past five years, this fund has outperformed 50 percent of all mutual funds; within its general category, it has done better than 95 percent of its peers. High-yield bond funds have averaged 3 percent annually over these same five years.

During the past five years, a $10,000 initial investment grew to $11,390 after taxes, assuming a 39.6 percent income tax bracket (state and federal combined) and a capital gains rate of 28 percent. This means that investors in this fund were able to preserve 41 percent of their total returns. Compared to other fixed-income funds, this fund's tax savings are considered to be very good.

Risk/Volatility   ★★★★★

Over the past five years, Lord Abbett has been safer than 95 percent of all high-yield bond funds. Over the past decade, the fund has had two negative years, while the Lehman Brothers Aggregate Bond Index has also had two (off 3 percent in 1994 and 1 percent in 1999); the Credit Suisse High-Yield Bond Index fell twice (off 1 percent in 1994 and 5 percent in 2000). The fund has underperformed the Lehman Brothers Aggregate Bond Index and the Credit Suisse High-Yield Bond Index twice in the past ten years.

	past 5 years		past 10 years	
worst year	-1%	2000	-4%	1994
best year	13%	1997	38%	1991

In the past, Lord Abbett has done better than 90 percent of its peer group in up markets and outperformed 80 percent of its competition in down markets.

Consistency, or predictability, of returns for Lord Abbett Bond-Debenture A can be described as excellent. This fund's risk-related return is excellent.

Management   ★★★★★
There are 320 fixed-income securities in this $2.1 billion portfolio. The average high-yield bond fund today is $250 million in size. Close to 90 percent of the fund's holdings are in bonds. The average maturity of the bonds in this account is six years; the weighted coupon rate averages 7.5 percent. The portfolio's fixed-income holdings can be categorized as intermediate-term and BBB-rated (barely investment grade).

Christopher J. Towle has managed this fund for the past ten years. Towle uses a bottom-up, value-oriented method when seeking out undervalued bonds. Selection is further refined by credit and yield spread analysis. Management also factors in interest-rate trends in order to reduce risk. The fund is required to have roughly 20 percent of its holdings in investment grade issues. There are eighty-seven funds besides Bond-Debenture A within the Lord Abbett family. Overall, the fund family's risk-adjusted performance can be described as good to very good.

Current Income   ★★★
Over the past year, Lord Abbett Bond-Debenture A had a twelve-month yield of 9.1 percent. During this same twelve-month period, the typical high-yield bond fund had a yield that averaged 11.6 percent.

Expenses   ★★★★★
Lord Abbett Bond-Debenture's expense ratio is 0.9 percent; it has also averaged 0.9 percent annually over the past three calendar years. The average expense ratio for the 350 funds in this category is 1.3 percent. This fund's turnover rate over the past year has been 65 percent, while its peer group average has been 85 percent.

Summary
Lord Abbett Bond-Debenture A is the only fund in its category that does a superb job during bear and bull markets, as well as having the most predictable results (and one of only four funds in the entire book that is classified as "excellent" in all three of these categories). It has the lowest risk, second-lowest expenses, lowest turnover, and is the best down-market performer. Risk-adjusted returns have been outstanding over the past decade. The fund ranks in the top quintile when it comes to growth persistence: the ability to consistently outperform equity funds over the previous five years. This offering also scores highly when it comes to superior risk-adjusted return persistence.

Profile
minimum initial investment $1,000	*IRA accounts available* . . . . yes
subsequent minimum investment $1	*IRA minimum investment* $250
available in all 50 states. . . . . yes	*date of inception* . . . . Apr. 1971
telephone exchanges. . . . . yes	*dividend/income paid.* . . . . monthly
number of funds in family 88	*average credit quality.* . . . . BBB

Strong H/Y Bond Fund-Investor Class

P.O. Box 2936
Milwaukee, WI 53201
(800) 368-1030
www.strongfunds.com

total return	★★★★★
risk reduction	★★★★
management	★★★★★
current income	★★★★★
expense control	★★★★
symbol STHYX	23 points
up-market performance	good
down-market performance	very good
predictability of returns	excellent

Total Return   ★★★★★

Over the past five years (ending 12/31/00), Strong H/Y Bond Fund-Investor Class
has taken $10,000 and turned it into $15,390 ($10,305 over three years). This trans-
lates into an annualized return of 9 percent over the past five years and 1 percent
over the past three years. Over the past five years, this fund has outperformed 99
percent of its peers. High-yield bond funds have averaged 3 percent annually over
these same five years.

During the past five years, a $10,000 initial investment grew to $13,235 after
taxes, assuming a 39.6 percent income tax bracket (state and federal combined) and
a capital gains rate of 28 percent. This means that investors in this fund were able
to preserve 60 percent of their total returns. Compared to other fixed-income funds,
this fund's tax savings are considered to be excellent.

Risk/Volatility   ★★★★

Over the past five years, Strong has been safer than 90 percent of all high-yield
bond funds. Over the past decade, the fund has had one negative year, while the
Lehman Brothers Aggregate Bond Index has had two (off 3 percent in 1994 and 1
percent in 1999); the Credit Suisse High-Yield Bond Index fell twice (off 1 percent
in 1994 and 5 percent in 2000). The fund has underperformed the Lehman Brothers
Aggregate Bond Index and the Credit Suisse High-Yield Bond Index once in the
past ten years.

	past 5 years		past 10 years	
worst year	-7%	2000	-7%	2000
best year	27%	1996	27%	1996

In the past, Strong has done better than 75 percent of its peer group in up markets and outperformed 80 percent of its competition in down markets. Consistency,
or predictability, of returns for Strong H/Y Bond Fund-Investor Class can be
described as excellent. This fund's risk-related return is also excellent.

Management   ★★★★★
There are 140 fixed-income securities in this $625 million portfolio. The average high-yield bond fund today is $250 million in size. Close to 87 percent of the fund's holdings are in bonds and the balance is in cash. The average maturity of the bonds in this account is 6.5 years; the weighted coupon rate averages 8.2 percent. The portfolio's fixed-income holdings can be categorized as intermediate-term, low-quality debt.

Jeffery A. Koch and Thomas M. Price have comanaged this fund for the past five years. Roughly two-thirds of the fund's assets are in single-B rated bonds. There are forty-five funds besides H/Y Bond Fund-Investor Class within the Strong family. Overall, the fund family's risk-adjusted performance can be described as good.

Current Income   ★★★★★
Over the past year, Strong H/Y Bond Fund-Investor Class had a twelve-month yield of 12.7 percent. During this same twelve-month period, the typical high-yield bond fund had a yield that averaged 11.6 percent.

Expenses   ★★★★
Strong H/Y Bond Fund's expense ratio is 0.8 percent; it has also averaged 0.8 percent annually over the past three calendar years. The average expense ratio for the 350 funds in this category is 1.3 percent. This fund's turnover rate over the past year has been 145 percent, while its peer group average has been 85 percent.

Summary
Strong H/Y Bond Fund-Investor Class has the highest overall score of any fund in its category. It is considered the best high-yield corporate bond fund. The fund is the best five-year performer and has the lowest expense ratio among its peers. Tax efficiency has also been outstanding. With a near-perfect 23 out of 25 possible points, this Strong offering has no peers and is rated higher than most funds, regardless of category. It is highly recommended.

Profile

minimum initial investment $2,500	*IRA accounts available* . . . . yes
subsequent minimum investment . . . $50	*IRA minimum investment* $250
available in all 50 states. . . . . yes	*date of inception.* . . . . Dec. 1995
telephone exchanges. . . . . yes	*dividend/income paid.* . . . . monthly
number of funds in family 46	*average credit quality* . . . . B

Metals and Natural Resources Funds

These funds purchase metals in one or more of the following forms: bullion, South African gold stocks, and non–South African mining stocks. The United States, Canada, and Australia are the three major stock-issuing producers of metals outside South Africa. Metals funds, also referred to as gold funds, often own minor positions in other precious metals stocks, such as silver and platinum.

The proportion and type of metal held by a fund can have a great impact on its performance and volatility. Outright ownership of gold bullion is almost always less volatile than owning stock in a gold mining company. Thus, much greater gains or losses occur in metals funds that purchase only gold stocks, compared to funds that hold high levels of bullion, coins, and stock. Silver, incidentally, has nearly twice the volatility of gold, yet has not enjoyed any greater returns over the long term.

Gold, or metals, funds can do well during periods of political uncertainty and inflationary concerns. Over the past several hundred years, gold and silver have served as hedges against inflation. Most readers will be surprised to learn that, historically, both metals have outperformed inflation by less than 1 percent annually.

Metals funds are the second riskiest category of mutual funds described in this book with a standard deviation of 38.9 (technology stocks are number one, with a standard deviation of 63.6). And yet, although this is certainly a high-risk investment when viewed on its own, ownership of a metals fund can sometimes reduce a portfolio's overall risk level. Why? Because gold usually has a negative correlation to other investments.

There are forty metals funds; total market capitalization is less than $2 billion. Turnover has averaged 85 percent. The p/e ratio for metals funds is 24, while dividend yield is a little less than 0.75 percent. Over the past three years, these funds have averaged -8.9 percent per year, -13.8 percent for the past five years, -5.4 percent for the past decade, and -0.8 percent for the past fifteen years.

Natural resources funds invest in the stocks of companies that deal in the ownership, production, transmission, transportation, refinement, and/or storage of oil, natural gas, and timber. These funds also invest in companies that either own or are involved in real estate.

There are sixty-five natural resources funds; total market capitalization is under $5.8 billion. This group has had a standard deviation of 33.9 percent over the past three years. Beta, or market-related risk, has been 0.8 percent, but do not let this low number fool you. As you can see by the standard deviation, few equity categories are riskier. Annual turnover has averaged 220 percent. The p/e ratio for natural resources funds is 29; dividend yield is 0.5 percent. Over the past three years, these funds have averaged 7.4 percent, 11.2 percent for the past five years, 10.7 percent for the past ten years, and 10.3 percent for the past fifteen years.

Metals and natural resources funds should be avoided by anyone who cannot tolerate wide price swings in any single part of the portfolio. These funds are designed as an integral part of a diversified portfolio, for investors who look at the overall return of their holdings. Despite the potential benefits of diversification, metals funds are still not recommended for the vast majority of investors. The track record for metals funds is simply terrible except for an occasional great year (for example, +81.1 percent in 1993) and variations of return are frequently wild.

Precious Metals Funds

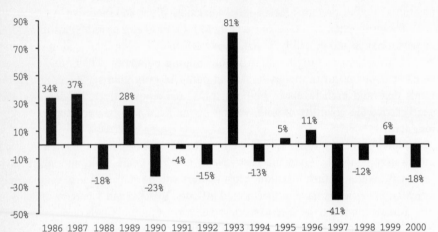

Natural Resources Funds

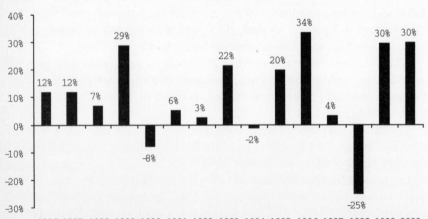

State Street Research Global Resources A

One Financial Center
Boston, MA 02111
(800) 882-0052
www.ssrfunds.com

total return	★★★★★
risk reduction	★★★★
management	★★★★★
tax minimization	★★★
expense control	★★★★
symbol SSGRX	22 points
up-market performance	excellent
down-market performance	good
predictability of returns	good

Total Return   ★★★★★

Over the past five years (ending 12/31/00), State Street Research Global Resources A has taken $10,000 and turned it into $20,115 ($10,930 over three years and $25,940 over the past ten years). This translates into an annualized return of 15 percent over the past five years, 3 percent over the past three years, and 10 percent for the decade. Over the past five years, this fund has outperformed 70 percent of all mutual funds; within its general category, it has done better than 80 percent of its peers. Metals and natural resources funds have averaged 0.25 percent annually over these same five years.

Risk/Volatility   ★★★★

Over the past five years, State Street Research has only been safer than 15 percent of all metals and natural resources funds. Over the past decade, the fund has had three negative years, while the S & P 500 has had one (off 9 percent in 2000). The fund has underperformed the S & P 500 seven times in the past ten years.

	past 5 years		past 10 years	
worst year	-48%	1998	-48%	1998
best year	84%	2000	84%	2000

In the past, State Street Research has done better than 80 percent of its peer group in up markets but outperformed just 30 percent of its competition in down markets. Consistency, or predictability, of returns for State Street Research Global Resources A can be described as good. This fund's risk-related return is poor.

Management   ★★★★★

There are seventy-five stocks in this $55 million portfolio. The average metals and natural resources fund today is $80 million in size. Close to 100 percent of the fund's holdings are in stocks. The stocks in this portfolio have an average price-earnings (p/e) ratio of 29 and a median market capitalization of $485 million. Roughly 90 percent of the stocks are from companies located in the United States or Canada. The portfolio's equity holdings can be categorized as small-cap and growth-oriented issues.

Daniel J. Rice III has managed this fund for the past eleven years. Prospective holdings include companies involved in the exploration, production, or distribution of oil and natural gas. Management mostly invests in developed markets around the world. Rice likes growth as well as value plays. There are eighty funds besides Global Resources within the State Street Research family. Overall, the fund family's risk-adjusted performance can be described as good.

Tax Minimization   ★★★
During the past five years, a $10,000 initial investment grew to $18,900 after taxes, assuming a 39.6 percent income tax bracket (state and federal combined) and a capital gains rate of 28 percent. This means that investors in this fund were able to preserve 88 percent of their total returns. Compared to other equity funds, this fund's tax savings are considered to be very good.

Expenses   ★★★★
State Street Research Global's expense ratio is 1.7 percent; it has averaged 1.6 percent annually over the past three calendar years. The average expense ratio for the 100 funds in this category is 2.0 percent. This fund's turnover rate over the past year has been 450 percent, while its peer group average has been 170 percent.

Summary
State Street Research Global Resources A ties for first place as the best five-year performing metals and natural resources fund in the book. In its category, it is also ranked the best performer during bull markets. The fund has outperformed 80 percent of its peers. Despite an incredibly high turnover rate, tax efficiency has been very good. This fund is a great choice for any investor who wishes to add natural resources to his or her portfolio for diversification.

Profile
minimum initial investment $2,500	*IRA accounts available* . . . . yes
subsequent minimum investment . . . $50	*IRA minimum investment* $2,000
available in all 50 states. . . . . yes	*date of inception*. . . . . Mar. 1990
telephone exchanges. . . . . yes	*dividend/income paid* . . . . annually
number of funds in family 81	*largest sector weighting*. . . . . . . energy

Vanguard Energy
Vanguard Financial Center
P.O. Box 2600
Valley Forge, PA 19482
(800) 662-7447
www.vanguard.com

total return	★★★★★
risk reduction	★★★★★
management	★★★★★
tax minimization	★★★★
expense control	★★★★★
symbol VGENX	24 points
up-market performance	good
down-market performance	excellent
predictability of returns	excellent

Total Return   ★★★★★

Over the past five years (ending 12/31/00), Vanguard Energy has taken $10,000 and turned it into $20,115 ($12,950 over three years and $33,950 over the past ten years). This translates into an annualized return of 15 percent over the past five years, 9 percent over the past three years, and 13 percent for the decade. Over the past five years, this fund has outperformed 80 percent of all mutual funds; within its general category, it has done better than 90 percent of its peers. Metals and natural resources funds have averaged 0.25 percent annually over these same five years.

Risk/Volatility   ★★★★★

Over the past five years, Vanguard has been safer than 75 percent of all metals and natural resources funds. Over the past decade, the fund has had two negative years, while the S & P 500 has had one (off 9 percent in 2000). The fund has underperformed the S & P 500 seven times in the past ten years.

	past 5 years		past 10 years	
worst year	-21%	1998	-21%	1998
best year	36%	2000	36%	2000

In the past, Vanguard has done better than 40 percent of its peer group in up markets and outperformed 48 percent of its competition in down markets. Consistency, or predictability, of returns for Vanguard Energy can be described as excellent. This fund's risk-related return is poor.

Management   ★★★★★

There are fifty stocks in this $1.2 billion portfolio. The average metals and natural resources fund today is $80 million in size. Close to 95 percent of the fund's holdings are in stocks. The stocks in this portfolio have an average price-earnings (p/e) ratio of 27 and a median market capitalization of $7.8 billion. The portfolio's equity holdings can be categorized as mid-cap and value-oriented issues.

Ernst H. von Metzsch has managed this fund for the past seventeen years. He believes it is difficult to find consistent growth in the energy sector, so von Metzsch tends to emphasize value over growth. Management has selected a diversified range of energy stocks, U.S. as well as foreign, and the portfolio is pretty evenly divided between oil and gas issues. The manager leans toward integrated companies as well as stand-alone producers and refiners. There are 101 funds besides Energy within the Vanguard family. Overall, the fund family's risk-adjusted performance can be described as very good.

Tax Minimization   ★★★★
During the past five years, a $10,000 initial investment grew to $19,005 after taxes, assuming a 39.6 percent income tax bracket (state and federal combined) and a capital gains rate of 28 percent. This means that investors in this fund were able to preserve 89 percent of their total returns. Compared to other equity funds, this fund's tax savings are considered to be very good.

Expenses   ★★★★★
Vanguard Energy's expense ratio is 0.5 percent; it has averaged 0.4 percent annually over the past three calendar years. The average expense ratio for the 100 funds in this category is 2.0 percent. This fund's turnover rate over the past year has been 15 percent, while its peer group average has been 170 percent.

Summary
Vanguard Energy has the highest overall score of any fund in its category. It ties for first place as the best five-year performer. It ranks first when it comes to three-year returns and has also exhibited the lowest risk and has the best bear market performance for its group. Finally, this Vanguard offering has lower expenses and the lowest turnover, and is the most tax-efficient natural resources fund in the book. Investors would be wise to check out other offerings from Vanguard.

Profile

minimum initial investment $3,000	IRA accounts available . . . . yes
subsequent minimum investment . . $100	IRA minimum investment $1,000
available in all 50 states. . . . . yes	date of inception. . . . . May 1984
telephone exchanges. . . . . yes	dividend/income paid . . . . annually
number of funds in family 102	largest sector weighting. . . . . . . energy

Money Market Funds

Money market funds invest in securities that mature in less than one year. They are made up of one or more of the following instruments: Treasury bills, certificates of deposit, commercial paper, repurchase agreements, Eurodollar CDs, and notes. There are four different categories of money market funds: all-purpose, government-backed, federally tax-free, and double tax-exempt.

All-purpose funds are the most popular and make up the bulk of the money market universe. Fully taxable, they are composed of securities such as CDs, commercial paper, and T-bills.

Government-backed money market funds invest only in short-term paper, directly or indirectly backed by the U.S. government. These funds are technically safer than the all-purpose variety, but only one money market fund has ever defaulted (a fund set up by a bank for banks). The yield on government-backed funds is somewhat lower than that of its all-purpose peers.

Federally tax-free funds are made up of municipal notes. Investors in these funds do not have to pay federal income taxes on the interest earned. The before-tax yield on federally tax-free funds is certainly lower than that of all-purpose and government-backed funds, but the after-tax return can be greater for the moderate- or high-tax-bracket investor.

Double tax-exempt funds invest in the municipal obligations of a specific state. You must be a resident of that state in order to avoid paying state income taxes on any interest earned. Nonresident investors will still receive a federal tax exemption.

All money market funds are safer than any other mutual fund or category of funds in this book. They have a perfect track record (if you exclude the one money market fund set up for banks)—investors can only make money in these interest-bearing accounts. The rate of return earned in a money market depends upon the average maturity of the fund's paper, the kinds of securities held, the quality rating of that paper, and how efficiently the fund is operated. A lean fund will almost always outperform a similar fund with high operating costs.

Investments such as U. S. Treasury bills and, for all practical purposes, money market funds, are often referred to as "risk-free." These kinds of investments are free from price swings and default risk because of their composition. However, as we have come to learn, there is more than one form of risk. Money market funds should never be considered as a medium- or long-term investment. The real return on this investment is poor. An investment's real return takes into account the effects of inflation and income taxes. During virtually every period of time, the after-tax, after-inflation return on all money market funds has been near zero or even negative.

Over the past fifty years, U.S. Treasury bills—an index often used as a substitute for money market funds—have outperformed inflation on average 80 percent of the time over 1-year periods, 80 percent of the time over 5-year periods, 78 percent of the time over 10-year periods, 92 percent of the time over 15-year periods, and 97 percent over any given 20-year period of time. These figures are not adjusted for income taxes. Money market funds have rarely, if ever, outperformed inflation on an after-tax basis when looking at 3-, 5-, 10-, 15-, or 20-year holding positions.

Investors often look back to the good old days of the early 1980s, when money market funds briefly averaged 18 percent, and wish such times would come again. Well, those were not good times. During the early 1980s the top tax bracket, state and federal combined, was 55 percent. If you began with an 18-percent return and deducted taxes, many taxpayers saw their 18-percent return knocked down to about 9 percent. This may look great, especially for a "risk-free" investment, but we are not through yet. During the partial year in which money market accounts paid 18 percent, inflation was 12 percent. Now, if you take the 9-percent return and subtract 12 percent for inflation; the real return was actually -3 percent for the year. So much for the good old days.

Money market funds are the best place to park your money while you are looking at other investment alternatives or if you will be using the money during the next year. These funds can provide the convenience of check writing and a yield that is highly competitive with interest rates in general. These incredibly safe funds should only be considered for short-term periods or for regular expenditures, the way you would use a savings or checking account.

Since money market funds only came into existence for the general public in the mid-1970s, Treasury bills are often used as a substitute by those who wish to analyze the performance of these funds over a long period of time. The results are instructive. Since the beginning of 1951, a dollar invested in T-bills grew to $12.87 by the end of 2000. By the end of 2000, you would have needed $6.96 to equal the purchasing power of $1 at the beginning of 1951.

To give you a better sense of the cumulative effects of inflation, consider what a $100,000 investment in a money market fund would have to yield at the beginning of 2000 to equal the same purchasing power as the interest (or yield) from a $100,000 investment in a money market fund twenty years ago (1981). At the beginning of 2000, for instance, a $100,000 account held since 1981 would need to generate $10,280 to equal the same purchasing power as a $100,000 account yielding approximately 5.3 percent in 1981 (the average interest rate for money market accounts that year). The reality, however, is that at the beginning of 2000, money market funds were yielding 5 percent ($5,000 a year versus the $10,280 that would be required to maintain purchasing power).

You may have avoided stock investing in the past because "stocks are too risky." Yet it all depends on how you define risk. As an example, in 1969 a $100,000 CD generated enough interest ($7,900) to buy a new, "fully loaded" Cadillac ($5,936) plus take a week-long cruise. As of the beginning of 1997, that same $100,000 CD would not generate enough income (CD rates were 4.95 percent) to buy one-eighth of the Cadillac ($4,950 versus $43,000 for the cost of a 1997 Cadillac Hardtop Sedan De Ville).

As a risk-reduction tool, the addition of a money market fund may be a worthwhile strategy. For the period between 1960 and 1996, a 50–50 mix of stocks and cash delivered 79 percent of the S & P's return, with half the volatility. A more aggressive mix of 60 percent stocks and 40 percent cash yielded 84 percent of the S & P's gains, with just 60 percent of the risk (as measured by standard deviation).

Over the past three years, taxable money market funds have had an average compound return of 5.2 percent per year. The annual return for the past five years has been 5.1 percent; and 4.7 percent for the past ten years (all periods ending December 31, 2000). During these same time periods, tax-free money market funds had the following average annual returns: 3.1 percent for the past 3- and 5-year period and 3.0 percent for the past ten years. The standard deviation for money market funds is lower than any other mutual fund category. This means that these funds have had fewer return variances than any other group. Close to 1,500 funds make up the money market category. Total market capitalization of this category close to $2 trillion.

Money Market Funds

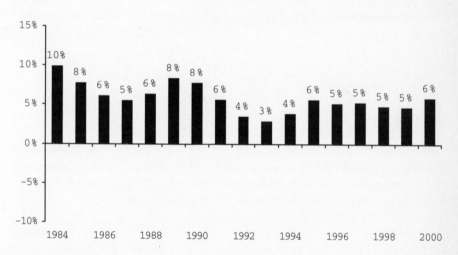

AON Money Market

6610 West Broad Street
Richmond, VA 23230
(800) 266-3637
www.aon.com

total return	★★★★★
risk reduction	★★★★★
management	★★★★★
expense control	★★★★★
symbol AONXX	20 points

Total Return   ★★★★★

Over the past five years, AON Money Market has taken $10,000 and turned it into $13,105 ($11,790 over three years). This translates into an annualized return of 5.7 percent over the past three years and 5.6 percent over the past five years. Money market funds have averaged 5.1 percent for the past three and five years (all periods ending 12/31/00).

Risk/Volatility   ★★★★★

During the past three and five years, the fund's standard deviation has been 0.15 percent.

	past 3 years		past 8 years	
worst year	5.1%	1999	3.4%	1993
best year	6.3%	2000	6.3%	2000

Management   ★★★★★

The average maturity of the paper in the portfolio is approximately thirty-three days. Keith Lemmer has managed the fund since 1992. The fund has outperformed its peer group average over the past one, three, and five years.

Expenses   ★★★★★

The expense ratio for this $1.4 billion fund is 0.19 percent. This means that for every $1,000 invested, $1.90 goes to paying overhead.

Summary

AON Money Market is highly recommended.

Profile

minimum initial investment $10,000	*IRA accounts available* . . . . yes
subsequent minimum investment . $1,000	*IRA minimum investment* 1,000
available in all 50 states . . . . yes	*date of inception* 1992
telephone exchanges . . . . yes	*dividend/income paid* . . . . daily
number of funds in family 3	

Elfun Money Market

3003 Summer Street, P.O. Box 120074
Stamford, CT 06912
(800) 242-0134
www.gefn.com/mutual funds

total return	★★★★★
risk reduction	★★★★★
management	★★★★★
expense control	★★★★★
symbol ELMXX	20 points

Total Return ★★★★★

Over the past five years, Elfun Money Market has taken $10,000 and turned it into $13,075 ($11,785 over three years). This translates into an annualized return of 5.6 percent over the past three years and 5.5 percent over the past five years. Money market funds have averaged 5.1 percent for the past three and five years (all periods ending 12/31/00).

Risk/Volatility ★★★★★

During the past three and five years, the standard deviation has been 0.15 percent.

	past 5 years		past 10 years	
worst year	5.1%	1999	3.3%	1993
best year	6.4%	2000	6.4%	2000

Management ★★★★★

The average maturity of the paper in the portfolio is approximately forty-two days. Robert MacDougall has managed the fund since 1990. The fund has outperformed its peer group average over the past one, three, five, and ten years.

Expenses ★★★★★

The expense ratio for this $320 million fund is 0.19 percent. This means that for every $1,000 invested, $1.90 goes to paying overhead.

Summary

Elfun Money Market is highly recommended.

Profile

minimum initial investment $500	*IRA accounts available* . . . . yes
subsequent minimum investment . . $100	*IRA minimum investment* $500
available in all 50 states . . . . yes	*date of inception* 1990
telephone exchanges . . . . yes	*dividend/income paid* . . . . daily
number of funds in family 23	

Federated Liquid Cash Trust

Federated Investors Tower
1001 Liberty Avenue
Pittsburgh, PA 15222
(800) 341-7400
www.federatedinvestors.com

total return	★★★★★
risk reduction	★★★★★
management	★★★★★
expense control	★★★★★
symbol LCTXX	20 points

Total Return   ★★★★★

Over the past five years, Federated Liquid Cash Trust has taken $10,000 and turned it into $13,100 ($11,780 over three years). This translates into an annualized return of 5.6 percent over the past three and five years. Money market funds have averaged 5.1 percent for the past three and five years (all periods ending 12/31/00).

Risk/Volatility   ★★★★★

During the past three and five years, the fund's standard deviation has been 0.15 percent.

	past 5 years		past 10 years	
worst year	5.0%	1999	3.1%	1993
best year	6.3%	2000	6.3%	2000

Management   ★★★★★

The average maturity of the paper in the portfolio is approximately three days. Susan R. Hill has managed the fund since 1993. The fund has outperformed its peer group average over the past one, three, five, and ten years.

Expenses   ★★★★★

The expense ratio for this $230 million fund is 0.16 percent. This means that for every $1,000 invested, $1.60 goes to paying overhead.

Summary

Federated Liquid Cash Trust is highly recommended.

Profile

minimum initial investment $25,000	*IRA accounts available* . . . . yes
subsequent minimum investment . . . $10	*IRA minimum investment* $250
available in all 50 states . . . . yes	*date of inception* 1983
telephone exchanges . . . . yes	*dividend/income paid* . . . . daily
number of funds in family 69	

Fidelity Spartan U.S. Government Money Market

82 Devonshire St.,
Mail Zone F 9A
Boston, MA 02109
(800) 544-8544
www.glenmede.com

total return	★★★★★
risk reduction	★★★★★
management	★★★★★
expense control	★★★★
symbol SPAXX	19 points

Total Return   ★★★★★

Over the past five years, Fidelity Spartan U.S. Government Money Market has taken $10,000 and turned it into $12,970 ($11,705 over three years). This translates into an annualized return of 5.4 percent over the past three years and 5.3 percent over the past five years. Government money market funds have averaged 5.0 percent for the past three and five years (all periods ending 12/31/00).

Risk/Volatility   ★★★★★

During the past three and five years, the standard deviation has been 0.14 percent.

	past 5 years		past 10 years	
worst year	4.9%	1999	2.8%	1993
best year	6.1%	2000	6.1%	1991

Management   ★★★★★

The average maturity of the paper in the portfolio is approximately forty-seven days. Robert Litterst has managed the fund since 1997. The fund has outperformed its peer group average over the past one, three, five, and ten years.

Expenses   ★★★★

The expense ratio for this $775 million fund is 0.45 percent. This means that for every $1,000 invested, $4.50 goes to paying overhead.

Summary

Fidelity Spartan U.S. Government Money Market is highly recommended.

Profile

minimum initial investment $20,000	*IRA accounts available* . . . . n/a
subsequent minimum investment . $1,000	*IRA minimum investment* . . . . n/a
available in all 50 states . . . . yes	*date of inception* 1990
telephone exchanges . . . . yes	*dividend/income paid* . . . . daily
number of funds in family 34	

Financial Square Money Market
4900 Sears Tower
Chicago, IL 60606
(800) 621-2550
www.gs.com

total return	★★★★★
risk reduction	★★★★★
management	★★★★★
expense control	★★★★★
symbol FSMXX	20 points

Total Return   ★★★★★
Over the past five years, Financial Square Money Market has taken $10,000 and turned it into $13,170 ($11,800 over three years). This translates into an annualized return of 5.7 percent over the past three and five years. Money market funds have averaged 5.1 percent for the past three and five years (all periods ending 12/31/00).

Risk/Volatility   ★★★★★
During the past three and five years, the fund's standard deviation has been 0.14 percent.

	past 3 years		inception	
worst year	5.2%	1999	5.2%	1999
best year	6.5%	2000	6.5%	2000

Management   ★★★★★
The average maturity of the paper in the portfolio is approximately forty-seven days. Goldman Sachs Asset Management has managed the fund since 1994. The fund has outperformed its peer group average over the past one, three, and five years.

Expenses   ★★★★★
The expense ratio for this $6.8 billion fund is 0.18 percent. This means that for every $1,000 invested, $1.80 goes to paying overhead.

Summary
Financial Square Money Market is highly recommended.

Profile
minimum initial investment	.... $1	
subsequent minimum investment	.... $1	
available in all 50 states	.... yes	
telephone exchanges	.... yes	
number of funds in family	 40	

IRA accounts available .... yes
IRA minimum investment $500
date of inception 1994
dividend/income paid .... daily

Lake Forest Money Market
One Westminster Pl.
Lake Forest, IL 60045
(800) 592-7722
www.lakeforestfunds.com

total return	★★★★★
risk reduction	★★★★★
management	★★★★★
expense control	★★★★★
symbol LFMXX	20 points

Total Return   ★★★★★
Over the past five years, Lake Forest Money Market has taken $10,000 and turned it into $13,025 ($11,730 over three years). This translates into an annualized return of 5.5 percent over the past three years and 5.4 percent over the past five years. Government money market funds have averaged 5.0 percent for the past three and five years (all periods ending 12/31/00).

Risk/Volatility   ★★★★★
During the past three and five years, the standard deviation has been 0.20 percent.

	past 3 years		inception	
worst year	4.8%	1999	4.8%	1999
best year	6.1%	2000	6.1%	2000

Management   ★★★★★
The average maturity of the paper in the portfolio is approximately one day. Irving Boberski has managed the fund since 1995. The fund has outperformed its peer group average over the past one, three, and five years.

Expenses   ★★★★★
The expense ratio for this $800 million fund is 0.13 percent. This means that for every $1,000 invested, $1.30 goes to paying overhead.

Summary
Lake Forest Money Market is highly recommended.

Profile
minimum initial investment $2,500	*IRA accounts available* . . . . yes
subsequent minimum investment . . $500	*IRA minimum investment* $1,000
available in all 50 states . . . . yes	*date of inception* 1995
telephone exchanges . . . . yes	*dividend/income paid* . . . . daily
number of funds in family 2	

Strong Heritage Money
W140 N9001 Lily Road
Menomonee Falls, WI 53051
(800) 368-3863
www.strong.com

total return	★★★★★
risk reduction	★★★★★
management	★★★★★
expense control	★★★★
symbol SHMXX	19 points

Total Return   ★★★★★
Over the past five years, Strong Heritage Money has taken $10,000 and turned it into $13,130 ($11,760 over three years). This translates into an annualized return of 5.6 percent over the past three and five years. Money market funds have averaged 5.1 percent for the past three and five years (all periods ending 12/31/00).

Risk/Volatility   ★★★★★
During the past three and five years, the fund's standard deviation has been 0.16 percent.

	past 3 years		inception	
worst year	5.0%	1999	5.0%	1999
best year	6.2%	2000	6.2%	2000

Management   ★★★★★
The average maturity of the paper in the portfolio is approximately forty-two days. Jay N. Mueller has managed the fund since 1995. The fund has outperformed its peer group average over the past one, three, and five years.

Expenses   ★★★★
The expense ratio for this $1.5 billion fund is 0.40 percent. This means that for every $1,000 invested, $4.00 goes to paying overhead.

Summary
Strong Heritage Money is highly recommended.

Profile
minimum initial investment $25,000	IRA accounts available . . . . yes
subsequent minimum investment . $1,000	IRA minimum investment $250
available in all 50 states . . . . yes	date of inception 1995
telephone exchanges . . . . yes	dividend/income paid . . . . daily
number of funds in family 46	

Strong Municipal Money Market
W140 N9001 Lily Road
Menomonee Falls, WI 53051
(800) 368-3863
www.strong.com

total return	★★★★★
risk reduction	★★★★★
management	★★★★★
expense control	★★★★
symbol SXFXX	19 points

Total Return   ★★★★★
Over the past five years, Strong Municipal Money Market has taken $10,000 and turned it into $11,960 ($11,145 over three years). This translates into an annualized return of 3.7 percent over the past three years and 3.6 percent over the past five years. Tax-free money market funds have averaged 3.1 percent for the past three and five years (all periods ending 12/31/00).

Risk/Volatility   ★★★★★
During the past three and five years, the fund's standard deviation has been 0.15 percent.

	past 5 years		past 10 years	
worst year	3.3%	1999	2.5%	1993
best year	4.2%	2000	4.2%	2000

Management   ★★★★★
The average maturity of the paper in the portfolio is approximately thirty-seven days. John Bonnell has managed the fund since 2000. The fund has outperformed its peer group average over the past one, three, five, and ten years.

Expenses   ★★★★
The expense ratio for this $2.9 billion fund is 0.60 percent. This means that for every $1,000 invested, $6.00 goes to paying overhead.

Summary
Strong Municipal Money Market is highly recommended.

Profile
minimum initial investment $2,500	*IRA accounts available* . . . . yes
subsequent minimum investment . . . $50	*IRA minimum investment* $250
available in all 50 states . . . . yes	*date of inception* 1986
telephone exchanges . . . . yes	*dividend/income paid* . . . . daily
number of funds in family 46	

USAA Tax-Exempt Money Market

USAA Building, 9800 Fredericksberg Road
San Antonio, TX 78288
(800) 531-8722
www.usaa.com

total return	★★★★★
risk reduction	★★★★★
management	★★★★★
expense control	★★★★
symbol USEXX	19 points

Total Return ★★★★★
Over the past five years, USAA Tax-Exempt Money Market has taken $10,000 and turned it into $11,840 ($11,080 over three years). This translates into an annualized return of 3.5 percent over the past three years and 3.4 percent over the past five years. Tax-free money market funds have averaged 3.1 percent for the past three and five years (all periods ending 12/31/00).

Risk/Volatility ★★★★★
During the past three and five years, the standard deviation has been 0.14 percent.

	past 5 years		past 10 years	
worst year	3.1%	1999	2.4%	1993
best year	3.9%	2000	4.8%	1991

Management ★★★★★
The average maturity of the paper in the portfolio is approximately thirty-seven days. Anthony Era has managed the fund since 1984. The fund has outperformed its peer group average over the past one, three, five, and ten years.

Expenses ★★★★
The expense ratio for this $1.9 billion fund is 0.38 percent. This means that for every $1,000 invested, $3.80 goes to paying overhead.

Summary
USAA Tax-Exempt Money Market is highly recommended.

Profile

minimum initial investment $3,000	*IRA accounts available* . . . . yes
subsequent minimum investment . . . $50	*IRA minimum investment* $1
available in all 50 states . . . . yes	*date of inception* 1984
telephone exchanges . . . . yes	*dividend/income paid* . . . . daily
number of funds in family 29	

U.S. Global Investors U.S. Gov't Securities
525 Market Street, 12th Floor, MAC 0103-121
San Francisco, CA 94105
(800) 222-8222
www.wellsfargo.com

total return	★★★★★
risk reduction	★★★★★
management	★★★★★
expense control	★★★★
symbol SCCME	19 points

Total Return ★★★★★
Over the past five years, U.S. Global Investors U.S. Gov't Securities has taken $10,000 and turned it into $12,975 ($11,695 over three years). This translates into an annualized return of 5.4 percent over the past three years and 5.3 percent over the past five years. Government money market funds have averaged 5.0 percent for the past three and five years (all periods ending 12/31/00).

Risk/Volatility ★★★★★
During the past three and five years, the standard deviation has been 0.14 percent.

	past 5 years		past 10 years	
worst year	4.9%	1999	3.4%	1993
best year	6.0%	2000	6.3%	1991

Management ★★★★★
The average maturity of the paper in the portfolio is approximately fifty-nine days. U.S. Global Investors, Inc. has managed the fund since 1986. The fund has outperformed its peer group average over the past one, three, five, and ten years.

Expenses ★★★★
The expense ratio for this $790 million fund is 0.40 percent. This means that for every $1,000 invested, $4.00 goes to paying overhead.

Summary
U.S. Global Investors U.S. Gov't Securities is highly recommended.

Profile
minimum initial investment $1,000	*IRA accounts available* . . . . yes
subsequent minimum investment . . . $50	*IRA minimum investment* $50
available in all 50 states . . . . yes	*date of inception* 1986
telephone exchanges . . . . yes	*dividend/income paid* . . . . daily
number of funds in family 11	

Municipal Bond Funds

Municipal bond funds invest in securities issued by municipalities, political subdivisions, and U.S. territories. The type of security issued is either a note or bond, both of which are interest-bearing instruments that are exempt from federal income taxes. There are three different categories of municipal bond funds: national, state-free, and high-yield.

National municipal bond funds are made up of debt instruments issued by a wide range of states. These funds are exempt from federal income taxes only. To determine what small percentage is also exempt from state income taxes, consult the fund's prospectus and look for the weighting of U.S. territory issues (U.S. Virgin Islands, Guam, Puerto Rico), District of Columbia items, and obligations from your state of residence.

State-free funds, sometimes referred to as "double tax-free funds," invest only in bonds and notes issued in a particular state. You must be a legal resident of that state in order to avoid paying state income taxes on the fund's return. For example, most California residents who are in a high tax bracket will only want to consider purchasing a municipal bond fund that has the name "California" in it. Residents of New York who purchase a California tax-free fund will escape federal income taxes but not state taxes.

High-yield tax-free funds invest in the same kinds of issues found in a national municipal bond fund but with one important difference. By seeking higher returns, high-yield funds look for lower-rated or nonrated notes and bonds. A municipality may decide not to obtain a rating for its issue because of the costs involved compared to the relatively small size of the bond or note being floated. Many nonrated issues are very safe. High-yield municipal bond funds are relatively new but should not be overlooked by the tax-conscious investor. These kinds of tax-free funds have demonstrated less volatility and higher return than their other tax-free counterparts.

Prospective investors need to compare tax-free bond yields to after-tax yields on corporate or government bond funds. To determine which of these three fund categories is best for you, use your marginal tax bracket, subtract this amount from one, and multiply the resulting figure by the taxable investment. For instance, suppose you were in the 35-percent bracket, state and federal combined. By subtracting this figure from 1, you are left with 0.65. Multiply 0.65 by the fully taxable yield you could get; let us say, 9 percent. Sixty-five percent of 9 percent is 5.85 percent. The 5.85 percent represents what you get on a 9-percent investment after you have paid state and federal income taxes on it. This means that if you can get 5.85 percent or higher from a tax-free investment, take it.

Interest paid on tax-free investments is generally lower than interest paid on taxable investments like corporate bonds and bank CDs. But you should compare the yields on tax-free investments to taxable investments only after you have considered the municipal bond fund's tax-free advantage. The result will be the taxable equivalent yield—the yield you will have to get on a similar taxable investment to equal the tax-free yield. If the example was not clear enough, look at the next table.

2000 Federal Income Tax Rates Plus Tax-Free Yields Versus Equivalent Taxable Yields

As you can see from the table, if you're in the 36-percent federal tax bracket, a taxable investment would have to yield 7.8 percent to give you the same after-tax income as a tax-free yield of 5.0 percent.

Municipal bond funds are not for investors who are in a low tax bracket. If such investors want to be in bonds, they would be better off in corporates or government issues. Furthermore, municipals should never be used in a retirement plan. There is only one way to make tax-free income taxable and that is to put it into a traditional IRA, pension, or profit-sharing plan. Everything that comes out of these plans is fully taxable by the federal government.

Over the past three and five years, the typical municipal bond fund has had an average compounded annual return of 3.5 and 4.5 percent, respectively. They have averaged a total annual return (current yield plus bond appreciation or minus bond depreciation) of 6.4 percent over the past ten years and 7.1 percent annually for the

Municipal Bond Funds

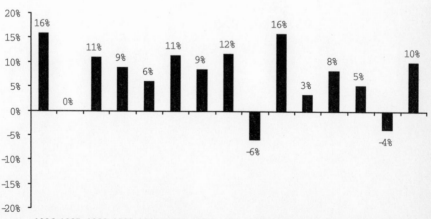

past fifteen years. Municipal bond fund returns have been fairly stable over the past three years, having a standard deviation of 3.5 percent.

Nineteen-hundred funds make up the municipal bond category. Total market capitalization of all municipal bond funds is $280 billion. Close to 99 percent of a typical municipal bond fund's portfolio is in tax-free bonds, with the balance in tax-free money market instruments. Close to 1,350 of the 1,900 municipal bond funds offered are single-state funds.

The typical municipal bond fund yields 4.6 percent in tax-free income each year. The average weighted maturity is thirteen years. Expenses for this category are 1.0 percent each year.

As you read through the descriptions of the municipal bond funds selected, you will notice a paragraph in each describing the tax efficiency of the portfolio. This may surprise you, because municipal bonds are supposed to be tax-free. Keep in mind that only the income (current yield) from these instruments is free from federal income taxes (and often state income taxes, depending on the fund in question and your state of residence). Since bond funds generally have a high turnover rate (which triggers a potential capital gain or loss upon each sale of a security by the portfolio manager), there are capital gains considerations with municipal bonds.

Franklin NY Tax-Free Income A

777 Mariners Island Boulevard
San Mateo, CA 94404
(800) 342-5236
www.franklin-templeton.com

total return	★★★★★
risk reduction	★★★★★
management	★★★★★
current income	★★★★★
expense control	★★★★
symbol FNYTX	24 points
up-market performance	good
down-market performance	poor
predictability of returns	excellent

Total Return   ★★★★★

Over the past five years (ending 12/31/00), Franklin NY Tax-Free Income A has taken $10,000 and turned it into $13,385 ($11,580 over three years and $19,675 over the past ten years). This translates into an annualized return of 6 percent over the past five years, 5 percent over the past three years, and 7 percent for the decade. Over the past five years, this fund has outperformed 45 percent of all mutual funds; within its general category, it has done better than 99 percent of its peers. Municipal bond funds have averaged 5 percent annually over these same five years.

During the past five years, a $10,000 initial investment grew to $13,350 after taxes, assuming a 39.6 percent income tax bracket (state and federal combined) and a capital gains rate of 28 percent. This means that investors in this fund were able to preserve 99 percent of their total returns. Compared to other fixed-income funds, this fund's tax savings are considered to be excellent.

Risk/Volatility   ★★★★★

Over the past five years, Franklin has been safer than 95 percent of all municipal bond funds. Over the past decade, the fund has had two negative years, while the Lehman Brothers Aggregate Bond Index has also had two (off 3 percent in 1994 and 1 percent in 1999); the Lehman Brothers Municipal Bond Index also fell twice (off 5 percent in 1994 and 2 percent in 1999). The fund has underperformed the Lehman Brothers Aggregate Bond Index and the Lehman Brothers Municipal Bond Index twice in the past ten years.

	past 5 years		past 10 years	
worst year	-2%	1999	-4%	1994
best year	11%	2000	14%	1995

In the past, Franklin has done better than 95 percent of its peer group in up markets but outperformed just 35 percent of its competition in down markets. Consistency, or predictability, of returns for Franklin NY Tax-Free Income A can be described as excellent. This fund's risk-related return is very good.

Management   ★★★★★
There are 500 fixed-income securities in this $4.4 billion portfolio. The average municipal bond fund today is $150 million in size. Close to 100 percent of the fund's holdings are in bonds. The average maturity of the bonds in this account is eighteen years; the weighted coupon rate averages 6.1 percent. The portfolio's fixed-income holdings can be categorized as long-term, high-quality debt.

A team has managed this fund for the past nine years. The primary goal of the fund is to provide the highest possible level of current income that is exempt from federal and New York State income taxes, while preserving underlying principal. No more than 5 percent of the portfolio is in any one issue. The average credit quality rating for the portfolio is AA. There are 165 funds besides NY Tax-Free Income within the Franklin-Templeton family. Overall, the fund family's risk-adjusted performance can be described as very good.

Current Income   ★★★★★
Over the past year, Franklin NY Tax-Free Income A had a twelve-month yield of 5.4 percent. During this same twelve-month period, the typical municipal bond fund had a yield that averaged 4.5 percent.

Expenses   ★★★★
Franklin NY Tax-Free Income's expense ratio is 0.6 percent; it has also averaged 0.6 percent annually over the past three calendar years. The average expense ratio for the 2,000 funds in this category is 1.1 percent. This fund's turnover rate over the past year has been 25 percent, while its peer group average has been 45 percent.

Summary
Franklin NY Tax-Free Income A ties for first as having the highest overall score of any fund in its category and ranks number two for current income. The fund also ties for first for having the best five-year returns and lowest risk. Risk-adjusted returns for the past five and ten years have been excellent. The portfolio usually ends up in the top quartile for performance on an annual basis. The fund ranks in the top quintile when it comes to growth persistence: the ability to consistently out-perform equity funds over the previous five years. This offering also excels when it comes to superior risk-adjusted return persistence. Investors would be wise to check out other offerings from Franklin-Templeton.

Profile

minimum initial investment $1,000	*IRA accounts available* . . . . yes
subsequent minimum investment . . . $50	*IRA minimum investment* $1
available in all 50 states. . . . . yes	*date of inception* . . . . Sept. 1982
telephone exchanges. . . . . yes	*dividend/income paid*. . . . . monthly
number of funds in family 166	*average credit quality*. . . . . AA

JP Morgan Tax-Exempt Bond
60 State Street, Suite 1300
Boston, MA 02109
(800) 521-5411
www.jpmorgan.com/mutualfunds

total return	★★★★
risk reduction	★★★★★
management	★★★★
current income	★★★
expense control	★★★★
symbol PPTBX	20 points
up-market performance	very good
down-market performance	good
predictability of returns	excellent

Total Return   ★★★★
Over the past five years (ending 12/31/00), JP Morgan Tax-Exempt Bond has taken $10,000 and turned it into $12,765 ($11,580 over three years and $17,910 over the past ten years). This translates into an annualized return of 5 percent over the past three and five years, and 6 percent for the decade. Over the past five years, this fund has outperformed 35 percent of all mutual funds; within its general category, it has done better than 80 percent of its peers. Municipal bond funds have averaged 5 percent annually over these same five years.

During the past five years, a $10,000 initial investment grew to $12,680 after taxes, assuming a 39.6 percent income tax bracket (state and federal combined) and a capital gains rate of 28 percent. This means that investors in this fund were able to preserve 97 percent of their total returns. Compared to other fixed-income funds, this fund's tax savings are considered to be excellent.

Risk/Volatility   ★★★★★
Over the past five years, JP Morgan has been safer than 70 percent of all municipal bond funds. Over the past decade, the fund has had two negative years, while the Lehman Brothers Aggregate Bond Index has also had two (off 3 percent in 1994 and 1 percent in 1999); the Lehman Brothers Municipal Bond Index also fell twice (off 5 percent in 1994 and 2 percent in 1999). The fund has underperformed the Lehman Brothers Aggregate Bond Index and the Lehman Brothers Municipal Bond Index twice in the past ten years.

	past 5 years		past 10 years	
worst year	-1%	1999	-3%	1994
best year	9%	2000	13%	1995

In the past, JP Morgan has done better than 95 percent of its peer group in up markets and outperformed 65 percent of its competition in down markets. Consistency, or predictability, of returns for JP Morgan Tax-Exempt Bond can be described as excellent. This fund's risk-related return is good.

Management   ★★★★
There are 140 fixed-income securities in this $355 million portfolio. The average municipal bond fund today is $150 million in size. Close to 97 percent of the fund's holdings are in bonds. The average maturity of the bonds in this account is six years; the weighted coupon rate averages 5.9 percent. The portfolio's fixed-income holdings can be categorized as very high quality.

A team has managed this fund for the past six years. They are required to invest at least 90 percent of the portfolio's assets in bonds rated BBB or higher; the balance must be in bonds rated B or better. Management relies on internal research to find attractive individual issues. The managers also consider interest-rate and yield-curve conditions. There are eighteen funds besides Tax-Exempt Bond within the JP Morgan family. Overall, the fund family's risk-adjusted performance can be described as excellent.

Current Income   ★★★
Over the past year, JP Morgan Tax-Exempt Bond had a twelve-month yield of 4.4 percent. During this same twelve-month period, the typical municipal bond fund had a yield that averaged 4.5 percent.

Expenses   ★★★★
JP Morgan Tax-Exempt's expense ratio is 0.7 percent; it has also averaged 0.7 percent annually over the past three calendar years. The average expense ratio for the 2,000 funds in this category is 1.1 percent. This fund's turnover rate over the past year has been 20 percent, while its peer group average has been 45 percent.

Summary
JP Morgan Tax-Exempt Bond is the second most predictable municipal fund in the book. It ties for first place as having the lowest risk. The fund has outperformed 80 percent of its peers. Risk-adjusted returns for the past three years have been superb. Over 95 percent of the portfolio is in bonds rated A or better. Investors are strongly encouraged to check out other funds from JP Morgan.

Profile
minimum initial investment . . . . . $2,500   *IRA accounts available* . . . . yes
subsequent minimum investment . . $500   *IRA minimum investment* $1
available in all 50 states. . . . . yes   *date of inception* . . . . Oct. 1984
telephone exchanges. . . . . yes   *dividend/income paid*. . . . . monthly
number of funds in family 19   *average credit quality* . . . . AAA

Scudder High-Yield Tax-Free S

Two International Place
Boston, MA 02110
(800) 225-2470
www.scudder.com

total return	★★★★★
risk reduction	★★★★
management	★★★★★
current income	★★★★★
expense control	★★★★★
symbol SHYTX	24 points
up-market performance	excellent
down-market performance	excellent
predictability of returns	very good

Total Return   ★★★★★

Over the past five years (ending 12/31/00), Scudder High-Yield Tax-Free S has taken $10,000 and turned it into $13,385 ($11,250 over three years and $21,590 over the past ten years). This translates into an annualized return of 6 percent over the past five years, 4 percent over the past three years, and 8 percent for the decade. Over the past five years, this fund has outperformed 40 percent of all mutual funds; within its general category, it has done better than 90 percent of its peers. Municipal bond funds have averaged 5 percent annually over these same five years.

During the past five years, a $10,000 initial investment grew to $13,385 after taxes, assuming a 39.6 percent income tax bracket (state and federal combined) and a capital gains rate of 28 percent. This means that investors in this fund were able to preserve 100 percent of their total returns. Compared to other fixed-income funds, this fund's tax savings are considered to be excellent.

Risk/Volatility   ★★★★

Over the past five years, Scudder has been safer than 96 percent of all municipal bond funds. Over the past decade, the fund has had two negative years, while the Lehman Brothers Aggregate Bond Index has also had two (off 3 percent in 1994 and 1 percent in 1999); the Lehman Brothers Municipal Bond Index also fell twice (off 5 percent in 1994 and 2 percent in 1999). The fund has underperformed the Lehman Brothers Aggregate Bond Index and the Lehman Brothers Municipal Bond Index twice in the past ten years.

	past 5 years		past 10 years	
worst year	-2%	1999	-8%	1994
best year	12%	1997	19%	1995

In the past, Scudder has done better than 90 percent of its peer group in up markets and outperformed 95 percent of its competition in down markets. Consistency, or predictability, of returns for Scudder High-Yield Tax-Free S can be described as very good. This fund's risk-related return is good.

Management   ★★★★★

There are 1,510 fixed-income securities in this $475 million portfolio. The average municipal bond fund today is $150 million in size. Close to 100 percent of the fund's holdings are in bonds. The average maturity of the bonds in this account is twelve years; the weighted coupon rate averages 5.7 percent. The portfolio's fixed-income holdings can be categorized as intermediate-term, medium-to-high-quality debt.

Philip G. Condon and Rebecca L. Wilson have comanaged this fund for the past nine years. Management concentrates on bonds with a maturity range of ten to twenty years; call protection is stressed in order to maintain stable income and low turnover. Although this is a "high-yield" offering, close to two-thirds of the portfolio is in investment grade bonds. The comanagers are more concerned with credit analysis and yield curve positioning than interest-rate predictions. There are thirty-five funds besides High-Yield Tax-Free S within the Scudder family. Overall, the fund family's risk-adjusted performance can be described as good.

Current Income   ★★★★★

Over the past year, Scudder High-Yield Tax-Free S had a twelve-month yield of 5.5 percent. During this same twelve-month period, the typical municipal bond fund had a yield that averaged 4.5 percent.

Expenses   ★★★★★

Scudder High-Yield Tax-Free's expense ratio is 0.8 percent; it has also averaged 0.8 percent annually over the past three calendar years. The average expense ratio for the 2,000 funds in this category is 1.1 percent. This fund's turnover rate over the past year has been 7 percent, while its peer group average has been 45 percent.

Summary

Scudder High-Yield Tax-Free S ties for first as having the highest overall score of any fund in its category. It has the highest current income, is the most tax efficient, and has the lowest turnover rate of any fund in its 2,000-plus member group. It is only one of three funds in its category that does a superb job during bear as well as bull markets. Among its peers, it is also rated as the best down-market performer. Risk-adjusted returns over the past three, five, and ten years have been outstanding. The fund ranks in the top quintile when it comes to growth persistence: the ability to consistently outperform equity funds over the previous five years. This offering also scores highly when it comes to superior risk-adjusted return persistence.

Profile

minimum initial investment $2,500	*IRA accounts available* . . . . yes
subsequent minimum investment . . $100	*IRA minimum investment* $1,000
available in all 50 states. . . . . yes	*date of inception* . . . . Jan. 1987
telephone exchanges. . . . . yes	*dividend/income paid.* . . . . monthly
number of funds in family 36	*average credit quality* . . . . A

Scudder Managed Municipal Bond S

Two International Place
Boston, MA 02110
(800) 225-2470
www.scudder.com

total return	★★★★★
risk reduction	★★★★
management	★★★★★
current income	★★★★★
expense control	★★★★
symbol SCMBX	23 points
up-market performance	excellent
down-market performance	very good
predictability of returns	very good

Total Return   ★★★★★

Over the past five years (ending 12/31/00), Scudder Managed Municipal Bond S has taken $10,000 and turned it into $13,385 ($11,580 over three years and $19,675 over the past ten years). This translates into an annualized return of 6 percent over the past five years, 5 percent over the past three years, and 7 percent for the decade. Over the past five years, this fund has outperformed 45 percent of all mutual funds; within its general category, it has done better than 95 percent of its peers. Municipal bond funds have averaged 5 percent annually over these same five years.

During the past five years, a $10,000 initial investment grew to $13,350 after taxes, assuming a 39.6 percent income tax bracket (state and federal combined) and a capital gains rate of 28 percent. This means that investors in this fund were able to preserve 99 percent of their total returns. Compared to other fixed-income funds, this fund's tax savings are considered to be excellent.

Risk/Volatility   ★★★★

Over the past five years, Scudder has been safer than 90 percent of all municipal bond funds. Over the past decade, the fund has had two negative years, while the Lehman Brothers Aggregate Bond Index has also had two (off 3 percent in 1994 and 1 percent in 1999); the Lehman Brothers Municipal Bond Index also fell twice (off 5 percent in 1994 and 2 percent in 1999). The fund has underperformed the Lehman Brothers Aggregate Bond Index and the Lehman Brothers Municipal Bond Index twice in the past ten years.

	past 5 years		past 10 years	
worst year	-2%	1999	-6%	1994
best year	11%	2000	17%	1995

In the past, Scudder has done better than 96 percent of its peer group in up markets and outperformed 95 percent of its competition in down markets. Consistency, or predictability, of returns for Scudder Managed Municipal Bond S can be described as very good. This fund's risk-related return is very good.

Management   ★★★★★
There are 565 fixed-income securities in this $790 million portfolio. The average municipal bond fund today is $150 million in size. Close to 100 percent of the fund's holdings are in bonds. The average maturity of the bonds in this account is nine years; the weighted coupon rate averages 4.6 percent. The portfolio's fixed-income holdings can be categorized as intermediate-term, high-quality debt.

Phillip G. Condon and Ashton P. Goodfield have comanaged this fund for the past eight years. Management focuses on bonds with maturities in the the ten to fifteen year range and looks for call protection whenever possible. Risk reduction is further enhanced by selecting bonds from numerous geographical areas across the country. There are thirty-five funds besides Managed Municipal Bond within the Scudder family. Overall, the fund family's risk-adjusted performance can be described as good.

Current Income   ★★★★★
Over the past year, Scudder Managed Municipal Bond S had a twelve-month yield of 5 percent. During this same twelve-month period, the typical municipal bond fund had a yield that averaged 4.5 percent.

Expenses   ★★★★
Scudder Managed Municipal's expense ratio is 0.7 percent; it has averaged 0.6 percent annually over the past three calendar years. The average expense ratio for the 2,000 funds in this category is 1.1 percent. This fund's turnover rate over the past year has been 45 percent, while its peer group average has been 45 percent.

Summary
Scudder Managed Municipal Bond S tied for first as the best five-year performer. Risk-adjusted returns over the past three and five years have been excellent. Close to 90 percent of the fund's holdings are in tax-free bonds rated AAA. The fund ranks in the top quintile when it comes to growth persistence: the ability to consistently outperform equity funds over the previous five years. This offering also excels when it comes to superior risk-adjusted return persistence.

Profile
minimum initial investment $2,500
subsequent minimum investment . . $100
available in all 50 states. . . . . yes
telephone exchanges. . . . . yes
number of funds in family 36

IRA accounts available . . . . yes
IRA minimum investment $1,000
date of inception . . . . Oct. 1976
dividend/income paid. . . . . monthly
average credit quality . . . . AAA

Tax-Exempt Bond of America

333 South Hope Street
Los Angeles, CA 90071
(800) 421-4120
www.americanfunds.com

total return	★★★★
risk reduction	★★★★★
management	★★★★★
current income	★★★★★
expense control	★★★★
symbol AFTEX	23 points
up-market performance	good
down-market performance	good
predictability of returns	excellent

Total Return   ★★★★

Over the past five years (ending 12/31/00), Tax-Exempt Bond of America has taken $10,000 and turned it into $12,765 ($11,250 over three years and $19,675 over the past ten years). This translates into an annualized return of 5 percent over the past five years, 4 percent over the past three years, and 7 percent for the decade. Over the past five years, this fund has outperformed 45 percent of all mutual funds; within its general category, it has done better than 95 percent of its peers. Municipal bond funds have averaged 5 percent annually over these same five years.

During the past five years, a $10,000 initial investment grew to $12,710 after taxes, assuming a 39.6 percent income tax bracket (state and federal combined) and a capital gains rate of 28 percent. This means that investors in this fund were able to preserve 98 percent of their total returns. Compared to other fixed-income funds, this fund's tax savings are considered to be excellent.

Risk/Volatility   ★★★★★

Over the past five years, Tax-Exempt has been safer than 55 percent of all municipal bond funds. Over the past decade, the fund has had two negative years, while the Lehman Brothers Aggregate Bond Index has also had two (off 3 percent in 1994 and 1 percent in 1999); the Lehman Brothers Municipal Bond Index also fell twice (off 5 percent in 1994 and 2 percent in 1999). The fund has underperformed the Lehman Brothers Aggregate Bond Index twice and the Lehman Brothers Municipal Bond Index twice in the past ten years.

	past 5 years		past 10 years	
worst year	-2%	1999	-5%	1994
best year	10%	2000	17%	1995

In the past, Tax-Exempt has done better than 75 percent of its peer group in up markets and outperformed 55 percent of its competition in down markets. Consistency, or predictability, of returns for Tax-Exempt Bond of America can be described as excellent. This fund's risk-related return is good.

Management   ★★★★★
There are 575 fixed-income securities in this $1.9 billion portfolio. The average municipal bond fund today is $150 million in size. Close to 98 percent of the fund's holdings are in bonds. The average maturity of the bonds in this account is eleven years; the weighted coupon rate averages 6.1 percent. The portfolio's fixed-income holdings can be categorized as intermediate-term, medium-quality debt.

A team has managed this fund for the past fifteen years. Management invests at least two-thirds of the portfolio in tax-free bonds rated AAA, AA, or A. The fund may not invest in issues subject to the Alternative Minimum Tax (AMT). The managers rely heavily on in-house research, which looks at fundamental as well as technological analysis. The fund favors noncallable bonds. There are twenty-nine funds besides Tax-Exempt Bond of America within the American Funds family. Overall, the fund family's risk-adjusted performance can be described as very good.

Current Income   ★★★★★
Over the past year, Tax-Exempt Bond of America had a twelve-month yield of 5.1 percent. During this same twelve-month period, the typical municipal bond fund had a yield that averaged 4.5 percent.

Expenses   ★★★★
Tax-Exempt Bond of America's expense ratio is 0.7 percent; it has also averaged 0.7 percent annually over the past three calendar years. The average expense ratio for the 2,000 funds in this category is 1.1 percent. This fund's turnover rate over the past year has been 25 percent, while its peer group average has been 45 percent.

Summary
Tax-Exempt Bond of America tied for first as the lowest-risk municipal fund in the book. Risk-adjusted returns for the past three, five, and ten years have been very good. Over the past six years, the fund has finished in the top quartile of performance five times. It has outperformed 95 percent of its 2,000-plus peer group. The fund ranks in the top quintile when it comes to growth persistence: the ability to consistently outperform equity funds over the previous five years. This offering also excels when it comes to superior risk-adjusted return persistence. Investors would be smart to check out other offerings from American Funds.

Profile
minimum initial investment $1,000
subsequent minimum investment . . . $50
available in all 50 states. . . . . yes
telephone exchanges. . . . . yes
number of funds in family 30

IRA accounts available . . . . yes
IRA minimum investment $1
date of inception . . . . Oct. 1979
dividend/income paid. . . . . monthly
average credit quality . . . . A

USAA CA Bond

USAA Building
San Antonio, TX 78288
(800) 382-8722
www.usaa.com

total return	★★★★★
risk reduction	★★★
management	★★★★★
current income	★★★★★
expense control	★★★★★
symbol USCBX	23 points
up-market performance	good
down-market performance	very good
predictability of returns	good

Total Return   ★★★★★

Over the past five years (ending 12/31/00), USAA CA Bond has taken $10,000 and turned it into $13,385 ($11,580 over three years and $19,675 over the past ten years). This translates into an annualized return of 6 percent over the past five years, 5 percent over the past three years, and 7 percent for the decade. Over the past five years, this fund has outperformed 55 percent of all mutual funds; within its general category, it has done better than 96 percent of its peers. Municipal bond funds have averaged 5 percent annually over these same five years.

During the past five years, a $10,000 initial investment grew to $13,385 after taxes, assuming a 39.6 percent income tax bracket (state and federal combined) and a capital gains rate of 28 percent. This means that investors in this fund were able to preserve 100 percent of their total returns. Compared to other fixed-income funds, this fund's tax savings are considered to be excellent.

Risk/Volatility   ★★★

Over the past five years, USAA has been safer than 90 percent of all municipal bond funds. Over the past decade, the fund has had two negative years, while the Lehman Brothers Aggregate Bond Index has also had two (off 3 percent in 1994 and 1 percent in 1999); the Lehman Brothers Municipal Bond Index also fell twice (off 5 percent in 1994 and 2 percent in 1999). The fund has underperformed the Lehman Brothers Aggregate Bond Index and the Lehman Brothers Municipal Bond Index twice in the past ten years.

	past 5 years		past 10 years	
worst year	-5%	1999	-9%	1994
best year	14%	2000	22%	1995

In the past, USAA has done better than 95 percent of its peer group in up markets and outperformed 96 percent of its competition in down markets. Consistency, or predictability, of returns for USAA CA Bond can be described as good. This fund's risk-related return is very good.

Management   ★★★★★

There are 100 fixed-income securities in this $650 million portfolio. The average municipal bond fund today is $150 million in size. Close to 100 percent of the fund's holdings are in bonds. The average maturity of the bonds in this account is nineteen years; the weighted coupon rate averages 5.5 percent. The portfolio's fixed-income holdings can be categorized as long-term, high-quality debt.

Robert R. Pariseau has managed this fund for the past six years. He is required to invest at least 80 percent of the portfolio in bonds that are exempt from federal and California state income taxes. Close to half the fund is in bonds rated AAA, another quarter is in AA-rated bonds, and roughly a fifth is in issues rated single-A. Pariseau favors long-term securities with the highest possible safe yield. There are twenty-eight funds besides CA Bond within the USAA family. Overall, the fund family's risk-adjusted performance can be described as good.

Current Income   ★★★★★

Over the past year, USAA CA Bond had a twelve-month yield of 5.2 percent. During this same twelve-month period, the typical municipal bond fund had a yield that averaged 4.5 percent.

Expenses   ★★★★★

USAA CA Bond's expense ratio is 0.4 percent; it has also averaged 0.4 percent annually over the past three calendar years. The average expense ratio for the 2,000 funds in this category is 1.1 percent. This fund's turnover rate over the past year has been 45 percent, while its peer group average has been 45 percent.

Summary

USAA CA Bond ties for first as the best five-year performer. It is also the most tax-efficient municipal bond fund in the book. Risk-adjusted returns for the past five years have been superb. Over the past six years, the fund has finished in the top quartile five times. This fund has outperformed 96 percent of its 2,000-plus peer group. It is highly recommended and turns in a near-perfect score of 23 out of a possible 25 points.

Profile

minimum initial investment $3,000	*IRA accounts available* . . . . yes
subsequent minimum investment . . . $50	*IRA minimum investment* $1
available in all 50 states. . . . . yes	*date of inception* . . . . Aug. 1989
telephone exchanges. . . . . yes	*dividend/income paid.* . . . . monthly
number of funds in family 29	*average credit quality.* . . . . AA

Vanguard CA Insured Long-Term Tax-Exempt
Vanguard Financial Center, P.O. Box 260
Valley Forge, PA 19482
(800) 662-7447
www.vanguard.com

total return	★★★★★
risk reduction	★★★
management	★★★★★
current income	★★★★
expense control	★★★★★
symbol VCITX	22 points
up-market performance	excellent
down-market performance	excellent
predictability of returns	good

Total Return   ★★★★★
Over the past five years (ending 12/31/00), Vanguard CA Insured Long-Term Tax-Exempt has taken $10,000 and turned it into $13,385 ($11,910 over three years and $21,590 over the past ten years). This translates into an annualized return of 6 percent over the past three and five years, and 8 percent for the decade. Over the past five years, this fund has outperformed 55 percent of all mutual funds; within its general category, it has done better than 98 percent of its peers. Municipal bond funds have averaged 5 percent annually over these same five years.

During the past five years, a $10,000 initial investment grew to $13,320 after taxes, assuming a 39.6 percent income tax bracket (state and federal combined) and a capital gains rate of 28 percent. This means that investors in this fund were able to preserve 98 percent of their total returns. Compared to other fixed-income funds, this fund's tax savings are considered to be excellent.

Risk/Volatility   ★★★
Over the past five years, Vanguard has been safer than 75 percent of all municipal bond funds. Over the past decade, the fund has had two negative years, while the Lehman Brothers Aggregate Bond Index has also had two (off 3 percent in 1994 and 1 percent in 1999); the Lehman Brothers Municipal Bond Index also fell twice (off 5 percent in 1994 and 2 percent in 1999). The fund has underperformed the Lehman Brothers Aggregate Bond Index and the Lehman Brothers Municipal Bond Index twice in the past ten years.

	past 5 years		past 10 years	
worst year	-3%	1999	-6%	1994
best year	15%	2000	19%	1995

In the past, Vanguard has done better than 98 percent of its peer group in up markets and outperformed 95 percent of its competition in down markets. Consistency, or predictability, of returns for Vanguard CA Insured Long-Term Tax-Exempt can be described as good. This fund's risk-related return is very good.

Management ★★★★★

There are 240 fixed-income securities in this $1.7 billion portfolio. The average municipal bond fund today is $150 million in size. Close to 96 percent of the fund's holdings are in bonds. The average maturity of the bonds in this account is eleven years; the weighted coupon rate averages 5.4 percent. The portfolio's fixed-income holdings can be categorized as long-term, high-quality debt.

A team has managed this fund for the past seven years. Over half the portfolio is in bonds rated AAA. The remaining half is evenly divided among issues rated AA, A, and BBB. Management makes use of call-protected issues whenever possible. The managers rotate between high- and low-coupon issues when modifying duration (maturity). There are 101 funds besides CA Insured Long-Term Tax-Exempt within the Vanguard family. Overall, the fund family's risk-adjusted performance can be described as very good.

Current Income ★★★★

Over the past year, Vanguard CA Insured Long-Term Tax-Exempt had a twelve-month yield of 4.9 percent. During this same twelve-month period, the typical municipal bond fund had a yield that averaged 4.5 percent.

Expenses ★★★★★

Vanguard CA Insured's expense ratio is 0.2 percent; it has averaged 0.2 percent annually over the past three calendar years. The average expense ratio for the 2,000 funds in this category is 1.1 percent. This fund's turnover rate over the past year has been 10 percent, while its peer group average has been 45 percent.

Summary

Vanguard CA Insured Long-Term Tax-Exempt ties for first place (with another Vanguard municipal bond fund) as having the best three- and five-year track record. Over the past three years, it has finished in the top quartile each year. Risk-adjusted returns have been super for the past three, five, and ten years. The fund ties for first as having the lowest expenses. Among its large peer group, it is the best up-market performer and has the second-best down-market track record. It is only one of two funds in its category that does a superb job during bear and bull markets. The fund ranks in the top quintile when it comes to growth persistence: the ability to consistently outperform equity funds over the previous five years. It excels when it comes to superior risk-adjusted return persistence. As mentioned, investors would be smart to check out other offerings from Vanguard, particularly bond funds.

Profile

minimum initial investment $3,000	IRA accounts available . . . . yes
subsequent minimum investment . . $100	IRA minimum investment $1,000
available in all 50 states. . . . . yes	date of inception. . . . . Apr. 1986
telephone exchanges. . . . . yes	dividend/income paid. . . . . monthly
number of funds in family 102	average credit quality . . . . AAA

Vanguard FL Insured Long-Term Tax-Exempt
Vanguard Financial Center
P.O. Box 260
Valley Forge, PA 19482
(800) 662-7447
www.vanguard.com

total return	★★★★★
risk reduction	★★★
management	★★★★★
current income	★★★★
expense control	★★★★★
symbol VFLTX	22 points
up-market performance	excellent
down-market performance	excellent
predictability of returns	good

Total Return   ★★★★★
Over the past five years (ending 12/31/00), Vanguard FL Insured Long-Term Tax-Exempt has taken $10,000 and turned it into $13,385 ($11,910 over three years). This translates into an annualized return of 6 percent over the past three and five years. Over the past five years, this fund has outperformed 50 percent of all mutual funds; within its general category, it has done better than 97 percent of its peers. Municipal bond funds have averaged 5 percent annually over these same five years.

During the past five years, a $10,000 initial investment grew to $13,350 after taxes, assuming a 39.6 percent income tax bracket (state and federal combined) and a capital gains rate of 28 percent. This means that investors in this fund were able to preserve 99 percent of their total returns. Compared to other fixed-income funds, this fund's tax savings are considered to be excellent.

Risk/Volatility   ★★★
Over the past five years, Vanguard has been safer than 55 percent of all municipal bond funds. Over the past decade, the fund has had two negative years, while the Lehman Brothers Aggregate Bond Index has also had two (off 3 percent in 1994 and 1 percent in 1999); the Lehman Brothers Municipal Bond Index also fell twice (off 5 percent in 1994 and 2 percent in 1999). The fund has underperformed the Lehman Brothers Aggregate Bond Index and the Lehman Brothers Municipal Bond Index twice in the past ten years.

	past 5 years		past 10 years	
worst year	-3%	1999	-5%	1994
best year	13%	2000	18%	1995

In the past, Vanguard has done better than 97 percent of its peer group in up markets and outperformed 95 percent of its competition in down markets.

Consistency, or predictability, of returns for Vanguard FL Insured Long-Term Tax-Exempt can be described as good. This fund's risk-related return is very good.

Management   ★★★★★

There are 155 fixed-income securities in this $920 million portfolio. The average municipal bond fund today is $150 million in size. Close to 100 percent of the fund's holdings are in bonds. The average maturity of the bonds in this account is twelve years; the weighted coupon rate averages 5.6 percent. The portfolio's fixed-income holdings can be categorized as long-term, high-quality debt.

Ian A. MacKinnon and Reid Smith have comanaged this fund for the past nine years. Most of the bonds in the portfolio are insured. Over 93 percent of the holdings are AAA-rated. The managers take large positions in issues that are call-protected in order to preserve the fund's current income stream. At least 80 percent of the fund's assets must be in Florida tax-free bonds and notes. There are 101 funds besides FL Insured Long-Term Tax-Exempt within the Vanguard family. Overall, the fund family's risk-adjusted performance can be described as very good.

Current Income   ★★★★

Over the past year, Vanguard FL Insured Long-Term Tax-Exempt had a twelve-month yield of 4.9 percent. During this same twelve-month period, the typical municipal bond fund had a yield that averaged 4.5 percent.

Expenses   ★★★★★

Vanguard FL Insured's expense ratio is 0.2 percent; it has also averaged 0.2 percent annually over the past three calendar years. The average expense ratio for the 2,000 funds in this category is 1.1 percent. This fund's turnover rate over the past year has been 15 percent, while its peer group average has been 45 percent.

Summary

Vanguard FL Insured Long-Term Tax-Exempt ties for first place (with another Vanguard municipal bond fund) as having the best three- and five-year track record. It also ties for first with another Vanguard offering as having the lowest expenses. It is one of only three funds in its entire category (2,000 funds) that does a superb job during bear as well as bull markets. It has outperformed 97 percent of all state and national tax-free funds. The fund ranks in the top quintile when it comes to growth persistence: the ability to consistently outperform equity funds over the previous five years. This offering also excels when it comes to superior risk-adjusted return persistence. Investors would be wise to check out other offerings from Vanguard.

Profile

minimum initial investment $3,000	*IRA accounts available* . . . . yes
subsequent minimum investment . . $100	*IRA minimum investment* $1,000
available in all 50 states. . . . . yes	*date of inception* . . . . Sept. 1992
telephone exchanges. . . . . yes	*dividend/income paid.* . . . . monthly
number of funds in family 102	*average credit quality* . . . . AAA

Vanguard Insured Long-Term Tax-Exempt
Vanguard Financial Center
P.O. Box 260
Valley Forge, PA 19482
(800) 662-7447
www.vanguard.com

total return	★★★★★
risk reduction	★★★
management	★★★★★
current income	★★★★★
expense control	★★★★★
symbol VILPX	23 points
up-market performance	excellent
down-market performance	very good
predictability of returns	good

Total Return   ★★★★★
Over the past five years (ending 12/31/00), Vanguard Insured Long-Term Tax-Exempt has taken $10,000 and turned it into $13,385 ($11,580 over three years and $19,675 over the past ten years). This translates into an annualized return of 6 percent over the past five years, 5 percent over the past three years, and 7 percent for the decade. Over the past five years, this fund has outperformed 45 percent of all mutual funds; within its general category, it has done better than 96 percent of its peers. Municipal bond funds have averaged 5 percent annually over these same five years.

During the past five years, a $10,000 initial investment grew to $13,320 after taxes, assuming a 39.6 percent income tax bracket (state and federal combined) and a capital gains rate of 28 percent. This means that investors in this fund were able to preserve 98 percent of their total returns. Compared to other fixed-income funds, this fund's tax savings are considered to be excellent.

Risk/Volatility   ★★★
Over the past five years, Vanguard has been safer than 75 percent of all municipal bond funds. Over the past decade, the fund has had two negative years, while the Lehman Brothers Aggregate Bond Index has also had two (off 3 percent in 1994 and 1 percent in 1999); the Lehman Brothers Municipal Bond Index also fell twice (off 5 percent in 1994 and 2 percent in 1999). The fund has underperformed the Lehman Brothers Aggregate Bond Index and the Lehman Brothers Municipal Bond Index twice in the past ten years.

	past 5 years		past 10 years	
worst year	-3%	1999	-6%	1994
best year	14%	2000	19%	1995

In the past, Vanguard has done better than 98 percent of its peer group in up markets and outperformed 80 percent of its competition in down markets.

Consistency, or predictability, of returns for Vanguard Insured Long-Term Tax-Exempt can be described as good. This fund's risk-related return is very good.

Management   ★★★★★

There are 260 fixed-income securities in this $2.3 billion portfolio. The average municipal bond fund today is $150 million in size. Close to 99 percent of the fund's holdings are in bonds. The average maturity of the bonds in this account is eleven years; the weighted coupon rate averages 5.3 percent. The portfolio's fixed-income holdings can be categorized as long-term, high-quality debt.

Ian A.MacKinnon and Reid Smith have comanaged this fund for the past eleven years. There are 101 funds besides Insured Long-Term Tax-Exempt within the Vanguard family. Overall, the fund family's risk-adjusted performance can be described as very good.

Current Income   ★★★★★

Over the past year, Vanguard Insured Long-Term Tax-Exempt had a twelve-month yield of 5.2 percent. During this same twelve-month period, the typical municipal bond fund had a yield that averaged 4.5 percent.

Expenses   ★★★★★

Vanguard Insured's expense ratio is 0.2 percent; it has also averaged 0.2 percent annually over the past three calendar years. The average expense ratio for the 2,000 funds in this category is 1.1 percent. This fund's turnover rate over the past year has been 15 percent, while its peer group average has been 45 percent.

Summary

Vanguard Insured Long-Term Tax-Exempt is tied for first as the best five-year performer, tied for first as having the lowest expenses, and had the second-best up-market performer. The fund ranks in the top quintile when it comes to growth persistence: the ability to consistently outperform equity funds over the previous five years. This offering also excels when it comes to superior risk-adjusted return persistence. Investors would be wise to check out other offerings from Vanguard.

Profile

minimum initial investment $3,000	*IRA accounts available* . . . . yes
subsequent minimum investment . . . $10	*IRA minimum investment* $1,000
available in all 50 states. . . . . yes	*date of inception* . . . . Oct. 1984
telephone exchanges. . . . . yes	*dividend/income paid*. . . . . monthly
number of funds in family 102	*average credit quality* . . . . AAA

Vanguard Intermediate-Term Tax-Exempt
Vanguard Financial Center
P.O. Box 260
Valley Forge, PA 19482
(800) 662-7447
www.vanguard.com

total return	★★★★
risk reduction	★★★★★
management	★★★★★
current income	★★★★
expense control	★★★★★
symbol VWITX	23 points
up-market performance	excellent
down-market performance	good
predictability of returns	excellent

Total Return　　★★★★
Over the past five years (ending 12/31/00), Vanguard Intermediate-Term Tax-Exempt has taken $10,000 and turned it into $12,765 ($11,580 over three years and $19,675 over the past ten years). This translates into an annualized return of 5 percent over the past three and five years, and 7 percent for the decade. Over the past five years, this fund has outperformed 45 percent of all mutual funds; within its general category, it has done better than 96 percent of its peers. Municipal bond funds have averaged 5 percent annually over these same five years.

During the past five years, a $10,000 initial investment grew to $12,740 after taxes, assuming a 39.6 percent income tax bracket (state and federal combined) and a capital gains rate of 28 percent. This means that investors in this fund were able to preserve 99 percent of their total returns. Compared to other fixed-income funds, this fund's tax savings are considered to be excellent.

Risk/Volatility　　★★★★★
Over the past five years, Vanguard has been safer than 75 percent of all municipal bond funds. Over the past decade, the fund has had two negative years, while the Lehman Brothers Aggregate Bond Index has also had two (off 3 percent in 1994 and 1 percent in 1999); the Lehman Brothers Municipal Bond Index also fell twice (off 5 percent in 1994 and 2 percent in 1999). The fund has underperformed the Lehman Brothers Aggregate Bond Index and the Lehman Brothers Municipal Bond Index twice in the past ten years.

	past 5 years		past 10 years	
worst year	-1%	1999	-2%	1994
best year	9%	2000	14%	1995

In the past, Vanguard has done better than 97 percent of its peer group in up markets but outperformed just 40 percent of its competition in down markets.

Consistency, or predictability, of returns for Vanguard Intermediate-Term Tax-Exempt can be described as excellent. This fund's risk-related return is very good.

Management   ★★★★★
There are 900 fixed-income securities in this $8.7 billion portfolio. The average municipal bond fund today is $150 million in size. Close to 98 percent of the fund's holdings are in bonds. The average maturity of the bonds in this account is seven years; the weighted coupon rate averages 5.7 percent. The portfolio's fixed-income holdings can be categorized as intermediate-term, high-quality debt.

Ian A. MacKinnon and Christopher M. Ryon have comanaged this fund for the past fifteen years. Two-thirds of the fund is in bonds rated AAA. Another 25 percent of the holdings are rated AA. Management likes to keep weighted maturity in the seven- to twelve-year range. Maturities do vary quite a bit. No more than 5 percent of the holdings may be in bonds rated below investment grade. There are 101 funds besides Intermediate-Term Tax-Exempt within the Vanguard family. Overall, the fund family's risk-adjusted performance can be described as very good.

Current Income   ★★★★
Over the past year, Vanguard Intermediate-Term Tax-Exempt had a twelve-month yield of 4.9 percent. During this same twelve-month period, the typical municipal bond fund had a yield that averaged 4.5 percent.

Expenses   ★★★★★
Vanguard Intermediate-Term's expense ratio is 0.2 percent; it has also averaged 0.2 percent annually over the past three calendar years. The average expense ratio for the 2,000 funds in this category is 1.1 percent. This fund's turnover rate over the past year has been 15 percent, while its peer group average has been 45 percent.

Summary
Vanguard Intermediate-Term Tax-Exempt has had outstanding risk-adjusted returns for the past three, five, and ten years. Intermediate-term bonds offer the best trade-off between return and low volatility, and the folks at Vanguard have taken full advantage of this fact. The fund ties for first as having the lowest overhead costs and the lowest risk. Even with such low risk, the portfolio has managed to outperform 96 percent of its peer group, regardless of maturity or quality. The fund is also the most predictable of its group. As noted numerous times in this book, investors would be smart to check out other Vanguard funds.

Profile
minimum initial investment $3,000	IRA accounts available . . . . yes
subsequent minimum investment . . $100	IRA minimum investment $1,000
available in all 50 states. . . . . yes	date of inception . . . . Sept. 1977
telephone exchanges. . . . . yes	dividend/income paid. . . . . monthly
number of funds in family 102	average credit quality. . . . . AA

Technology Funds

Consider the following statistics: the first desktop PC was introduced in 1984, the World Wide Web was invented in Switzerland in 1989, 46 million U.S. adults had Net access in 1997, 98 million U.S. adults had Net access in 1999, and the World Wide Web surpassed 1 billion unique pages in the year 2000. Just five years ago, it would have taken forty-seven minutes to download 1,000 pages; today this transmission takes just forty seconds. Experts anticipate that by 2003 Internet commerce will become a $1 trillion industry, and that more than 600 million users will be online worldwide.

Around the world, consumers who are rapidly embracing existing hardware and software in areas such as electronics, information technology, and cellular technology are driving the burgeoning need for technology. Technologies once considered highly advanced are now seen as household essentials—with progressively lower prices as a result of mass marketing. Because of intense global competition, lack of pricing flexibility, and tight labor markets, corporations seeking to maintain their profit margins are increasingly investing in technology to enhance productivity.

The technology sector has emerged as one of the principal drivers of both the global economy and the U.S. stock markets, as it produced staggering returns in 1999. For example, the Pacific Stock Exchange Tech 100 Index gained 116 percent and the average technology mutual fund gained 136 percent in 1999, followed by a loss of 33 percent in 2000.

However, technology stocks are also inherently more volatile and, consequently, riskier than the broad market as well as most, if not all, industry sectors. To demonstrate, let us examine standard deviation, the most common measure of performance volatility, or its tendency to move up or down. The higher the fund's standard deviation, the greater the fund's swings in performance. According to Morningstar, Inc., the standard deviation of returns for technology funds typically is roughly twice that of the S & P 500 Index.

Not all tech stocks are created equal. At the very basic level, Internet-related companies and general, non-Internet tech companies, such as those that make computers, chips, hard drives, or software, are at very different stages in their evolution. Internet companies are where regular technology companies were ten to fifteen years ago. The instability of Internet companies is what has made these stocks so volatile and so susceptible to momentum. As an example, Morgan Stanley's MOX Index of Internet stocks gained a staggering 514 percent between the end of 1998 and its peak on March 9, 2000, only to give up close to half of those gains over the next several weeks.

Technology stocks represent one of the fastest growing and largest contributors to the S & P 500 Index. At year-end 1999, technology stocks represented 30 percent of the S & P 500 Index (dropping to less than 20 percent by the middle of 2000) and accounted for 80 percent of the Index's overall growth. As you can see below, eight of the ten largest contributors to the S & P 500's 1999 return were technology companies:

Largest Technology Contributors to the S & P 500's 1999 Return

company	percentage of S & P 500's return	rank (by size)
Microsoft	11.9	1
Cisco	10.1	2
Oracle	5.7	5
Qualcomm	5.4	6
Nortel Networks	4.9	7
Sun Microsystems	4.2	8
America Online	4.0	9
Yahoo! Inc.	4.0	10

Technology fund investing can be quite complex. Not only are there over 125 funds that are specifically in the technology sector, but there are hundreds more in other categories that are heavily technology oriented. According to Morningstar, Inc. data, of the 670 largest growth funds, 125 hold 50 percent or more in technology-related stocks by the middle of 2000. And this may not be the whole story. Just defining technology can be a challenging endeavor.

There are 275 funds in this $145 billion category. Since 1986, the technology sector has underperformed the S & P 500 in the following years: 1986 by 11.1 percent, 1987 by 5.7 percent, 1988 by 9.8 percent, 1989 by 10.0 percent, 1995 by 2.3 percent, 1996 by 5.9 percent, and 1997 by 22.2 percent. In 1999, technology stocks outperformed the S & P 500 by 109 percent.

The typical technology fund is divided as follows: 83 percent in technology stocks, 9 percent in service, and 3 percent in industrials. The average technology fund is divided as follows: 84 percent in common stocks, 9 percent in foreign equities, and 7 percent in cash. The typical price-earnings (p/e) ratio for stocks in this category is 45 and they have a standard deviation of 63.6 percent.

Technology Funds

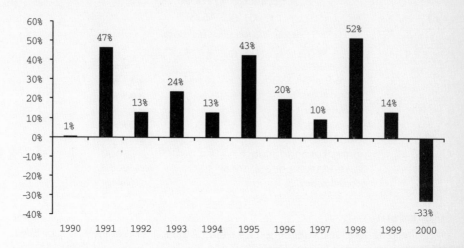

Alliance Technology A
P.O. Box 1520
Secaucus, NJ 07096
(800) 227-4618
www.alliancecapital.com

total return	★★★
risk reduction	★★★★★
management	★★★★★
tax minimization	★★★★★
expense control	★★★★
symbol ALTFX	22 points
up-market performance	good
down-market performance	very good
predictability of returns	excellent

Total Return   ★★★
Over the past five years (ending 12/31/00), Alliance Technology A has taken $10,000 and turned it into $25,940 ($20,975 over three years and $109,155 over the past ten years). This translates into an annualized return of 21 percent over the past five years, 28 percent over the past three years, and 27 percent for the decade. Over the past five years, this fund has outperformed 95 percent of all mutual funds; within its general category, it has done better than 50 percent of its peers. Technology funds have averaged 22 percent annually over these same five years.

Risk/Volatility   ★★★★★
Over the past five years, Alliance has been safer than 85 percent of all technology funds. Over the past decade, the fund has had one negative year, while the NASDAQ Index has had two (off 3 percent in 1994 and 39 percent in 2000); the Russell 2000 fell three times (off 2 percent in 1994, 3 percent in 1998, and 3 percent in 2000). The fund has underperformed the NASDAQ Index four times and the Russell 2000 three times in the past ten years.

	past 5 years		past 10 years	
worst year	-25%	2000	-25%	2000
best year	72%	1999	72%	1999

In the past, Alliance has done better than 40 percent of its peer group in up markets and outperformed 55 percent of its competition in down markets. Consistency, or predictability, of returns for Alliance Technology A can be described as excellent. This fund's risk-related return is excellent.

Management   ★★★★★
There are sixty stocks in this $2.8 billion portfolio. The average technology fund today is $450 million in size. Close to 90 percent of the fund's holdings are in stocks. The stocks in this portfolio have an average price-earnings (p/e) ratio of 41

and a median market capitalization of $16 billion. The portfolio's equity holdings can be categorized as large-cap and growth-oriented issues.

Peter Anastos and Gerald T. Malone have comanaged this fund for the past nine years. Management looks for companies that are on the leading edge of technology. The comanagers seek out corporations that are large and high quality. They are particularly concerned with profitability and valuations. The industry groups management likes include semiconductors, computer hardware, software, services, communications equipment, and services. There are 146 funds besides Technology A within the Alliance family. Overall, the fund family's risk-adjusted performance can be described as good.

Tax Minimization   ★★★★★
During the past five years, a $10,000 initial investment grew to $24,985 after taxes, assuming a 39.6 percent income tax bracket (state and federal combined) and a capital gains rate of 28 percent. This means that investors in this fund were able to preserve 94 percent of their total returns. Compared to other equity funds, this fund's tax savings are considered to be excellent.

Expenses   ★★★★
Alliance Technology's expense ratio is 1.7 percent; it has also averaged 1.7 percent annually over the past three calendar years. The average expense ratio for the 280 funds in this category is 1.8 percent. This fund's turnover rate over the past year has been 50 percent, while its peer group average has been 210 percent.

Summary
Alliance Technology A is the most predictable technology fund in the book. It also has the lowest risk and the second-lowest turnover rate (a real cost savings), and it is tied for first as being the most tax efficient. Risk-adjusted returns for the past three and ten years have been excellent. The fund ranks in the top quintile when it comes to growth persistence: the ability to consistently outperform equity funds over the previous five years. There are other funds that have turned in better than 28 percent annual returns over the past three years, but few, if any, with less risk.

Profile
minimum initial investment $250	*IRA accounts available* . . . . yes
subsequent minimum investment . . . $50	*IRA minimum investment* $250
available in all 50 states. . . . . yes	*date of inception*. . . . . Mar. 1982
telephone exchanges. . . . . yes	*dividend/income paid* . . . . annually
number of funds in family 147	*largest sector weighting* . . . technology

Firsthand Technology Value
101 Park Center Plaza, Suite 1300
San Jose, CA 95113
(888) 884-2675
www.firsthandfunds.com

total return	★★★★★
risk reduction	★★★★
management	★★★★★
tax minimization	★★★★★
expense control	★★★★
symbol TVFQX	23 points
up-market performance	excellent
down-market performance	fair
predictability of returns	fair

Total Return   ★★★★★
Over the past five years (ending 12/31/00), Firsthand Technology Value has taken $10,000 and turned it into $55,735 ($32,420 over three years). This translates into an annualized return of 41 percent over the past five years and 48 percent over the past three years. Over the past five years, this fund has outperformed 99 percent of all mutual funds; within its general category, it has done better than 75 percent of its peers. Technology funds have averaged 22 percent annually over these same five years.

Risk/Volatility   ★★★★
Over the past five years, Firsthand has been safer than 35 percent of all technology funds. Over the past decade, the fund has had one negative year, while the NASDAQ Index has had two (off 3 percent in 1994 and 39 percent in 2000); the Russell 2000 fell three times (off 2 percent in 1994, 3 percent in 1998, and 3 percent in 2000). The fund has underperformed the NASDAQ Index three times and the Russell 2000 twice in the past ten years.

	past 5 years		past 10 years	
worst year	-10%	2000	-10%	2000
best year	190%	1999	190%	1999

In the past, Firsthand has done better than 98 percent of its peer group in up markets but outperformed just 15 percent of its competition in down markets. Consistency, or predictability, of returns for Firsthand Technology Value can be described as fair. This fund's risk-related return is excellent.

Management   ★★★★★
There are sixty stocks in this $4.6 billion portfolio. The average technology fund today is $450 million in size. Close to 95 percent of the fund's holdings are in stocks. The stocks in this portfolio have an average price-earnings (p/e) ratio of 48

and a median market capitalization of $7 billion. The portfolio's equity holdings can be categorized as mid-cap and growth-oriented issues.

Kevin M. Landis has managed this fund for the past seven years. Due to concentration, the fund is considered to be "nondiversified." Landis does look for undervalued technology plays that are in electronics or medical technology. With its Silicon Valley residence, management has an edge over its competitors. The fund looks at a company's vision, marketing skills, and ability to respond quickly to changes. Issues selected vary from small-cap to mega-cap in size. There are five funds besides Technology Value within the Firsthand family.

Tax Minimization   ★★★★★
During the past five years, a $10,000 initial investment grew to $52,990 after taxes, assuming a 39.6 percent income tax bracket (state and federal combined) and a capital gains rate of 28 percent. This means that investors in this fund were able to preserve 94 percent of their total returns. Compared to other equity funds, this fund's tax savings are considered to be excellent.

Expenses   ★★★★
Firsthand Technology's expense ratio is 1.9 percent; it has also averaged 1.9 percent annually over the past three calendar years. The average expense ratio for the 280 funds in this category is 1.8 percent. This fund's turnover rate over the past year has been 40 percent, while its peer group average has been 210 percent.

Summary
Firsthand Technology Value has the highest overall score of any fund in its category. Overall, it is the recommended choice for the technology investor. Risk-adjusted returns have been outstanding over the past three and five years. It has outperformed 99 percent of all other mutual funds. It has performed better than any other tech fund during bull market periods. This Firsthand offering ties for first as being the most tax efficient. It has the best three- and five-year returns by a wide margin. Finally, the fund sports the lowest turnover rate in its 280-member group. This fund is highly recommended.

Profile
minimum initial investment $10,000	*IRA accounts available* . . . . yes
subsequent minimum investment . . . $50	*IRA minimum investment* $2,000
available in all 50 states. . . . . yes	*date of inception*. . . . . May 1994
telephone exchanges. . . . . yes	*dividend/income paid* . . . . annually
number of funds in family 6	*largest sector weighting* . . . technology

Hancock Technology A
101 Huntington Avenue
Boston, MA 02199
(800) 225-5291
www.jhancock.com

total return	★★★
risk reduction	★★★★
management	★★★★
tax minimization	★★★★
expense control	★★★★
symbol NTTFX	19 points
up-market performance	very good
down-market performance	excellent
predictability of returns	very good

Total Return   ★★★
Over the past five years (ending 12/31/00), (John) Hancock Technology A has taken $10,000 and turned it into $25,940 ($21,970 over three years and $79,260 over the past ten years). This translates into an annualized return of 21 percent over the past five years, 30 percent over the past three years, and 23 percent for the decade. Over the past five years, this fund has outperformed 95 percent of all mutual funds; within its general category, it has done better than 45 percent of its peers. Technology funds have averaged 22 percent annually over these same five years.

Risk/Volatility   ★★★★
Over the past five years, Hancock has been safer than 30 percent of all technology funds. Over the past decade, the fund has had one negative year, while the NASDAQ Index has had two (off 3 percent in 1994 and 39 percent in 2000); the Russell 2000 fell three times (off 2 percent in 1994, 3 percent in 1998, and 3 percent in 2000). The fund has underperformed the NASDAQ Index four times and the Russell 2000 five times in the past ten years.

	past 5 years		past 10 years	
worst year	-37%	2000	-37%	2000
best year	132%	1999	132%	1999

In the past, Hancock has done better than 65 percent of its peer group in up markets and outperformed 60 percent of its competition in down markets. Consistency, or predictability, of returns for Hancock Technology A can be described as very good. This fund's risk-related return is excellent.

Management   ★★★★
There are 110 stocks in this $715 million portfolio. The average technology fund today is $450 million in size. Close to 95 percent of the fund's holdings are in stocks. The stocks in this portfolio have an average price-earnings (p/e) ratio of 43

and a median market capitalization of $16 billion. The portfolio's equity holdings can be categorized as large-cap and growth-oriented issues.

Barry J. Gordon and Marc H. Klee have comanaged this fund for the past eighteen years. A bottom-up research approach is used. Management looks for companies that rely heavily on technology in their product development or operations. A stock is sold once it reaches management's predetermined price level. There are eighty-two funds besides Technology A within the John Hancock family. Overall, the fund family's risk-adjusted performance can be described as good to very good.

Tax Minimization   ★★★★
During the past five years, a $10,000 initial investment grew to $24,665 after taxes, assuming a 39.6 percent income tax bracket (state and federal combined) and a capital gains rate of 28 percent. This means that investors in this fund were able to preserve 92 percent of their total returns. Compared to other equity funds, this fund's tax savings are considered to be excellent.

Expenses   ★★★★
Hancock Technology's expense ratio is 1.4 percent; it has also averaged 1.4 percent annually over the past three calendar years. The average expense ratio for the 280 funds in this category is 1.8 percent. This fund's turnover rate over the past year has been 60 percent, while its peer group average has been 210 percent.

Summary
Hancock Technology A has had excellent risk-adjusted returns over the past three years. The fund has outperformed 95 percent of all mutual funds. It scores very well in every category and is ranked as the best down-market performer within the technology fund sector. After-tax returns have also been outstanding.

Profile
minimum initial investment $1,000	*IRA accounts available* . . . . yes
subsequent minimum investment $1	*IRA minimum investment* $250
available in all 50 states. . . . . yes	*date of inception* . . . . Jan. 1983
telephone exchanges. . . . . yes	*dividend/income paid* . . . . annually
number of funds in family 83	*largest sector weighting* . . . technology

RS Information Age
388 Market Street, Suite 200
San Francisco, CA 94111
(800) 270-5829
www.rsim.com

total return	★★★★
risk reduction	★★★★
management	★★★★
tax minimization	★★★★★
expense control	★★★
symbol RSIFX	20 points
up-market performance	very good
down-market performance	very good
predictability of returns	very good

Total Return   ★★★★
Over the past five years (ending 12/31/00), RS Information Age has taken $10,000 and turned it into $30,520 ($22,485 over three years). This translates into an annualized return of 25 percent over the past five years and 31 percent over the past three years. Over the past five years, this fund has outperformed 98 percent of all mutual funds; within its general category, it has done better than 65 percent of its peers. Technology funds have averaged 22 percent annually over these same five years.

Risk/Volatility   ★★★★
Over the past five years, RS has been safer than 35 percent of all technology funds. Over the past decade, the fund has had one negative year, while the NASDAQ Index has had two (off 3 percent in 1994 and 39 percent in 2000); the Russell 2000 fell three times (off 2 percent in 1994, 3 percent in 1998, and 3 percent in 2000). The fund has underperformed the NASDAQ Index once and the Russell 2000 twice in the past ten years.

	past 5 years		past 10 years	
worst year	-35%	2000	-35%	2000
best year	126%	1999	126%	1999

In the past, RS has done better than 65 percent of its peer group in up markets but outperformed just 45 percent of its competition in down markets. Consistency, or predictability, of returns for RS Information Age can be described as very good. This fund's risk-related return is excellent.

Management   ★★★★
There are thirty-five stocks in this $230 million portfolio. The average technology fund today is $450 million in size. Close to 95 percent of the fund's holdings are in stocks. The stocks in this portfolio have an average price-earnings (p/e) ratio of

37 and a median market capitalization of $39 billion. The portfolio's equity holdings can be categorized as large-cap and a blend of growth and value stocks.

Ronald E. Elijah and Roderick R. Berry have comanaged this fund for the past five years. The fund invests in information-technology stocks (companies that are mostly involved with the development, production, or distribution of products or services related to information). The comanagers first start their selection process by identifying a theme and then finding companies that are poised to benefit from such a theme. Management relies heavily on in-house research and visits with company managers whose stocks are, or may be, in the portfolio. There are ten funds besides Information Age within the RS family. Overall, the fund family's risk-adjusted performance can be described as good.

Tax Minimization   ★★★★★
During the past five years, a $10,000 initial investment grew to $29,290 after taxes, assuming a 39.6 percent income tax bracket (state and federal combined) and a capital gains rate of 28 percent. This means that investors in this fund were able to preserve 94 percent of their total returns. Compared to other equity funds, this fund's tax savings are considered to be excellent.

Expenses   ★★★
RS Information Age's expense ratio is 1.7 percent; it has also averaged 1.7 percent annually over the past three calendar years. The average expense ratio for the 280 funds in this category is 1.8 percent. This fund's turnover rate over the past year has been 180 percent, while its peer group average has been 210 percent.

Summary
RS Information Age scores highest when it comes to tax efficiency, but its pre-tax returns are also impressive; it has outperformed 98 percent of all mutual funds while having a low risk level. It is one of only four funds in the entire book that does a very good job when it comes to predictability of returns, up-market performance, and down-market returns. Risk-adjusted returns over the past three years have been great.

Profile
minimum initial investment $5,000	*IRA accounts available* . . . . yes
subsequent minimum investment . . $100	*IRA minimum investment* $1,000
available in all 50 states. . . . . yes	*date of inception* . . . . Nov. 1995
telephone exchanges. . . . . yes	*dividend/income paid* . . . . annually
number of funds in family 11	*largest sector weighting* . . . technology

Utility Stock Funds

Utility stock funds look for both growth and income, investing in common stocks of utility companies across the country. Somewhere between one-third and one-half of these funds' total returns come from common stock dividends. Utility funds normally stay away from speculative issues, focusing instead on well established companies with solid histories of paying good dividends. The goal of most of these funds is long-term growth.

Utility, metals, natural resources, and technology funds are the only four sector, or specialty, fund categories in this book. Funds that invest in a single industry, or sector, should be avoided by most investors for two reasons. First, you limit the fund manager's ability to find attractive stocks or bonds if he or she is only able to choose securities from one particular geographic area or industry. Second, the track record of sector funds as a whole is pretty bad. In fact, as a general category, these specialty funds represent the worst of both worlds: above-average risk and substandard returns. If you find the term "aggressive growth" unappealing, then the words "sector fund" should positively appall you.

Utility funds are the one exception. They sound safe and they are safe. In fact, over the past ten years, this category has only experienced one down year (-9.0 percent in 1994). Any category of stocks that somewhat relies on dividends generated automatically has a built-in safety cushion. A comparatively high dividend income means that you have to worry less about the appreciation of the underlying issues.

Four factors generally determine the profitability of a utility company: (1) how much it pays for energy, (2) the general level of interest rates, (3) its expected use of nuclear power, and (4) the political climate.

The prices of oil and gas are passed directly on to the consumer, but the utility companies are sensitive to this issue. Higher fuel prices mean that the utility industry has less latitude to increase its profit margins. Thus, higher fuel prices can mean smaller profits and/or dividends to investors.

Next to energy costs, interest expense is the industry's greatest expense. Utility companies are heavily debt-laden. Their interest costs directly affect their profitability. When rates go down and companies are able to refinance their debt, the savings can be staggering. Paying 7 percent interest on a couple of hundred million dollars, worth of bonds each year is much more appealing than having to pay 9 percent on the same amount of debt. A lower-interest-rate environment translates into more money being left over for shareholders.

Depending on how you look at it, nuclear power has been an issue or problem for the United States for a few decades now. Other countries seem to have come to grips with the matter, yet we remain divided. Although new power plants have not been successfully proposed or built in this country for several years, no one knows what the future may hold. Venturing into nuclear power always seems to be much more expensive than anticipated by the utility companies and the independent experts they rely on for advice. Because of these uncertainties, mutual fund managers try to seek out utility companies that have no foreseeable plans to develop any or more nuclear power facilities. Whether this will help the nation in the long term remains to be seen, but such avoidance keeps share prices more stable and predictable.

Finally, the political climate is an important concern when calculating whether utility funds should be part of your portfolio. The Public Utilities Commission (PUC) is a political animal and can directly reflect the views of a state's government. Utility bills are something most of us are concerned with and aware of; the powers that be are more likely to be re-elected if they are able to keep rate increases to a minimum. Modest, or minimum, increases can be healthy for the utility companies; freezing rates for a couple of years is a bad sign.

One hundred funds make up the utilities category. Total market capitalization of this category is over $29 billion. Over 85 percent of a typical utility fund's portfolio is in common stocks, with the balance in bonds, convertibles, and money market instruments. The typical utility fund has about 9 percent of its holdings in foreign stocks.

Over the past three years, utility funds have had an average compound return of 13.4 percent per year; the annual return for the past five years has been 15.2 percent. For the past ten and fifteen years, these funds have averaged 13.7 percent and 13.1 percent, respectively. The standard deviation for utility funds has been 17.5 percent over the past three years. This means that these funds have been less volatile than any other stock category except equity-income funds, which have exhibited almost identical volatility. The average annual expense ratio for this category is 1.4 percent.

Standard Deviation of the Different Stock (Equity) Categories over the Past Three Years (Ending December 31, 2000)

category	standard deviation	category	standard deviation
technology	63.6%	growth	27.6%
aggressive growth	34.4%	world stock	25.2%
metals	38.9%	growth & income	19.6%
health care	37.6%	utilities	17.4%
natural resources	33.9%		

Usually, utility stock prices closely follow the long-term bond market. If long-term interest rates go up, utility stock prices are likely to go down. Utility stocks are also vulnerable to a general stock market decline, although they are considered less risky than other types of common stock because of their dividends and the monopoly position of most utilities. Typically, utilities have fallen about two-thirds as much as other common stocks during market downturns.

Worldwide, there is a tremendous opportunity for growth in this industry. The average per-capita production of electricity in many developing countries is only one-fifth that of the United States. The electrical output per capita in the United States is 12,100 kilowatt hours, compared to 2,500 kilowatt hours for developing nations. This disparity may well be on the way out. All over the world, previously underdeveloped countries are making economic strides as they move toward free market systems.

When emerging countries become developed economically, their citizens demand higher standards of living. As a result, their requirements for electricity, water, and telephones tend to rise dramatically. Moreover, many countries are selling their utility companies to public owners, opening a new arena for investors. The net result of all of this for you, the investor, is that fund groups are beginning to offer global utility funds. This increased diversification—allowing a fund to invest in utility companies all over the world instead of just in the United States, coupled with tremendous long-term growth potential—should make this a dynamic industry group. Utility funds are a good choice for the investor who wants a hedge against inflation but is still afraid or distrustful of the stock market in general.

Beta, which measures the market-related risk of a stock, is only 0.5 percent for utility funds as a group (compared to 1.0 for the S & P 500). This means that when it comes to stock market risk, utilities have only 50 percent the risk of the Dow Jones Industrial Average (DJIA) or the S & P 500. Keep in mind, however, that there are other risks, such as rising interest rates, that also need to be considered whenever utilities are being considered.

Utility Stock Funds

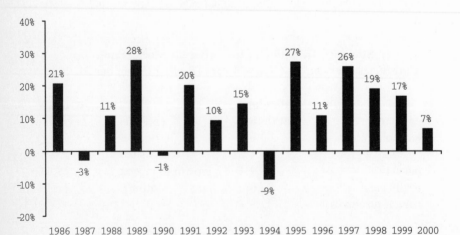

American Gas Index

4922 Fairmont Avenue
Bethesda, MD 20814
(800) 343-3355
www.fbr.com

total return	★★★★
risk reduction	★★★★
management	★★★★★
tax minimization	★★★★
expense control	★★★★★
symbol GASFX	22 points
up-market performance	very good
down-market performance	excellent
predictability of returns	very good

Total Return   ★★★★

Over the past five years (ending 12/31/00), American Gas Index has taken $10,000 and turned it into $23,865 ($15,610 over three years and $37,075 over the past ten years). This translates into an annualized return of 19 percent over the past five years, 16 percent over the past three years, and 14 percent for the decade. Over the past five years, this fund has outperformed 90 percent of all mutual funds; within its general category, it has done better than 88 percent of its peers. Utility stock funds have averaged 15 percent annually over these same five years.

Risk/Volatility   ★★★★

Over the past five years, American has been safer than 65 percent of all utility stock funds. Over the past decade, the fund has had two negative years, while the S & P 500 has had one (off 9 percent in 2000). The fund has underperformed the S & P 500 seven times in the past ten years.

	past 5 years		past 10 years	
worst year	-4%	1999	-10%	1994
best year	56%	2000	56%	2000

In the past, American has done better than 40 percent of its peer group in up markets and outperformed 98 percent of its competition in down markets. Consistency, or predictability, of returns for American Gas Index can be described as very good. This fund's risk-related return is excellent.

Management   ★★★★★

There are eighty-five stocks in this $320 million portfolio. The average utility stock fund today is $290 million in size. Close to 100 percent of the fund's holdings are in stocks. The stocks in this portfolio have an average price-earnings (p/e) ratio of 29 and a median market capitalization of $8 billion. The portfolio's equity holdings can be categorized as large-cap and value-oriented issues.

A team has managed this fund for the past twelve years. Management tries to replicate return results of an index of common stocks that are members of the American Gas Association. Proportional index weighting is used to determine the size of a stock's position in the fund. There are three funds besides American Gas Index within the Rushmore family. Overall, the fund family's risk-adjusted performance can be described as good.

Tax Minimization   ★★★★
During the past five years, a $10,000 initial investment grew to $22,200 after taxes, assuming a 39.6 percent income tax bracket (state and federal combined) and a capital gains rate of 28 percent. This means that investors in this fund were able to preserve 88 percent of their total returns. Compared to other equity funds, this fund's tax savings are considered to be very good.

Expenses   ★★★★★
American Gas Index's expense ratio is 0.9 percent; it has also averaged 0.9 percent annually over the past three calendar years. The average expense ratio for the 100 funds in this category is 1.4 percent. This fund's turnover rate over the past year has been 15 percent, while its peer group average has been 55 percent.

Summary
American Gas Index has a very low correlation with the S & P 500, making it an excellent choice for any investor looking for equity diversification. Risk-adjusted returns for the past three and five years have been very good. The fund ties for first as having the highest overall score of any portfolio in its 100-member category. It also has lower turnover (a real cost saver) than any of its peers and is rated as the best bear market performer. Even though this is a real niche play, the fund has been able to outperform 90 percent of all other mutual funds, regardless of category.

Profile
minimum initial investment $2,500	*IRA accounts available* . . . . yes
subsequent minimum investment $1	*IRA minimum investment* $500
available in all 50 states . . . . yes	*date of inception* . . . . May 1989
telephone exchanges . . . . yes	*dividend/income paid* . . . . quarterly
number of funds in family 4	*largest sector weighting* . . . . . . utilities

AXP Utilities Income A

IDS Tower 10
Minneapolis, MN 55440
(800) 328-8300
www.americanexpress.com

total return	★★★★
risk reduction	★★★★
management	★★★★
tax minimization	★★★
expense control	★★★★
symbol INUTX	19 points
up-market performance	very good
down-market performance	very good
predictability of returns	excellent

Total Return   ★★★★

Over the past five years (ending 12/31/00), AXP Utilities Income A has taken $10,000 and turned it into $22,880 ($15,610 over three years and $44,115 over the past ten years). This translates into an annualized return of 18 percent over the past five years, 16 percent over the past three years, and 16 percent for the decade. Over the past five years, this fund has outperformed 90 percent of all mutual funds; within its general category, it has done better than 85 percent of its peers. Utility stock funds have averaged 15 percent annually over these same five years.

Risk/Volatility   ★★★★

Over the past five years, AXP has been safer than 85 percent of all utility stock funds. Over the past decade, the fund has had one negative year, while the S & P 500 has also had one (off 9 percent in 2000). The fund has underperformed the S & P 500 seven times in the past ten years.

	past 5 years		past 10 years	
worst year	9%	1999	-7%	1994
best year	29%	1997	29%	1997

In the past, AXP has done better than 65 percent of its peer group in up markets and outperformed 70 percent of its competition in down markets. Consistency, or predictability, of returns for AXP Utilities Income A can be described as excellent. This fund's risk-related return is very good.

Management   ★★★★

There are seventy stocks in this $1.7 billion portfolio. The average utility stock fund today is $290 million in size. Close to 90 percent of the fund's holdings are in stocks. The stocks in this portfolio have an average price-earnings (p/e) ratio of 26 and a median market capitalization of $16 billion. The portfolio's equity holdings can be categorized as large-cap and value-oriented issues.

Bern Fleming has managed this fund for the past six years. Fleming invests in stocks of public utility companies and includes stocks from a wide range: those that produce or supply natural gas, water, telecommunications, or electric power. He prefers well established and large-cap companies that have low price-to-book and low p/e multiples. Management will sometimes have as much as a fifth of the portfolio in foreign issues. There are 104 funds besides Utilities Income A within the American Express Financial family. Overall, the fund family's risk-adjusted performance can be described as good.

Tax Minimization   ★★★
During the past five years, a $10,000 initial investment grew to $20,690 after taxes, assuming a 39.6 percent income tax bracket (state and federal combined) and a capital gains rate of 28 percent. This means that investors in this fund were able to preserve 83 percent of their total returns. Compared to other equity funds, this fund's tax savings are considered to be good.

Expenses   ★★★★
AXP Utilities Income's expense ratio is 0.9 percent; it has also averaged 0.9 percent annually over the past three calendar years. The average expense ratio for the 100 funds in this category is 1.4 percent. This fund's turnover rate over the past year has been 70 percent, while its peer group average has been 55 percent.

Summary
AXP Utilities Income A has had very good risk-adjusted returns for the past three, five, and ten years. It has outperformed 85 percent of its peers and 90 percent of all mutual funds. Within its category, it has the most predictable returns and the lowest expense ratio. The fund ranks in the top two quintiles when it comes to growth persistence: the ability to consistently outperform equity funds over the previous five years. This offering excels when it comes to superior risk-adjusted return persistence.

Profile
minimum initial investment $2,000	*IRA accounts available* . . . . yes
subsequent minimum investment . . $100	*IRA minimum investment* $1
available in all 50 states . . . . yes	*date of inception* . . . . Aug. 1988
telephone exchanges . . . . yes	*dividend/income paid* . . . . quarterly
number of funds in family 105	*largest sector weighting* . . . . . . utilities

MFS Utilities A

P.O. Box 2281
Boston, MA 02107
(800) 637-2929
www.mfs.com

total return	★★★★★
risk reduction	★★★★★
management	★★★★★
tax minimization	★★
expense control	★★★
symbol MMUFX	20 points
up-market performance	excellent
down-market performance	poor
predictability of returns	excellent

Total Return   ★★★★★

Over the past five years (ending 12/31/00), MFS Utilities A has taken $10,000 and turned it into $25,940 ($16,430 over three years). This translates into an annualized return of 21 percent over the past five years and 18 percent over the past three years. Over the past five years, this fund has outperformed 96 percent of all mutual funds; within its general category, it has done better than 99 percent of its peers. Utility stock funds have averaged 15 percent annually over these same five years.

Risk/Volatility   ★★★★★

Over the past five years, MFS has been safer than 99 percent of all utility stock funds. Over the past decade, the fund has had one negative year, while the S & P 500 has also had one (off 9 percent in 2000). The fund has underperformed the S & P 500 five times in the past eight years.

	past 5 years		past 8 years	
worst year	7%	2000	-5%	1994
best year	32%	1999	32%	1995

In the past, MFS has done better than 90 percent of its peer group in up markets and outperformed 50 percent of its competition in down markets. Consistency, or predictability, of returns for MFS Utilities A can be described as excellent. This fund's risk-related return is excellent.

Management   ★★★★★

There are 115 stocks in this $760 million portfolio. The average utility stock fund today is $290 million in size. Close to 80 percent of the fund's holdings are in stocks, the balance is in bonds. The stocks in this portfolio have an average price-earnings (p/e) ratio of 26 and a median market capitalization of $18 billion. The portfolio's equity holdings can be categorized as large-cap and value-oriented issues.

Maura Shaughnessy has managed this fund for the past nine years. She is a bottom-up equity picker who emphasizes fundamentals in order to reduce risk. Management likes to keep roughly a fifth of the portfolio in bonds or convertibles in order to further reduce risk. Management is allowed to have up to a third of its holdings in foreign and emerging markets. There are 191 funds besides Utilities A within the MFS family. Overall, the fund family's risk-adjusted performance can be described as very good.

Tax Minimization   ★★
During the past five years, a $10,000 initial investment grew to $21,955 after taxes, assuming a 39.6 percent income tax bracket (state and federal combined) and a capital gains rate of 28 percent. This means that investors in this fund were able to preserve 75 percent of their total returns. Compared to other equity funds, this fund's tax savings are considered to be fair.

Expenses   ★★★
MFS Utilities's expense ratio is 1.1 percent; it has also averaged 1.1 percent annually over the past three calendar years. The average expense ratio for the 100 funds in this category is 1.4 percent. This fund's turnover rate over the past year has been 130 percent, while its peer group average has been 55 percent.

Summary
MFS Utilities A boasts the highest five-year returns of any fund in its category. It scores as the second most predictable in its group when it comes to returns. It has the lowest risk of any utilities fund in the book, yet has been the best performer during bull markets. The fund ranks in the top quintile when it comes to growth persistence: the ability to consistently outperform equity funds over the previous five years. This offering also excels when it comes to superior risk-adjusted return persistence. Risk-adjusted returns over the past five years have been excellent. Investors should check out other mutual fund offerings from MFS.

Profile
minimum initial investment $1,000	*IRA accounts available* . . . . yes
subsequent minimum investment . . . $50	*IRA minimum investment* $250
available in all 50 states. . . . . yes	*date of inception* . . . . Feb. 1992
telephone exchanges. . . . . yes	*dividend/income paid.* . . . . monthly
number of funds in family 192	*largest sector weighting* . . . . . . utilities

MSDW Global Utilities B

Two World Trade Center, 72nd Floor
New York, NY 10048
(800) 869-3863
www.deanwitter.com/funds

total return	★★★★★
risk reduction	★★★★★
management	★★★★★
tax minimization	★★★★
expense control	★★★
symbol GUTBX	22 points
up-market performance	excellent
down-market performance	poor
predictability of returns	excellent

Total Return   ★★★★★

Over the past five years (ending 12/31/00), MSDW Global Utilities B has taken $10,000 and turned it into $24,885 ($18,160 over three years). This translates into an annualized return of 20 percent over the past five years and 22 percent over the past three years. Over the past five years, this fund has outperformed 95 percent of all mutual funds; within its general category, it has done better than 94 percent of its peers. Utility stock funds have averaged 15 percent annually over these same five years.

Risk/Volatility   ★★★★★

Over the past five years, MSDW has been safer than 65 percent of all utility stock funds. Over the past decade, the fund has had no negative years, while the S & P 500 has had one (off 9 percent in 2000). The fund has underperformed the S & P 500 three times in the past six years.

	past 3 years		past 6 years	
worst year	7%	2000	7%	2000
best year	38%	1998	38%	1998

In the past, MSDW has done better than 95 percent of its peer group in up markets but outperformed just 20 percent of its competition in down markets. Consistency, or predictability, of returns for MSDW Global Utilities B can be described as excellent. This fund's risk-related return is excellent.

Management   ★★★★★

There are eighty-five stocks in this $960 million portfolio. The average utility stock fund today is $290 million in size. Close to 95 percent of the fund's holdings are in stocks. The stocks in this portfolio have an average price-earnings (p/e) ratio of 27 and a median market capitalization of $16 billion. The portfolio's equity holdings can be categorized as large-cap and value-oriented issues.

Edward F. Gaylor has managed this fund for the past seven years. The fund invests in stocks of companies that either produce, distribute, or sell electricity, natural gas, or telecommunications. Gaylor looks around the world for possible candidates; roughly 15 to 20 percent of the portfolio is in foreign issues. There are 220 funds besides Global Utilities B within the Morgan Stanley Dean Witter family. Overall, the fund family's risk-adjusted performance can be described as good.

Tax Minimization   ★★★★
During the past five years, a $10,000 initial investment grew to $23,250 after taxes, assuming a 39.6 percent income tax bracket (state and federal combined) and a capital gains rate of 28 percent. This means that investors in this fund were able to preserve 89 percent of their total returns. Compared to other equity funds, this fund's tax savings are considered to be very good.

Expenses   ★★★
MSDW Global's expense ratio is 1.7 percent; it has also averaged 1.7 percent annually over the past three calendar years. The average expense ratio for the 100 funds in this category is 1.4 percent. This fund's turnover rate over the past year has been 50 percent, while its peer group average has been 55 percent.

Summary
The Morgan Stanley Dean Witter (MSDW) Global Utilities B ties for first as having the highest overall score of any fund in its category. It has the best three-year performance figures and is number two over the past five years. It has lower risk than any other utility fund in the book. During bull markets it has been the best performer, yet it has had lower risk than any portfolio in its group. The fund ranks in the top two quintiles when it comes to growth persistence: the ability to consistently outperform equity funds over the previous five years. This offering excels when it comes to superior risk-adjusted return persistence.

Profile
minimum initial investment $1,000	IRA accounts available . . . . yes
subsequent minimum investment . . $100	IRA minimum investment $1,000
available in all 50 states. . . . . yes	date of inception. . . . . June 1994
telephone exchanges. . . . . yes	dividend/income paid . . . . quarterly
number of funds in family 221	largest sector weighting . . . . . . utilities

Strong American Utilities

P.O. Box 2936
Milwaukee, WI 53201
(800) 368-1030
www.strongfunds.com

total return	★★★
risk reduction	★★★★
management	★★★★
tax minimization	★★★
expense control	★★★★
symbol SAMUX	18 points
up-market performance	very good
down-market performance	excellent
predictability of returns	excellent

Total Return   ★★★

Over the past five years (ending 12/31/00), Strong American Utilities has taken $10,000 and turned it into $21,005 ($15,610 over three years). This translates into an annualized return of 16 percent over the past five years and 16 percent over the past three years. Over the past five years, this fund has outperformed 85 percent of all mutual funds; within its general category, it has done better than 60 percent of its peers. Utility stock funds have averaged 15 percent annually over these same five years.

Risk/Volatility   ★★★★

Over the past five years, Strong has been safer than 60 percent of all utility stock funds. Over the past decade, the fund has had one negative year, while the S & P 500 has also had one (off 9 percent in 2000). The fund has underperformed the S & P 500 six times in the past seven years.

	past 3 years		past 7 years	
worst year	1%	1999	-3%	1994
best year	28%	1997	37%	1995

In the past, Strong has done better than 60 percent of its peer group in up markets and outperformed 95 percent of its competition in down markets. Consistency, or predictability, of returns for Strong American Utilities can be described as excellent. This fund's risk-related return is very good.

Management   ★★★★

There are forty-five stocks in this $300 million portfolio. The average utility stock fund today is $290 million in size. Close to 96 percent of the fund's holdings are in stocks. The stocks in this portfolio have an average price-earnings (p/e) ratio of 24 and a median market capitalization of $17 billion. The portfolio's equity holdings can be categorized as large-cap and value-oriented issues.

A team has managed this fund for the past eight years. Management must invest at least two-thirds of the portfolio in domestic utility companies; the remaining third may be invested in any type of security in any industry (although almost all of this is invested in utilities). The managers look for companies that have 12 to 15 percent or more returns-on-equity along with an increasing dividend stream. The fund does not invest in a company before visiting it. There are forty-five funds besides American Utilities within the Strong family. Overall, the fund family's risk-adjusted performance can be described as good.

Tax Minimization ★★★
During the past five years, a $10,000 initial investment grew to $19,355 after taxes, assuming a 39.6 percent income tax bracket (state and federal combined) and a capital gains rate of 28 percent. This means that investors in this fund were able to preserve 85 percent of their total returns. Compared to other equity funds, this fund's tax savings are considered to be good.

Expenses ★★★★
Strong American Utilities's expense ratio is 1 percent; it has also averaged 1 percent annually over the past three calendar years. The average expense ratio for the 100 funds in this category is 1.4 percent. This fund's turnover rate over the past year has been 75 percent, while its peer group average has been 55 percent.

Summary
Strong American Utilities has had very good three- and five-year risk-adjusted returns. Within its category, it has been the second-best performer during bear stock markets. It has outperformed 85 percent of all mutual funds. The fund scores well in every category. This offering also excels when it comes to superior risk-adjusted return persistence.

Profile
minimum initial investment $2,500	*IRA accounts available* . . . . yes
subsequent minimum investment . . . $50	*IRA minimum investment* $250
available in all 50 states. . . . . yes	*date of inception* . . . . July 1993
telephone exchanges. . . . . yes	*dividend/income paid* . . . . quarterly
number of funds in family 46	*largest sector weighting* . . . . . . utilities

World Bond Funds

Global, or world, funds invest in securities issued all over the world, including the United States. A global bond fund usually invests in bonds issued by stable governments from a handful of countries. These funds try to avoid purchasing foreign government debt instruments from politically or economically unstable nations. Foreign, also known as international, bond funds invest in debt instruments from countries other than the United States.

International funds purchase securities issued in a foreign currency, such as the Japanese yen or the British pound. Prospective investors need to be aware of the potential changes in the value of the foreign currency relative to the U.S. dollar. As an example, if you were to invest in U.K. pound-denominated bonds with a yield of 15 percent and the British currency appreciated 12 percent against the U.S. dollar, your total return for the year would be 27 percent. If the British pound declined by 20 percent against the U.S. dollar, your total return would be -5 percent (15 percent yield minus 20 percent).

Since foreign markets do not necessarily move in tandem with U.S. markets, each country represents varying investment opportunities at different times. According to Salomon Brothers, the current value of the world bond market is estimated to be over $24 trillion. About 40 percent of this bond marketplace is made up of U.S. bonds; Japan ranks a distant second.

Assessing the economic environment to evaluate its effects on interest rates and bond values requires an understanding of two important factors—inflation and supply. During inflationary periods, when there is too much money chasing too few goods, government tightening of the money supply helps create a balance between an economy's cash resources and its available goods. Money supply refers to the amount of cash made available for spending, borrowing, or investing. Controlled by the central banks of each nation, it is a primary tool used to manage inflation, interest rates, and economic growth.

A prudent tightening of the money supply can help bring on disinflation— decelerated loan demand, reduced durable goods orders, and falling prices. During disinflationary times, interest rates also fall, strengthening the underlying value of existing bonds. While such factors ultimately contribute to a healthier economy, they also mean lower yields for government bond investors. A trend toward disinflation currently exists in markets around the world.

As the United States and other governments implement policies designed to reduce inflation, interest rates are stabilizing. This disinflation can be disquieting to the individual who specifically invests for high monthly income. In reality, falling interest rates mean higher bond values, and investors seeking long-term growth or high total returns can therefore benefit from declining rates. Inflation, which drives interest rates higher, is the true enemy of bond investors. It diminishes bond values and, in addition, erodes the buying power of the interest income investors receive.

Income-seeking investors need to find economies where inflation is coming under control, yet where interest rates are still high enough to provide favorable bond yields. An investor who has only U.S. bonds is not taking advantage of such opportunities. If global disinflationary trends continue, those who remain invested only in the United States can lose out on opportunities for high income and total return elsewhere. The gradually decreasing yields on U.S. bonds compel the investor who seeks high income to think globally.

While not all bond markets will peak at the same level, they do tend to follow patterns. Targeting those countries where interest rates are at peak levels and inflation is falling not only results in higher income but also creates significant potential for capital appreciation as rates ultimately decline and bond prices increase.

Each year since 1984, at least three government bond markets have provided yields higher than those available in the United States. With over 60 percent of the world's bonds found outside the United States, investors must look beyond U.S. borders to find bonds offering yields and total returns that meet their investment objectives.

According to Salomon Brothers, over the past three years, international bonds have underperformed U.S. bonds by an average of 3.5 percent per year; the figure increases to 4.8 percent over the past five years. Over the past ten years, the figure drops to an average of 1.2 percent per year and then falls down to just 0.9 percent per year over the past fifteen years (all periods ending December 31, 2000).

Even with high income as the primary goal (these funds have a typical yield of roughly 6.7 percent annually), investors must consider credit and market risk. By investing primarily in mutual funds that purchase government-guaranteed bonds from the world's most creditworthy nations, you can get an extra measure of credit safety for payment of interest and repayment of principal. By diversifying across multiple markets, fund managers can significantly reduce market risk as well. Diversification is a proven technique for controlling market risk.

The long-term success of a global bond manager depends on expertise in assessing economic trends from country to country, as well as protecting the U.S. valuation of foreign holdings. The most effective way to protect the U.S. dollar value of international holdings is through active currency management. Although its effects over a 10-year period are nominal at best, currency fluctuations can help returns over a 1-, 3-, or 5-year period.

In the simplest terms, effective currency management provides exposure to bond markets worldwide, while reducing the effects of adverse currency changes that can lower bond values. If a portfolio manager anticipates that the U.S. dollar will strengthen, he or she can lock in a currency exchange rate to protect the fund against a decline in the value of its foreign holdings. (A strong dollar means that other currencies are declining in value.) This strategy is commonly referred to as hedging the exposure of the portfolio. If, on the other hand, the manager expects the U.S. dollar to weaken, the fund can stay unhedged to allow it to benefit from the increasing value of foreign currencies. As good as hedging sounds, there is a cost to hedging and, on balance, this cost over time more than wipes out any benefit.

Investing in global bonds gives you the potential for capital appreciation during periods of declining interest rates. An inverse relationship exists between bond values and interest rates. When interest rates fall, as is the case in most bond markets in the world today, existing bond values climb. Conversely, as interest rates rise, the value of existing bonds declines (they are less desirable since "new" bonds have a higher current yield).

Over the past three and five years, global bond funds have had an average compound return of 2.6 and 5.0 percent per year, respectively; the annual returns for the past ten and fifteen years have been 5.4 and 8.5 percent, respectively. The standard deviation for global bond funds has been 10 percent over the past three years. This means that these funds have been less volatile than any equity fund but more volatile than government bond funds (standard deviation of 3 percent). Just 220 funds make up the global bond category. Total market capitalization of this category is approximately $21 billion.

Global bond funds, particularly those with high concentrations in foreign issues, are an excellent risk-reduction tool that should be utilized by a wide range of investors.

World Bond Funds

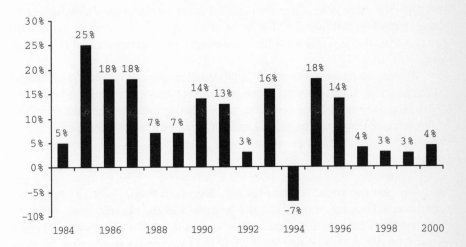

Alliance Global Dollar Government A

P.O. Box 1520
Secaucus, NJ 07096
(800) 227-4618
www.alliancecapital.com

total return	★★★★
risk reduction	★★
management	★★★
current income	★★★★★
expense control	★★★
symbol AGDAX	17 points
up-market performance	excellent
down-market performance	poor
predictability of returns	good

Total Return ★★★★

Over the past five years (ending 12/31/00), Alliance Global Dollar Government A has taken $10,000 and turned it into $17,625 ($11,250 over three years). This translates into an annualized return of 12 percent over the past five years and 4 percent over the past three years. Over the past five years, this fund has outperformed 75 percent of all mutual funds; within its general category, it has done better than 70 percent of its peers. World bond funds have averaged 5 percent annually over these same five years.

During the past five years, a $10,000 initial investment grew to $13,280 after taxes, assuming a 39.6 percent income tax bracket (state and federal combined) and a capital gains rate of 28 percent. This means that investors in this fund were able to preserve 43 percent of their total returns. Compared to other fixed-income funds, this fund's tax savings are considered to be good.

Risk/Volatility ★★

Over the past five years, Alliance has only been safer than 25 percent of all world bond funds. Over the past decade, the fund has had one negative year, while the Lehman Brothers Aggregate Bond Index has had two (off 3 percent in 1994 and 1 percent in 1999); the Salomon Brothers World Government Bond Index fell three times (off 4 percent in 1997, 5 percent in 1999, and 3 percent in 2000). The fund has underperformed the Lehman Brothers Aggregate Bond Index once and the Salomon Brothers World Government Bond Index three times in the past ten years.

	past 5 years		past 10 years	
worst year	-22%	1998	-22%	1998
best year	39%	1996	39%	1996

In the past, Alliance has done better than 99 percent of its peer group in up markets but outperformed just 10 percent of its competition in down markets. Consistency, or predictability, of returns for Alliance Global Dollar Government A can be described as good. This fund's risk-related return is good.

Management   ★★★
There are fifty-five fixed-income securities in this $65 million portfolio. The average world bond fund today is $95 million in size. Close to 95 percent of the fund's holdings are in bonds. The average maturity of the bonds in this account is twelve years; the weighted coupon rate averages 9.6 percent. The portfolio's fixed-income holdings can be categorized as high quality and somewhat long term.

Paul J. DeNoon and Wayne D. Lyski have managed this fund for the past five years. Brady bonds comprise a substantial portion of the portfolio, which has half its assets in emerging markets securities. Management uses the J. P. Morgan Emerging Markets Bond Index as a reference, but it does not hesitate to venture off into other areas if a favorable opportunity arises. Performance swings in some years have been wild and extreme. There are 146 funds besides Global Dollar Government A within the Alliance family. Overall, the fund family's risk-adjusted performance can be described as good.

Current Income   ★★★★★
Over the past year, Alliance Global Dollar Government A had a twelve-month yield of 11.4 percent. During this same twelve-month period, the typical world bond fund had a yield that averaged 6.7 percent.

Expenses   ★★★
Alliance Global Dollar Government's expense ratio is 1.8 percent; it has averaged 1.6 percent annually over the past three calendar years. The average expense ratio for the 220 funds in this category is 1.4 percent. This fund's turnover rate over the past year has been 170 percent, while its peer group average has been 185 percent.

Summary
Alliance Global Dollar Government A ties for first as being the best up-market performer within its 220-member category, world bonds. This fund is particularly attractive for the current income investor; few funds in any category have had such a high yield. It has outperformed 75 percent of all mutual funds and has done so with fairly acceptable risk. Over two-thirds of the fund is in bonds rated B or BB.

Profile
minimum initial investment $250	*IRA accounts available* .... yes
subsequent minimum investment ... $50	*IRA minimum investment* $250
available in all 50 states. .... yes	*date of inception* .... Feb. 1994
telephone exchanges. .... yes	*dividend/income paid.* .... monthly
number of funds in family 147	*average credit quality* .... AAA

Alliance North American Government Income B

P.O. Box 1520
Secaucus, NJ 07096
(800) 227-4618
www.alliancecapital.com

total return	★★★★★
risk reduction	★★★★★
management	★★★★★
current income	★★★★★
expense control	★★
symbol ANABX	22 points
up-market performance	excellent
down-market performance	fair
predictability of returns	excellent

Total Return   ★★★★★

Over the past five years (ending 12/31/00), Alliance North American Government Income B has taken $10,000 and turned it into $19,255 ($13,310 over three years). This translates into an annualized return of 14 percent over the past five years and 10 percent over the past three years. Over the past five years, this fund has outperformed 85 percent of all mutual funds; within its general category, it has done better than 99 percent of its peers. World bond funds have averaged 5 percent annually over these same five years.

During the past five years, a $10,000 initial investment grew to $16,110 after taxes, assuming a 39.6 percent income tax bracket (state and federal combined) and a capital gains rate of 28 percent. This means that investors in this fund were able to preserve 66 percent of their total returns. Compared to other fixed-income funds, this fund's tax savings are considered to be very good.

Risk/Volatility   ★★★★★

Over the past five years, Alliance has been safer than 35 percent of all world bond funds. Over the past decade, the fund has had one negative year, while the Lehman Brothers Aggregate Bond Index has had two (off 3 percent in 1994 and 1 percent in 1999); the Salomon Brothers World Government Bond Index fell three times (off 4 percent in 1997, 5 percent in 1999, and 3 percent in 2000). The fund has underperformed the Lehman Brothers Aggregate Bond Index twice and the Salomon Brothers World Government Bond Index three times in the past ten years.

	past 5 years		past 10 years	
worst year	6%	1998	-31%	1994
best year	23%	1996	30%	1995

In the past, Alliance has done better than 95 percent of its peer group in up markets but outperformed just 25 percent of its competition in down markets. Consistency, or predictability, of returns for Alliance North American Government Income B can be described as excellent. This fund's risk-related return is excellent.

Management ★★★★★

There are twenty fixed-income securities in this $860 million portfolio. The average world bond fund today is $95 million in size. Close to 100 percent of the fund's holdings are in bonds. The average maturity of the bonds in this account is eleven years; the weighted coupon rate averages 10 percent. The portfolio's fixed-income holdings can be categorized as high quality and medium-to-long term in maturity.

Wayne D. Lyski has managed this fund for the past nine years. Over half the fund is in bonds rated AAA. Management may invest up to a third of the portfolio's assets in Latin American debt, although such exposure has been largely limited to Argentina. Lyski closely monitors economic and political trends that affect bond pricing around the world. There are 146 funds besides North American Government Income B within the Alliance family. Overall, the fund family's risk-adjusted performance can be described as good.

Current Income ★★★★★

Over the past year, Alliance North American Government Income B had a twelve-month yield of 10 percent. During this same twelve-month period, the typical world bond fund had a yield that averaged 6.7 percent.

Expenses ★★

Alliance North American Government's expense ratio is 2.1 percent; it has also averaged 2.1 percent annually over the past three calendar years. The average expense ratio for the 220 funds in this category is 1.4 percent. This fund's turnover rate over the past year has been 150 percent, while its peer group average has been 185 percent.

Summary

Alliance North American Government Income B has the highest overall score of any fund in its category. It is rated as the number one world or global bond fund. Within its category, it is the best three-year performer and has the second-best five-year return figures. Yet, this Alliance offering is more predictable in its returns than any of its peers. The fund also has the lowest risk by a wide margin. The fund ranks in the top quintile when it comes to growth persistence: the ability to consistently outperform equity funds over the previous five years. This offering also scores highly when it comes to superior risk-adjusted return persistence. Risk-adjusted returns over the past five years have been exceptional.

Profile

minimum initial investment $250	*IRA accounts available* . . . . yes
subsequent minimum investment . . . $50	*IRA minimum investment* $250
available in all 50 states. . . . . yes	*date of inception*. . . . . Mar. 1992
telephone exchanges. . . . . yes	*dividend/income paid*. . . . . monthly
number of funds in family 147	*average credit quality*. . . . . AA

Fidelity New Markets Income
82 Devonshire Street
Boston, MA 02109
(800) 544-8888
www.fidelity.com

total return	★★★★★
risk reduction	★★
management	★★★★
current income	★★★★★
expense control	★★★★
symbol FNMIX	20 points
up-market performance	excellent
down-market performance	excellent
predictability of returns	good

Total Return   ★★★★★
Over the past five years (ending 12/31/00), Fidelity New Markets Income has taken $10,000 and turned it into $21,005 ($12,600 over three years). This translates into an annualized return of 16 percent over the past five years and 8 percent over the past three years. Over the past five years, this fund has outperformed 85 percent of all mutual funds; within its general category, it has done better than 96 percent of its peers. World bond funds have averaged 5 percent annually over these same five years.

During the past five years, a $10,000 initial investment grew to $17,005 after taxes, assuming a 39.6 percent income tax bracket (state and federal combined) and a capital gains rate of 28 percent. This means that investors in this fund were able to preserve 70 percent of their total returns. Compared to other fixed-income funds, this fund's tax savings are considered to be excellent.

Risk/Volatility   ★★
Over the past five years, Fidelity has been safer than 75 percent of all world bond funds. Over the past decade, the fund has had two negative years, while the Lehman Brothers Aggregate Bond Index has also had two (off 3 percent in 1994 and 1 percent in 1999); the Salomon Brothers World Government Bond Index fell three times (off 4 percent in 1997, 5 percent in 1999, and 3 percent in 2000). The fund has underperformed the Lehman Brothers Aggregate Bond Index twice and the Salomon Brothers World Government Bond Index four times in the past ten years.

	past 5 years		past 10 years	
worst year	-21%	1998	-21%	1998
best year	37%	1999	41%	1996

In the past, Fidelity has done better than 96 percent of its peer group in up markets but outperformed just 40 percent of its competition in down markets.

Consistency, or predictability, of returns for Fidelity New Markets Income can be described as good. This fund's risk-related return is very good.

Management   ★★★★
There are ninety-five fixed-income securities in this $255 million portfolio. The average world bond fund today is $95 million in size. Close to 80 percent of the fund's holdings are in bonds. The average maturity of the bonds in this account is fifteen years; the weighted coupon rate averages 8.3 percent. The portfolio's fixed-income holdings can be categorized as long-term and below investment grade.

John H. Carlson has managed this fund for the past six years. Roughly 85 percent of the portfolio is in bonds rated BB and lower. Only 15 percent of the holdings are in BBB-rated issues. Most of the fund's assets are in bonds from emerging markets with the potential for high growth GNP per capita. Currency hedging is not needed for the most part since Brady bonds are the debt instrument of choice. Carlson is concerned with a country's average level of education, savings rate, infrastructure needs and capital markets. There are 148 funds besides New Markets Income within the Fidelity family. Overall, the fund family's risk-adjusted performance can be described as good to very good.

Current Income   ★★★★★
Over the past year, Fidelity New Markets Income had a twelve-month yield of 14.5 percent. During this same twelve-month period, the typical world bond fund had a yield that averaged 6.7 percent.

Expenses   ★★★★
Fidelity New Markets Income's expense ratio is 1.1 percent; it has also averaged 1.1 percent annually over the past three calendar years. The average expense ratio for the 220 funds in this category is 1.4 percent. This fund's turnover rate over the past year has been 270 percent, while its peer group average has been 185 percent.

Summary
Fidelity New Markets Income has bettered all other world bond funds when it comes to five-year returns. It also has the best after-tax returns. This Fidelity offering also boasts the lowest overhead costs of any of its peers. It has been its category's best bear market performer and tied for first as number one when it comes to bull market returns. The fund is only one of two funds in its category that does a superb job during up as well as down markets. Despite what has already been said, it is current income that really makes this fund shine. It has the highest yield, by a wide margin, of any fund, in any category in the book.

Profile

minimum initial investment $2,500	*IRA accounts available* . . . . yes
subsequent minimum investment . . $250	*IRA minimum investment* $500
available in all 50 states. . . . . yes	*date of inception*. . . . . May 1993
telephone exchanges. . . . . yes	*dividend/income paid*. . . . . monthly
number of funds in family 149	*average credit quality* . . . . BB

T. Rowe Price Emerging Markets Bond

100 East Pratt Street
Baltimore, MD 21202
(800) 638-5660
www.troweprice.com

total return	★★★★
risk reduction	★★
management	★★★★
current income	★★★★★
expense control	★★★★★
symbol PREMX	20 points
up-market performance	excellent
down-market performance	excellent
predictability of returns	good

Total Return   ★★★★

Over the past five years (ending 12/31/00), T. Rowe Price Emerging Markets Bond has taken $10,000 and turned it into $17,625 ($10,930 over three years). This translates into an annualized return of 12 percent over the past five years and 3 percent over the past three years. Over the past five years, this fund has outperformed 75 percent of all mutual funds; within its general category, it has done better than 80 percent of its peers. World bond funds have averaged 5 percent annually over these same five years.

During the past five years, a $10,000 initial investment grew to $14,270 after taxes, assuming a 39.6 percent income tax bracket (state and federal combined) and a capital gains rate of 28 percent. This means that investors in this fund were able to preserve 56 percent of their total returns. Compared to other fixed-income funds, this fund's tax savings are considered to be very good.

Risk/Volatility   ★★

Over the past five years, T. Rowe Price Emerging Markets Bond has been safer than 65 percent of all world bond funds. Over the past decade, the fund has had one negative year, while the Lehman Brothers Aggregate Bond Index has had two (off 3 percent in 1994 and 1 percent in 1999); the Salomon Brothers World Government Bond Index fell three times (off 4 percent in 1997, 5 percent in 1999, and 3 percent in 2000). The fund has underperformed the Lehman Brothers Aggregate Bond Index once and the Salomon Brothers World Government Bond Index three times in the past ten years.

	past 5 years		past 10 years	
worst year	-23%	1998	-23%	1998
best year	23%	1999	37%	1996

In the past, T. Rowe Price has done better than 50 percent of its peer group in up markets but outperformed just 40 percent of its competition in down markets.

Consistency, or predictability, of returns for T. Rowe Price Emerging Markets Bond can be described as good. This fund's risk-related return is fair.

Management   ★★★★
There are sixty fixed-income securities in this $160 million portfolio. The average world bond fund today is $95 million in size. Close to 96 percent of the fund's holdings are in bonds. The average maturity of the bonds in this account is seventeen years; the weighted coupon rate averages 7.7 percent. The portfolio's fixed-income holdings can be categorized as long-term, low-quality debt.

A team has managed this fund for the past seven years. All of the fund's assets are dollar denominated (Brady bonds); over half the fund is in emerging markets. Management looks at a country's political and economic conditions prior to making any selections. Two-thirds of the fund is in issues rated BB and lower. Lead manager Mike Conelius will not commit more than 20 percent of his portfolio to any one country. There are eighty funds besides Emerging Markets Bond within the T. Rowe Price family. Overall, the fund family's risk-adjusted performance can be described as good.

Current Income   ★★★★★
Over the past year, T. Rowe Price Emerging Markets Bond had a twelve-month yield of 9.9 percent. During this same twelve-month period, the typical world bond fund had a yield that averaged 6.7 percent.

Expenses   ★★★★★
T. Rowe Price Emerging Markets Bond's expense ratio is 1.3 percent; it has also averaged 1.3 percent annually over the past three calendar years. The average expense ratio for the 220 funds in this category is 1.4 percent. This fund's turnover rate over the past year has been 50 percent, while its peer group average has been 185 percent.

Summary
T. Rowe Price Emerging Markets Bond is one of only two funds in its category that does a superb job during bear as well as bull markets. Within its group, it has the second-lowest overhead plus the lowest turnover by a wide margin. Out of all world bond funds, this one has had the second-best results during bear markets. Despite its specialty, this portfolio has outperformed 75 percent of all mutual funds. Tax efficiency has also been quite good.

Profile
minimum initial investment $2,500	*IRA accounts available* . . . . yes
subsequent minimum investment . . $100	*IRA minimum investment* $1,000
available in all 50 states. . . . . yes	*date of inception*. . . . . Dec. 1994
telephone exchanges. . . . . yes	*dividend/income paid*. . . . . monthly
number of funds in family 81	*average credit quality* . . . . BB

XII.
Summary

Aggressive Growth Funds
Bridgeway Aggressive Growth
Citizens Emerging Growth Fund
INVESCO Dynamics Fund-
 Investor Shares
MFS Mid-Cap Growth B
Oppenheimer Capital
 Appreciation A
Royce Total Return
Smith Barney Aggressive Growth A
State Street Research Aurora A

Balanced Funds
Alleghany/Montag & Caldwell
 Balanced Fund N
Calamos Convertible A
Calamos Convertible Growth &
 Income A
Flag Investors Value Builder A
Green Century Balanced
Leuthold Core Investment
Nations Convertible Securities
 Investor A
Oppenheimer Global Growth &
 Income A
PaineWebber Tactical Allocation C
Vanguard Asset Allocation

Corporate Bond Funds
Eaton Vance Prime Rate Reserves
FPA New Income
Fremont Bond
Lebenthal Taxable Municipal Bond
Stein Roe Intermediate Bond
Strong Advantage Fund-Investor
 Class

Strong Corporate Bond Fund-
 Investor Class
Vanguard Short-Term Corporate

Global Equity Funds
Artisan International
Citizens Global Equity-Standard
 Shares
Julius Baer International Equity A
Merrill Lynch Global SmallCap D
New Perspective
Oppenheimer Global A
Pilgrim International SmallCap A
Tweedy, Browne Global Value
W&R International Growth C
William Blair International
 Growth N

Government Bond Funds
AIM Limited Maturity Treasury
 Fund-Retail Shares
American Century Target
 Maturities Trust 2020
Montgomery Short Duration
 Government Bond R
Pilgrim GNMA Income A
Vanguard GNMA

Growth Funds
Calamos Growth A
Franklin Growth & Income A
Growth Fund of America
Heritage Capital Appreciation A
Janus Mercury
Legg Mason Value Trust-Primary
 Class

Meridian Value
Thornburg Value A
White Oak Growth Stock

Growth and Income Funds
Alliance Growth & Income A
Ameristock
Burnham A
IPS Millennium
Oppenheimer Quest Balanced
Value A
Pioneer A
Selected American
Van Kampen Growth & Income A
Victory Diversified Stock A

Health Care Funds
Eaton Vance Worldwide Health A
Vanguard Health Care

High-Yield Corporate Bond Funds
Fidelity Capital & Income
Janus High-Yield
Lord Abbett Bond-Debenture A
Strong H/Y Bond Fund-Investor
Class

Metals and Natural Resources Funds
State Research Global Resources A
Vanguard Energy

Money Market Funds
AON Money Market
Elfun Money Market
Federated Liquid Cash Trust
Fidelity Spartan U.S. Government
Money Market
Financial Square Money Market
Lake Forest Money Market
Strong Heritage Money
Strong Municipal Money Market
USAA Tax-Exempt Money Market
U.S. Global Investors U.S. Gov't
Securities

Municipal Bond Funds
Franklin NY Tax-Free Income A
JP Morgan Tax-Exempt Bond
Scudder High-Yield Tax-Free S
Scudder Managed Municipal Bond S
Tax-Exempt Bond of America
USAA CA Bond
Vanguard CA Insured Long-Term
Tax-Exempt
Vanguard FL Insured Long-Term
Tax-Exempt
Vanguard Insured Long-Term
Tax-Exempt
Vanguard Intermediate-Term
Tax-Exempt

Technology Funds
Alliance Technology A
Firsthand Technology Value
Hancock Technology A
RS Information Age

Utility Stock Funds
American Gas Index
AXP Utilities Income A
MFS Utilities A
MSDW Global Utilities B
Strong American Utilities

World Bond Funds
Alliance Global Dollar
Government A
Alliance North American
Government Income B
Fidelity New Markets Income
T. Rowe Price Emerging Markets
Bond

Appendix A
Glossary of Mutual Fund Terms

Advisor—The individual or organization employed by a mutual fund to give professional advice on the fund's investments and asset management practices (also called the "investment advisor").

Asked or Offering Price—The price at which a mutual fund's shares can be purchased. The asked, or offering, price means the current net asset value per share plus sales charge, if any.

BARRA Growth Index—An index of 152 large-capitalization stocks that are all part of the S & P 500; specifically those with above-average sales and earnings growth.

BARRA Value Index—An index of 363 large-capitalization stocks that are all part of the S & P 500; specifically those with above-average dividend yields and relatively low prices considering their book values.

Bid or Sell Price—The price at which a mutual fund's shares are redeemed (bought back) by the fund. The bid or redemption price usually means the current net asset value per share.

Board Certified—Designation given to someone who has become certified in insurance, estate planning, income taxes, securities, mutual funds, or financial planning. To obtain additional information about the board certified programs or to get the name of a board certified advisor in your area, call (800) 848-2029.

Bottom Up—Refers to a type of security analysis. Management that follows the bottom-up approach is more concerned with the company than with the economy in general. (For a contrasting style, see **Top Down.**)

Broker/Dealer—A firm that buys and sells mutual fund shares and other securities to the public.

Capital Gains Distributions—Payments to mutual fund shareholders of profits (long-term gains) realized on the sale of the fund's portfolio securities. These amounts are usually paid once a year.

Capital Growth—An increase in the market value of a mutual fund's securities, as reflected in the net asset value of fund shares. This is a specific long-term objective of many mutual funds.

Cash Reserves—Short-term, interest-bearing securities that can easily and quickly be converted to cash. Some funds keep cash levels at a minimum and always remain in stocks and/or bonds; other funds hold up to 25 percent or more of their assets in cash reserves (money market instruments) as either a defensive play or as a buying opportunity to be used when securities become depressed in price.

CFS—Also known as Certified Fund Specialist, this is the only designation awarded to brokers, financial planners, CPAs, insurance agents, and other investment advisors who either recommend or sell mutual funds. Fewer than 7,000 people across the country have passed this certification program. To obtain additional information about the CFS program or to get the name of a CFS in your area, call (800) 848-2029.

CPI—The Consumer Price Index (CPI) is the most commonly used yardstick for measuring the rate of inflation in the United States.

Custodian—The organization (usually a bank) that keeps custody of securities and other assets of a mutual fund.

Derivatives—A financial contract whose value is based on, or "derived," from a traditional security, such as a stock or bond. The most common examples of derivatives are futures contracts and options.

Diversification—The policy of all mutual funds to spread investments among a number of different securities in order to reduce the risk inherent in investing.

Dollar-Cost Averaging—The practice of investing equal amounts of money at regular intervals regardless of whether securities markets are moving up or down. This procedure reduces average share costs to the investor, who acquires more shares in the periods of lower securities prices and fewer shares in periods of higher prices.

EAFE—An equity index (EAFE stands for Europe, Australia, and the Far East) used to measure stock market performance outside the United States. The EAFE is a sort of S & P 500 Index for overseas or foreign stocks. As of the middle of 1997, the EAFE was weighted as follows: 59.5% Europe, 28.8% Japan, 10.6% Pacific Rim, and 1.1% "other."

Exchange Privilege—An option enabling mutual fund shareholders to transfer their investment from one fund to another within the same fund family as their needs or objectives change. Typically, funds allow investors to use the exchange privilege several times a year for a low fee or no fee per exchange.

Expense Ratio—A figure expressed as a percentage of a fund's assets. The main element is the management fee. Administrative fees cover a fund's day-to-day operations, including printing materials, keeping records, paying staff, and renting office space. Sometimes administrative fees are included in the management fee; a number of funds list such fees separately. Roughly half of all funds charge a 12b-1 fee, which pays for a fund's distribution and advertising costs. The 12b-1 fee can be higher than the management or administrative fee.

Indexing—In contrast to the traditional approach to investing that tries to outperform market averages, index investing is a strategy that seeks to match the performance of a group of securities that form a recognized market measure, known as an index.

Investment Company—A corporation, trust, or partnership that invests pooled funds of shareholders in securities appropriate to the fund's objective. Among the benefits of investment companies, compared to direct investments, are professional management and diversification. Mutual funds (also known as open-ended and close-ended investment companies) are the most popular type of investment company.

Investment Objective—The goal that the investor and mutual fund pursue together (e.g., growth of capital or current income).

Large-Cap Stocks—Equities issued by companies with a net worth of at least $7.5 billion.

Long-Term Funds—An industry designation for funds that invest primarily in securities with remaining maturities of more than one year. In this book the term means fifteen years or more. Long-term funds are broadly divided into bond and income funds.

Management Fee—The amount paid by a mutual fund to the investment advisor for its services. The average annual fee industrywide is about 0.7 percent of fund assets.

"Market-Neutral" Funds—A strategy that seeks to neutralize market movements by running two portfolios simultaneously—one buys stocks that are predicted to rise, and the other invests an equal amount in a similar assortment of other stocks that are predicted to decline.

Mid-Cap Stocks—*Equities* issued by companies with a net worth between $1 billion and $7.5 billion.

Mutual Fund—An investment company that pools money from shareholders and invests in a variety of securities, including stocks, bonds, and money market instruments. A mutual fund stands ready to buy back (redeem) its shares at their current net asset value; this value depends on the market value of the fund's portfolio securities at the time of redemption. Most mutual funds continuously offer new shares to investors.

Net Asset Value Per Share—The market worth of one share of a mutual fund. This figure is derived by taking a fund's total assets—securities, cash, and any accrued earnings—deducting liabilities, and dividing by the number of shares outstanding.

No-Load Fund—A mutual fund selling its shares at net asset value without the addition of sales charges.

Passive Management—A portfolio that tries to match the performance of a target index, such as the S & P 500.

Portfolio—A collection of securities owned by an individual or an institution (such as a mutual fund). A fund's portfolio may include a combination of stocks, bonds, and money market securities.

Portfolio Diversification—The average U.S. stock fund has about 30 percent of its assets invested in its ten largest holdings.

Prospectus—The official booklet that describes a mutual fund, which must be furnished to all investors. It contains information required by the U.S. Securities and Exchange Commission on such subjects as the fund's investment objectives, services, and fees. A more detailed document, known as "Part B" of the prospectus or the "Statement of Additional Information," is available at no charge upon request.

Redemption Price—The amount per share (shown as the "bid" in newspaper tables) that mutual fund shareholders receive when they cash in the shares. The value of the shares depends on the market value of the fund's portfolio securities at the time. This value is the same as net asset value per share.

Reinvestment Privilege—An option available to mutual fund shareholders in which fund dividends and capital gains distributions are automatically turned back into the fund to buy new shares, without charge (meaning no sales fee or commission), thereby increasing holdings.

Russell 2000—An index that represents 2,000 small domestic companies (less than 8 percent of the U.S. equity market).

Sales Charge—An amount charged to purchase shares in many mutual funds sold by brokers or other sales agents. The maximum charge is 8.5 percent of the initial investment; the vast majority of funds now have a maximum charge of 4.75 percent or less. The charge is added to the net asset value per share when determining the offering price.

Short-Term Funds—An industry designation for funds that invest primarily in securities with maturities of less than one year; the term means five years or less in this book. Short-term funds include money market funds and certain municipal bond funds.

Small-Cap Stocks—Equities issued by companies with a net worth of less than $1 billion.

Top Down—Refers to a type of security analysis. Management that follows the top-down approach is very concerned with the general level of the economy and any fiscal policy being followed by the government.

Transfer Agent—The organization employed by a mutual fund to prepare and maintain records relating to the accounts of its shareholders. Some funds serve as their own transfer agents.

Turnover—The percentage of a fund's portfolio that is sold during the year, a percentage rate that can range from 0 to 300 percent or more. The average turnover rate for U.S. stock funds is approximately 80 percent (10 percent for domestic stock index funds).

12b-1 Fee—The distribution fee charged by some funds, named after a federal government rule. Such fees pay for marketing costs, such as advertising and dealer compensation. The fund's prospectus outlines 12b-1 fees, if applicable.

Underwriter—The organization that acts as the distributor of a mutual fund's shares to broker/dealers and investors.

Value Stocks—Stocks that most investors view as unattractive for some reason. They tend to be priced low relative to some measure of the company's worth, such as earnings, book value, or cash flow. Value stock managers try to identify companies whose prices are depressed for temporary reasons but that may bounce back strongly if investor sentiment improves.

■ ■ ■

The Securities Act of 1933 requires a fund's shares to be registered with the Securities and Exchange Commission (SEC) prior to their sale. In essence, the Securities Act ensures that the fund provides potential investors with a current prospectus. This law also limits the types of advertisements that may be used by a mutual fund.

The Securities Exchange Act of 1934 regulates the purchase and sale of all types of securities, including mutual fund shares.

The Investment Advisors Act of 1940 is a body of law that regulates certain activities of the investment advisors to mutual funds.

The Investment Company Act of 1940 is a highly detailed regulatory statute applying to mutual fund companies. This act contains numerous provisions designed to prevent self-dealing by employees of the mutual fund company, as well as other conflicts of interest. It also provides for the safekeeping of fund assets and prohibits the payment of excessive fees and charges by the fund and its shareholders.

Appendix B
Who Regulates Mutual Funds?

Mutual funds are highly regulated businesses that must comply with some of the toughest laws and rules in the financial services industry. All funds are regulated by the U.S. Securities and Exchange Commission (SEC). With its extensive rule-making and enforcement authority, the SEC oversees mutual fund compliance chiefly by relying on the four major federal securities statutes mentioned in Appendix A.

Fund assets must generally be held by an independent custodian. There are strict requirements for fidelity bonding to ensure against the misappropriation of shareholder monies. In addition to federal statutes, almost every state has its own set of regulations governing mutual funds.

Although federal and state laws cannot guarantee that a fund will be profitable, they are designed to ensure that all mutual funds are operated and managed in the interests of their shareholders. Here are some specific investor protections that every fund must follow:

- Regulations concerning what may be claimed or promised about a mutual fund and its potential.
- Requirements that vital information about a fund be made readily available (such as a prospectus, the "Statement of Additional Information," also known as "Part B" of the prospectus, and annual and semiannual reports).
- Requirements that a fund operate in the interest of its shareholders, rather than any special interests of its management.
- Rules dictating diversification of the fund's portfolio over a wide range of investments to avoid too much concentration in a particular security.

Appendix C
Dollar-Cost Averaging

Investors often believe that the market will go down as soon as they get in. For these people, and anyone concerned with reducing risk, the solution is dollar-cost averaging (DCA).

Dollar-cost averaging is a simple yet effective way to reduce risk, whether you are investing in stocks or bonds. The premise behind dollar-cost averaging is that if several purchases of a fund are made over an extended period of time, the unpredictable highs and lows will average out. The investor ends up buying some shares at a comparatively low price, others at perhaps a much higher price.

DCA assumes that investors are willing to sacrifice the possibility of having bought all of their shares at the lowest price in return for knowing that they did not also buy every share at the highest price. In short, investors are willing to accept a compromise—a sort of *risk-adjusted* decision.

DCA is based on investing a fixed amount of money in a given fund at specific intervals. Typically, an investor will add a few hundred dollars at the beginning of each month into the XYZ mutual fund. DCA works best if you invest and continue to invest on an established schedule, *regardless of price fluctuations*. You will be buying more shares when the price is down than when it is up. Most investors do not mind buying shares when prices are increasing, since this means that their existing shares are also going up. When this program is followed, losses during market declines are limited, while the ability to participate in good markets is maintained.

Another advantage of DCA is that it increases the likelihood that you will follow an investment program. As with other aspects of our life, it is important to have goals. However, DCA is not something that should be universally recommended. Your risk level determines whether you should use dollar-cost averaging.

From its beginnings well over one hundred years ago, there has been an upward bias in the performance of the stock market. More often than not, the market goes up, not down. Therefore, it hardly makes sense to apply dollar-cost averaging to an investment vehicle, knowing that historically one would be paying a higher and higher price per share over time.

Studies done by the Institute of Business & Finance (800-848-2029) show that over the past fifty years, a dollar-cost averaging program produced inferior returns compared to a lump-sum investment. The institute's studies conclude the following: (1) a DCA program is a good idea for a conservative investor (the person or couple who gives more weight or importance to risk than reward); (2) for investors whose risk level is anything but conservative, an immediate, one-time investment resulted in better returns the great majority of the time; and (3) there have certainly been periods of time when a DCA program would have benefited even the extremely aggressive investor, but such periods have not been very common over the past half century and have been quite rare over the past 20, 15, 10, 5, and 3 years.

Example of Dollar-Cost Averaging
($1,000 invested per period)

period (1)	cost per share (2)	number of shares bought with $1,000 (3)	total shares owned (4)	total amount invested (5)	current value of shares (2) x (4) (6)	net gain or loss (percentage) (6) x (5) (7)
1	$100	10.0	10.0	$1,000	$1,000	0
2	$80	12.5	22.5	$2,000	$1,800	−10.0%
3	$70	14.3	36.8	$3,000	$2,576	−14.1%
4	$60	16.7	53.5	$4,000	$3,210	−19.7%
5	$50	20.0	73.5	$5,000	$3,675	−26.5%
6	$70	14.3	87.8	$6,000	$6,146	+2.4%
7	$80	12.5	100.3	$7,000	$8,024	+14.6%
8	$100	10.0	110.3	$8,000	$11,030	+37.9%

Appendix D
Systematic Withdrawal Plan

A systematic withdrawal plan (SWP) allows you to have a check for a specified amount sent monthly or quarterly to you, or anyone you designate, from your mutual fund account. There is no charge for this service.

This method of getting monthly checks is ideal for the income-oriented investor. It is also a risk reduction technique—a kind of dollar-cost averaging in reverse. A set amount is sent to you each month. In order to send you a check for a set amount, shares of one or more of your mutual funds must be sold, which, in turn, will most likely trigger a taxable event, but only for those shares redeemed.

When the market is low, the number of mutual fund shares being liquidated will be higher than when the market is high because the fund's price per share will be lower. If you need $500 a month and the fund's price is $25 per share, twenty shares must be liquidated; if the price per share is $20 per share, twenty-five shares must be sold.

Shown below is an example of a SWP from the Investment Company of America (ICA), a conservative growth and income fund featured in previous editions of this book. The example assumes an initial investment of $100,000 in the fund at its inception, the beginning of 1934. A greater or smaller dollar amount could be used. The example shows what happens to the investor's principal over a sixty-seven-year period (January 1, 1934 through March 31, 2000). It assumes that $10,000 is withdrawn from the fund at the end of the first year. At the end of the first year, the $10,000 withdrawal is increased by 4 percent each year thereafter to offset the effects of inflation, which averaged less than 4 percent during this sixty-seven-year period. This means that the withdrawal for the second year was $10,400 ($10,000 multiplied by 1.04), for the third year $10,816 ($10,400 multiplied by 1.04), and so on.

Compare this example to what would have happened if the money had been placed in an average fixed-income account at a bank. The $100,000 depositor who took out only $9,000 each year would be in a far different situation. His (or her) original $100,000 was fully depleted by the end of 1948. All the principal and interest payments could not keep up with an annual withdrawal of $9,000.

The difference between ICA and the savings account is over $13 million. The savings account had a total return of $26,300 (plus distribution of the original $100,000 principal); the ICA account had a total return of $13,244,780 ($3,210,780 distributed over sixty-seven years plus a remaining principal, or account balance, of $10,034,000). This difference becomes even more disturbing when you consider that the bank depositor's withdrawals were not increasing each year to offset the effects of inflation. The interest rates used in this example came from the U.S. Savings & Loan League Fact Book.

SWP from the Investment Company of America (ICA)

initial investment: $100,000
annual withdrawals of: $10,000 (10%)
the first check is sent: 12/31/34
withdrawals annually increased by: 4%

date	amount withdrawn	value of remaining shares
12/31/34	$10,000	$109,000
12/31/35	$10,400	$185,000
12/31/40	$12,700	$153,000
12/31/45	$15,400	$247,000
12/31/50	$18,700	$212,000
12/31/55	$22,800	$374,000
12/31/60	$27,700	$465,000
12/31/65	$33,700	$679,000
12/31/70	$41,000	$742,000
12/31/75	$50,000	$669,000
12/31/80	$60,700	$1,007,000
12/31/85	$73,900	$1,790,000
12/31/86	$76,900	$2,104,000
12/31/87	$79,900	$2,136,000
12/31/88	$83,100	$2,336,000
12/31/89	$86,500	$2,936,000
12/31/90	$89,900	$2,865,000
12/31/91	$93,500	$3,525,000
12/31/92	$86,500	$3,673,000
12/31/93	$101,200	$3,997,000
12/31/94	$105,200	$3,897,000
12/31/95	$109,400	$4,981,000
12/31/96	$113,780	$5,830,000
12/31/97	$118,330	$7,448,000
12/31/98	$123,060	$9,026,000
12/31/99	$127,987	$10,386,000
12/31/00	$133,107	$10,649,000
3/31/01	------------	$10,034,000

If the ICA systematic withdrawal plan were 8 percent annually instead of 10 percent (but still increased by 4 percent each year to offset the effects of inflation), the investor would have ended up with remaining shares worth $99.5 million, plus withdrawals that totaled $2.6 million.

Next time some broker or banker tells you that you should be buying bonds or CDs for current income, tell them about a systematic withdrawal plan (SWP), a program designed to maximize your income and offset something the CD, T-bill, and bond advocates never mention: inflation.

Appendix E
Load or No-Load—Which Is Right for You?

As the amount of information available on mutual funds continues to grow almost exponentially, the load versus no-load debate has intensified. What makes the issue difficult to evaluate is the continued absence of neutrality on either side. Before you learn the real truth, let us first examine who is advocating what, what their biases are, and how each side argues its point.

A number of publications, including *Money, Forbes, Fortune, Kiplinger Personal Investor*, and *BusinessWeek*, favor the no-load camp. Although these publications appear neutral, they are not. First, each one derives the overwhelming majority of its mutual fund advertisements from funds that charge no commission. Second, all of these publications are trying to increase readership; they are in the business of selling copy, not information. A good way to increase or maintain a healthy circulation is by having their readership rely on them for advice—instead of going to a broker or investment advisor.

On the other side is the financial services industry, whose most vocal load supporters include the brokerage, banking, and insurance industries. That's not much of a surprise. These groups are also biased. Like the publication that only makes money by getting you to purchase a copy or having an editorial board whose policy favors no-load funds, much of the financial services community supports a sales charge because that is how they are compensated.

No-load proponents argue that a fund that charges any kind of commission or ongoing marketing fee (which is known as a 12b-1 charge) inherently cannot be as good as a similar investment that has no entry or exit fee or ongoing 12b-1 charge. On its surface, this argument appears logical. After all, if one investor starts off with a dollar invested and the other starts off with somewhere between 99 and 92 cents (commissions range from 1.0 to 8.5 percent; most are in the 3.0 to 5.0 percent range), all other things being equal, the person who has all of his money working for him will do better than someone who has an initial deduction. The press and the no-load funds say that there is no reason to pay a commission because you can do as well or better than the broker or advisor whose job it is to provide you with suggestions and guidance.

The commission-oriented community says you should pay a sales charge because you get what you pay for—good advice and ongoing service. After all, brokers, financial planners, banks that include mutual fund desks, and insurance agents are all highly trained professionals who know things you do not. Moreover, they study the markets on a continuous basis, ensuring that they have more information than any weekend investor. In short, they ask, do you want someone managing your money who has experience and works full-time in this area, or someone such as yourself who has no formal training and whose time and resources are limited?

There is no clear-cut solution. Valid points are raised by both sides. To gain more insight into what course of action (or type of fund) is best for you, let us take a neutral approach. I believe I can give you valid reasons both kinds of funds make sense, because I have no hidden agenda. True, I am a licensed broker and branch manager of a national securities firm; however, it is also true that the great majority of my compensation is based on a fee for service, meaning that clients who invest solely in no-load funds pay me an annual management fee.

First, you should never pay a commission to someone who knows no more about investing than you do. There is no value added in such a situation, except perhaps during uncertain or negative periods in the market. (This point will be discussed later.) After all, if your broker's advice and mutual fund experience are based solely on the same financial publications you have access to, you are not getting your money's worth by paying a sales charge. I raise this point first because the financial services industry is filled with a tremendous number of inexperienced and ignorant brokers. These people may make a lot of money, but this is usually the result of their connections (they know a lot of people) or marketing skills (they know how to get new business)—neither of which has anything to do with your money.

Brokerage firms, banks, and insurance companies hire stockbrokers based on their sales ability, not their knowledge or analytical ability. The financial analysts at the home office are the ones involved in research and managing money. The fact that your broker has a couple of dozen years of experience in the securities industry or is a vice president may actually be hazardous to your financial health. Extensive experience could mean that the advisor is less inclined to learn about new products or studies because he or she already has an established client base. Brokers obtain titles such as "vice president" because they outsell their peers. Contests (awards, trips, prizes, and enhanced payouts) are based on how much is sold, period. There has never been an instance of a brokerage firm, bank, or insurance company giving an award to someone based on knowledge or how well a client's account performed.

Second, if your investment time horizon is less than a couple of years, it is a mistake to pay anything more than a nominal fee, something in the 1 percent range. Even though the advice you are receiving may be great, it is hard to justify a 3 to 5 percent commission over the short haul. Sales charges in this range can only be rationalized if they can be amortized over a number of years. Thus, worthwhile advice becomes a bargain if you stay with the investment, or within the same family of mutual funds, for at least three years.

Third, if you are purchasing a fund that charges a fee, find out what you are getting for your money. Question the advisor; find out about his or her training, experience, education, and designations. Equally important, get a clear understanding of what you will be receiving on an ongoing basis. What kind of continuing education does the broker engage in (attending conferences, reading books, seeking a designation, and so forth)? Finally, make sure your advisor or broker tells you how your investments will be monitored. It is important to know how often you will be contacted and how a buy, hold, or sell decision will be made.

So far, it looks as if I've been pretty tough on my fellow brokers. Well, believe me, I'm even harder on about 99 percent of those do-it-yourself investors. I have been in this business for close to twenty years, and I can tell you that I have rarely met an investor who was better off on his or her own. Here's why.

First, it is extremely difficult to be objective about your own investments. Decisions based on what you have read from a newsletter or magazine or what you learned at a seminar are often a response to current news, such as trade relations with Japan, the value of the U.S. dollar, the state of the economy, or the direction of interest rates. This kind of knee-jerk reaction has proven to be wrong in most cases.

Mind you, out of fairness to those who manage their own investments, amateurs aren't the only ones who make investment errors. As an example, the majority of the major brokerage firms gave a sell signal just before the war in the Persian Gulf. It turned out that this would have been about the perfect time to buy. E.F. Hutton was forced to merge with another brokerage firm because they incorrectly predicted the direction of interest rates (and lost tens of millions of dollars in their own portfolio).

The mutual fund industry itself deserves a healthy part of the blame, as evidenced by their timing of new funds. Take my advice: When you see a number of new mutual funds coming out with the same timely theme (government plus or optioned-enhanced bond funds in the mid-1980s, Eastern European funds after German reunification, health care funds a few years ago, derivatives and hedge funds last year), run for cover. By the time these funds come out, the party is about to end. Investors who got into these funds often do well for a number of months but soon face devastating declines.

Your favorite financial publications are also to blame. Their advice is based on a herd instinct—What do our readers think? Instead of providing leadership, they simply reinforce what is most likely incorrect information. For example, for over a year after the 1987 stock market crash, the most popular of these mainstream publications, *Money*, had cover stories that recommended (and extolled the virtues of) safe investments. For almost a year and a half after the crash, this magazine was giving out bad advice. When something goes on sale (stocks, in this case), you should be a buyer, not a seller. Since *Money* routinely surveys (or polls) their readers for feature articles, such behavior (the herd instinct) is understandable but not forgivable.

Besides the lack of objectivity and the constant bombardment of what I call "daily noise" (what the market is doing at the moment, comments from the financial gurus, etc.), there is also the question of your competence. Presumably, you and I could figure out how to fix our own plumbing, sew our own clothes, fix the car when it breaks down, or avoid paying a lawyer by purchasing "do-it-yourself" books. The question then becomes whether it is worth going through the learning curve, and, even supposing we are successful, whether the task would have been better accomplished by someone else—perhaps for less money or better use of our own time. I think the answer is obvious. Each of us has his or her own area or areas of expertise or skill. You and I rely on others either because they know more than we do about the topic or task at hand or because having someone else help is a more efficient use of our time.

If you're going to seek the services of an investment advisor or broker, it should be because he or she knows more than you do, because he or she is more objective, or because you can make more money doing whatever you do than in taking the time to make complex investment decisions yourself. This is what makes sense. The fact that there are brokers and advisors who put their interests before yours is simply a reality that you must deal with. And the proper way to deal with these conflicts of interest or ignorant counselors is by doing your homework. Ask questions. Just as there are great plumbers, mechanics, lawyers, and doctors, so too are there exceptional investment advisors and brokers. Your job is to find them.

Eliminating load or no-load funds from your investing universe is not the answer. If you are determined never to pay a commission, then you may miss out on the next John Templeton (the Franklin Templeton family of funds), Peter Lynch (Fidelity Magellan Fund), or Jean-Marie Eveillard (SoGen Funds). You will also miss out on some of the very best mutual fund families: American Funds (large), Fidelity-Advisor (medium), and SoGen (small). A better way to proceed is to try to separate good funds from bad ones. After all, an investor is clearly far better off in a good load fund than in a bad no-load one.

The bottom line is that performance, as well as risk-adjusted returns, for load funds often exceeds the returns on no-load funds, and vice versa. The "top 10" list (or whatever number you want to use) for one period may have been dominated by funds that charge a commission, but in just a year or two the top 10 list may be heavily populated by mutual funds with no sales charge or commission.

It might seem strange to be questioning the benefits of financial planning when our society places professions like law and accountancy in such high regard. And certainly I am not suggesting that investors should consider only load funds. But with all the load-fund bashing in recent years, it is important to recognize that no-load funds are not the perfect answer for a large percentage of investors. Approaching the mutual fund industry with an us versus them mentality results in a great deal of misleading information and unfairly discredits the work of skilled financial planners and brokers.

Appendix F
U.S. Compared to Foreign Markets

Investing worldwide gives you exposure to different stages of economic market cycles, which has given international investors an advantage in the past. Foreign equities and bonds have generally offered higher levels of short-, intermediate-, and long-term growth than their domestic counterparts. Not once during the past thirteen years was the U.S. stock market the world's top performer.

Top-Performing World Stock Markets: A 13-Year Review: 1987–2000

year	1st	2nd	3rd	4th	5th
2000	Denmark 22%	Switzerland 16%	Venezuela 12%	Ireland 7%	Norway 2%
1999	Finland 153%	Malaysia 110%	Singapore 99%	Sweden 80%	Japan 62%
1998	Finland 121%	Belgium 68%	Italy 52%	Spain 50%	France 42%
1997	Portugal 47%	Switzerland 45%	Italy 36%	Denmark 35%	**USA 34%**
1996	Spain 37%	Sweden 35%	Finland 32%	Hong Kong 29%	Ireland 29%
1995	Switzerland 44%	**USA 37%**	Sweden 33%	Spain 30%	Netherlands 28%
1994	Finland 52%	Norway 24%	Japan 22%	Sweden 19%	Ireland 15%
1993	Malaysia 114%	Hong Kong 110%	Finland 101%	Singapore 62%	Ireland 60%
1992	Hong Kong 37%	Switzerland 17%	**USA 6%**	Singapore 6%	France 3%
1991	Hong Kong 43%	Australia 39%	**USA 30%**	Singapore 23%	France 16%
1990	United Kingdom 6%	Austria 5%	Hong Kong 4%	Norway (1%)	Denmark (2%)
1989	Austria 105%	Germany 49%	Norway 46%	Denmark 45%	Singapore 42%
1988	Belgium 54%	Denmark 53%	Sweden 48%	Norway 42%	France 38%
1987	Japan 43%	Spain 41%	United Kingdom 35%	Canada 14%	Denmark 13%

The U.S. stock market has ranked among the five top performers only four times in the past thirteen years. During this same period, the U.S. bond market has never claimed the number one spot against other world markets. For the 2000 calendar year, the five *worst* performing markets were: Indonesia (-56%), Thailand (-51%), Taiwan (-45%), Greece (-42%), and New Zealand (-32%).

Appendix G
The Power of Dividends

The following table shows how important common stock dividends can be. The figures assume a one-time investment of $100,000 in the S & P 500 at the beginning of 1977. The table shows that dividends have increased for fifteen of the past twenty-four years.

Viewed from a different perspective, if you were strictly income-oriented and invested $100,000 in the S & P 500 at the beginning of 1977, you would have received a 4.3 percent return on your investment ($4,310 divided by $100,000) for the calendar year. For the 1998 calendar year, this same investment returned 19.4 percent for the year ($19,440 divided by $100,000); for 1999, the figure decreases to 18.9 percent ($18,811 divided by $100,000). These figures assume that dividends received each year were spent and not reinvested. Moreover, these numbers do not include the over twelve-fold growth of capital (the original $100,000 grew to $1,228,880 without dividends) that also took place.

As a point of comparison for the figures described in the previous paragraph, consider what would have happened if the same investor had invested in a 23-year U.S. government bond in 1977. By the end of 2000, twenty-four years later, the original $100,000 worth of bonds would have matured and had an ending value of $100,000. Additionally, the investor would have received approximately 7 percent for each of these twenty-four years—a far cry from the increased dividend stream and capital appreciation the S & P 500 experienced over the same period. Perhaps more important, the bond investor could have taken his $100,000 at the beginning of 2001 and invested the money for another twenty to thirty years, getting a 6 percent return for each of those years (versus the S & P 500 investor who just finished receiving over 12.2 percent, based on $100,000, and presumably will be receiving even greater dividend returns for most of the next twenty years).

The reason the dividend income stream appears to be so large, even though it was just 1.1 percent in 2000, is that the yields are based on the yearly value of the S & P 500. Starting off with a negative return in 1977 (the S & P 500 was down 11.5 percent, excluding dividends), a $100,000 investment at the beginning of 1977 grew to $1,228,880 by the end of 2000. Thus, 1.36 percent (the actual dividend yield for 2000) multiplied by $1,228,880 equals $12,288 (shown in the table). As a side note, if no dividends were taken out, and instead reinvested, a $100,000 investment made at the beginning of 1999 in the S & P 500 grew to $2,855,300 by the end of 2000.

Annual Dividends from $100,000 Invested in the S & P 500

year	S & P 500 dividend
1977	$3,857
1978	$4,821
1979	$5,800
1980	$7,321
1981	$5,640
1982	$7,280
1983	$7,761
1984	$7,177
1985	$10,141
1986	$8,525
1987	$8,465
1988	$10,901
1989	$12,808
1990	$10,445
1991	$11,897
1992	$12,428
1993	$12,427
1994	$12,192
1995	$16,873
1996	$17,254
1997	$19,275
1998	$19,440
1999	$18,811
2000	$12,288

Appendix H
Growth Stocks Versus Value Stocks

Throughout the different equity sections (growth, growth and income, global equity, etc.), the end of each stock fund's "Management" paragraph often mentions whether the fund manager seeks out "growth" or "value" issues. The differences and possible consequences of these two forms of equity selection are shown in the following table.

Value means that the stocks are inexpensive relative to their earnings potential. Growth refers to stocks of companies whose earnings per share are expected to grow significantly faster than the market average.

As you can see by the table, the performance of these two types of stocks can vary from year to year. On a monthly or quarterly basis, the difference is often much more significant than on an annual basis.

The table shows performance of all growth stocks and all value stocks (dividends reinvested in both indexes). Over the past fifteen-plus years, an investment in *both* growth stocks and value stocks would have been less volatile than an investment in only one equity style.

year	growth stocks	value stocks
1986	12.2%	20.9%
1987	5.0%	-2.8%
1988	12.0%	25.4%
1989	34.3%	29.4%
1990	-1.1%	-15.0%
1991	43.9%	28.8%
1992	6.8%	24.3%
1993	3.4%	21.2%
1994	1.4%	-4.7%
1995	37.1%	35.8%
1996	20.1%	14.9%
1997	30.3%	32.9%
1998	33.1%	12.1%
1999	29.8%	5.4%
2000	-13.4%	0%

Source: S & P 500 Barra Value Index and the S & P 500 Barra Growth Index.

Appendix I
Stock Market Declines

If you are a relatively new investor, you may not have had firsthand experience with a bear market. Since corrections are a natural part of the stock market cycle, it is important to ask yourself how you would react. Would you panic or would you be patient? It is difficult to know for sure. Stock market fire drills do not really work, because it is one thing to ponder your reaction to a market meltdown—another to live through one with your financial goals at stake. However, a historical perspective may help you gain a better perspective and, more importantly, may help you remain patient.

The table shows all of the periods when the U.S. stock market dropped 15 percent or more from 1953 through the end of 2000 (a "bear market" is defined as a drop of 20 percent or more; a "correction" is a decline of 10 percent or more). Of these fourteen down markets, the worst took place during the 1973–74 recesssion, resulting in the greatest loss since the Great Depression. Surprisingly, half of the 48 percent loss that took place during the 1973–74 decline was recovered within five months after the drop.

During the 1998 calendar year, the S & P 500 dropped 15.4 percent from the end of June through the end of August. It took just four months (end of November) for the market to recover this loss and move on to yet another high.

U.S. Market Declines of 15% or More (1953–1999)

bear year	decline	# of down months	months to recovery
1953	15%	9	6
1956–57	16%	6	5
1957	20%	3	12
1961–62	29%	6	14
1966	22%	9	6
1968–70	37%	18	22
1973–74	48%	21	64
1975	15%	2	4
1977–78	18%	14	6
1978	17%	2	10
1980	22%	2	4
1981–82	22%	13	3
1987	34%	2	23
1990	20%	3	23
1998	15%	2	5
average	23%	7	14

One possible strategy for avoiding market declines is to sit on the sidelines until the volatility passes. According to a study by the University of Michigan, this is a bad idea. An investor who was on the sidelines during the best 1 percent of all trading days from 1963 to 2001 missed 95 percent of the market's gains.

These included investors who were sidelined in 1995 by the poor showing in 1994 for both stocks and bonds as well as those stock market investors who bailed out in 1996 because the 38 percent gain in 1995 made them nervous about a downturn. Those who bailed out in 1997 because the 23 percent gain in 1996 made them nervous missed a 29 percent gain in 1998 and a 21 percent gain in 1999.

Being in the market when it falls is not the greatest risk most stock investors face, it is being out of the market when it soars. The best strategy is to keep investing through any market environment.

The problem is that no one rings a bell when the market hits bottom. Similarly, you do not get any advance notice that the market is turning around. Stocks tend to gain significant ground in short periods; missing out on the first, brief phase of a recovery can be costly. For example, when the stock market took off in August 1982, ending years of mediocre performance, the market jumped 42 percent in just three months. From the October low of the 1987 crash to the end of December, just two months later, stocks rebounded 22 percent. And in the four months after the October 1990 Gulf War low, with the U.S. still mired in recession, the stock market shot up more than 30 percent.

Trying to get out of the market and get back in calls for two right decisions. There is no evidence that professional investors, market timers, brokers, financial analysts, or anyone else can get these calls right with any degree of consistency. One bad market timing call can seriously handicap lifetime performance.

The question then becomes, if stock prices fall hard, should you cut your losses and play it safe? Of all the options that investors have, this one may be the worst solution and the most devastating. An investment of $10,000 in common stocks, as measured by the S & P 500, on the day before the October 1987 crash would have fallen to $7,995 in a single day. Leaving the account intact would have resulted in a whopping 630 percent gain through December 31, 2000. Taking the $7,995 and reinvesting it in U.S. Treasury bills would have resulted in a gain of just 94 percent over the same period.

Appendix J
A Reason Not to Index

Appendix D showed a systematic withdrawal program (SWP) for Investment Company of America (ICA), a growth and income portfolio from the American Funds Group, starting with its first full year through the first three months of 2001. Let us now look at two more examples of a SWP, comparing results from Washington Mutual, another growth and income fund offered through the American Funds Group, with the S & P 500.

For this example, a different time frame (January 1, 1973 through March 31, 2001) will be used, showing radically different results. Like the ICA example, it is assumed that a single $100,000 investment is made and that all capital gains and dividend payments are automatically reinvested into the fund. Also, less money is taken out in this example (8 percent, or $8,000 per year).

As you can see, applying an SWP to the S & P 500 (or an index fund that matches the S & P 500) results in the investor being flat broke by December 1996 (all of the $100,000 and its resulting growth has been depleted). Yet, by using professional management like that found with Washington Mutual (abbreviated as WM), not only are the cumulative distributions greater ($224,000 versus $188,700), so is the remaining principal ($994,560 versus zero).

Systematic Withdrawal Program Using a
Growth & Income Fund (Washington Mutual) Versus the S & P 500
$100,000 Invested in Each Portfolio on January 1, 1973

date	cumulative withdrawal from WM	cumulative withdrawal from S & P 500	remaining value of Washington Mutual (WM)	remaining value of S & P 500
1/1/73	0	0	$100,000	$100,000
12/31/73	$8,000	$8,000	$79,280	$76,890
12/31/74	$16,000	$16,000	$57,460	$48,370
12/31/75	$24,000	$24,000	$74,830	$58,050
12/31/80	$64,000	$64,000	$89,980	$52,930
12/31/85	$104,000	$104,000	$170,740	$42,890
12/31/90	$144,000	$144,000	$260,020	$28,520
12/31/95	$184,000	$184,000	$503,180	$3,910
12/31/96	$192,000	$188,700	$596,530	$0
12/31/97	$200,000		$787,050	
12/31/98	$208,000		$931,140	
12/31/99	$216,000		$933,800	
12/31/00	$224,000		$1,009,930	
3/31/01	------------		$994,560	

For the S & P 500, the average annual total return for this illustration was 6.0 percent (January 1, 1973 through December 15, 1996, when the money ran out) and 17.5 percent for the past ten years. For Washington Mutual Fund (WM), the average annual total return for this illustration was 12.3 percent (January 1, 1973 through March 31, 2001) and 14.3 percent for the past ten years.

Two conclusions can be reached from this illustration. First, there is a benefit to professional management versus a passively managed portfolio such as the S & P 500 (which as an index fund is also considered to be a growth and income fund). Second, moderate gains or advances in some early years can make a great difference later on (compare the value of both portfolios at the end of 1974 and 1975 versus what happened in later years, such as 1980 and 1985, when the gaps become huge due to earlier gains by Washington Mutual).

Appendix K
A Benefit of Balanced Funds

Prudence can pay off. Even though stocks usually outperform bonds, there have been extensive periods of time when a balanced portfolio (30 percent to 70 percent in bonds and the balance in stocks) can be a better way to go than a pure stock portfolio (represented by the S & P 500)—especially when current income is needed.

The table below shows a systematic withdrawal program (SWP) for Income Fund of America (a balanced portfolio from the American Funds Group) versus a similar SWP using the S & P 500. Both withdrawal programs assume a one-time investment of $200,000 made on January 1, 1974, annual withdrawals made at the end of each year, and a first-year withdrawal of $15,000 (7.5 percent of $200,000) that is then increased by 3.5 percent for each subsequent year (to offset the effects of inflation). As you can see, the balanced fund comes out ahead.

Systematic Withdrawal Program
Using a Balanced Fund (IFA) and the S & P 500
$200,000 Invested in Each Portfolio on January 1, 1972

date	cumulative withdrawal from IFA	cumulative withdrawal from S & P 500	remaining value of IFA	remaining value of S & P 500
1/1/74	0	0	$200,000	$200,000
12/31/74	$15,000	$15,000	$165,240	$131,834
12/31/75	$30,525	$30,525	$208,287	$164,740
12/31/76	$46,593	$46,593	$265,307	$187,368
12/31/80	$116,691	$116,691	$248,709	$191,095
12/31/85	$219,029	$219,029	$488,588	$221,773
12/31/90	$340,574	$340,574	$632,843	$257,400
12/31/95	$484,932	$484,932	$1,067,108	$347,972
12/31/96	$516,905	$516,905	$1,197,075	$394,987
12/31/97	$549,997	$549,997	$1,428,937	$493,109
12/31/98	$584,247	$584,247	$1,529,268	$597,424
12/31/99	$619,696	$619,696	$1,501,077	$686,033
12/31/00	$656,385	$656,385	$1,612,601	$586,516
3/31/01	-----------	-----------	$1,619,619	$517,140

For the S & P 500, the average annual total return for this illustration was 11.5 percent (January 1, 1974 through March 31, 2001) and 14.4 percent for the last 10 years. For Income Fund of America (IFA), the average annual total return for this illustration was 13.1 percent and 11.3 percent for the last ten years.

Appendix L
Stock Gains, Losses, and Averages

In the five calendar years ending December 1932, the S & P 500 had a cumulative loss of almost 49 percent. Although this is quite a depressing figure (particularly since similar losses took place during the 1973–74 recession), basing your stock market strategy on a couple of terrible periods is foolish.

To get a better feel for the likely range of returns you will experience, let us examine what happens when you throw out the worst 10 percent and best 10 percent of the years and then look at performance for the remaining 80 percent of the time. Here is what you would find, looking at rolling calendar year periods from 1871 through 1998 (all figures are from *Stocks for the Long Run* by Jeremy Siegel and the Institute of Business and Finance):

- for 5-year periods (124 observations) and then eliminating the 12 best and 12 worst such periods, annualized returns ranged from 0.1 percent to 18.5 percent;
- for 10-year periods (119 observations), annualized returns ranged from 2.8 percent to 15.9 percent;
- for 20-year periods (109 observations), annualized returns ranged from 5.3 percent to 13.8 percent;
- for 30-year periods (99 observations), annualized returns ranged from 6.0 percent to 11.8 percent.

Note: If you earned 5.3 percent a year for 20 years, your money would grow 181 percent. If you earned 6.0 percent a year for 30 years, you would end up with a growth of 474 percent.

Looking at returns and variability from a different perspective Jeffrey Schwartz, a senior consultant at Ibbotson, provides an even wider range of returns. According to his figures, since the end of World War II (throwing out the best 5 percent and the worst 5 percent of the years):

- 5-year returns vary from 2.5 percent to 22.7 percent a year;
- 10-year returns vary from 4.0 percent to 20.4 percent a year;
- 20-year returns vary from 6.0 percent to 15.8 percent a year.

Appendix M
The 20 Largest Mutual Funds
Versus Category Averages

The table below lists the 20 largest equity mutual funds, the ten largest fixed-income funds, their size, and average annual return figures for the past 3, 5, and 10 years, ending 12/31/00.

The 20 Largest Mutual Funds:
Total Return Figures through December 31, 2000

	assets (billions)	3 years	5 years	10 years
Fidelity Magellan Fund	$93	15.4%	16.7	17.9
Vanguard 500 Index; Inv.	88	13.2	18.3	17.3
ICA	56	14.7	18.0	16.0
Washington Mutual Inv.	47	10.2	16.0	16.2
Fidelity Contrafund	40	13.9	16.6	19.4
Fidelity Growth & Income	40	10.5	15.7	17.8
Janus Fund	39	22.4	21.5	18.9
Growth Fund of America	37	28.7	25.1	20.1
Amer Century: AC Ultra; Inv.	34	16.3	17.4	19.5
Janus Worldwide	33	20.0	21.5	n/a
Europacific Growth	31	14.4	14.2	13.8
New Perspective Fund	31	19.0	17.9	16.0
Fidelity Growth Co.	30	27.6	23.2	20.8
Fidelity Blue Chip Grow	27	14.7	17.3	19.7
Vanguard Instl. Index; Ins	26	13.3	18.5	17.4
Vanguard Windsor II	25	9.0	15.2	16.2
Janus Twenty	24	24.5	26.3	21.6
Vanguard Wellington	23	9.3	13.0	13.8
Fidelity Equity-Inc.	22	9.9	15.0	16.8
Vanguard PRIMECAP	22	23.1	25.6	21.9

The 10 Largest Bond Mutual Funds
Average Annualized Return Figures Through 12/31/00

	assets (billions)	3 years	5 years	10 years
PIMCO: Total Ret; Inst.	$30	7.0%	7.3%	9.3%
Vanguard GNMA	14	6.5	6.9	7.8
Franklin CA Tax-Free	13	4.7	5.6	6.8
Vanguard Total Bond	11	6.4	6.6	7.9
Bond Fund of America	9	5.1	6.3	8.9
Vanguard Int-Tm. Tx-Ex	9	5.0	5.2	6.8
Vanguard Sh.-Tm. Corp.	7	6.2	6.1	7.0
Franklin Gov't	7	6.1	6.5	7.3
Franklin Fed. IF Inc.	6	4.3	5.4	7.0
Vanguard Hi Yield Corp.	5	3.4	6.4	10.8

Appendix N
Decades at a Glance (1930–2000)

The text and figures below cover the past seven decades (1930–2000). The summary information is useful in gaining a historic perspective of the market. Perhaps more important, it shows that despite a number of catastrophic events, the U.S. stock market has continued to trend upward.

Decade at a Glance (the 1930s)
Economic distress swept the nation after the October 1929 stock market crash. The Great Depression, which lasted from 1930 to 1936, bottomed in 1933, when one-fourth of the civilian labor force was unemployed.

Index	Average annual total return
Standard & Poor's 500 Index	-0.1%
Long-term U.S. government bonds	4.9%
U.S. Treasury bills	0.6%
	Average for the decade
Short-term interest rates	1.5%
Annual inflation rate	-2.1%
Unemployment rate	18.2%

Decade at a Glance (the 1940s)
Japan's attack on Pearl Harbor on December 7, 1941, thrust the United States into World War II and a wartime economy. In the midst of price controls and consumer goods shortages, upward trends marked the stock market from 1943 to 1946, with a vigorous bull market in 1945 as the war ended.

Index	Average annual total return
Standard & Poor's 500 Index	9.2%
Long-term U.S. government bonds	3.2%
U.S. Treasury bills	0.4%
	Average for the decade
Short-term interest rates	1.6%
Annual inflation rate	5.4%
Unemployment rate	5.2%

Decade at a Glance (the 1950s)

While Eisenhower guided America through the early years of the Cold War, the stock market made gains and by year-end 1954 stock prices had reached their highest levels since 1929. This exuberance was followed by a bear market lasting eighteen months, from April 1956 through October 1957, during which the S & P 500 declined 19.4 percent.

Index	Average annual total return
Standard & Poor's 500 Index	19.4%
Long-term U.S. government bonds	0.1%
U.S. Treasury bills	1.9%
	Average for the decade
Short-term interest rates	3.2%
Annual inflation rate	2.2%
Unemployment rate	4.5%

Decade at a Glance (the 1960s)

American culture, long restrained by the sense of team spirit and conformity induced by the crises of depression, war, and the ongoing Cold War, broke loose in a multitude of swift changes. The economy was equally turbulent, and the stock market cycles recorded three bear markets. In 1963, President Kennedy submitted a federal budget with the largest deficit in history, $10 billion.

Index	Average annual total return
Standard & Poor's 500 Index	7.8%
Long-term U.S. government bonds	1.5%
U.S. Treasury bills	3.9%
	Average for the decade
Short-term interest rates	5.3%
Annual inflation rate	2.5%
Unemployment rate	4.8%

Decade at a Glance (the 1970s)

When The Organization of the Petroleum Exporting Countries (OPEC) quintupled oil prices in 1973, a deep recession hit America. The stock market plunged 45.1 percent, from January 1973 through December 1974. Unemployment reached 8.7 percent in March 1975, the highest level since 1941. In 1979, commercial banks raised their prime rates to a whopping 15.7 percent.

Index	Average annual total return
Standard & Poor's 500 Index	5.9%
Long-term U.S. government bonds	5.5%
U.S. Treasury bills	6.3%
	Average for the decade
Short-term interest rates	8.1%
Annual inflation rate	7.4%
Unemployment rate	6.2%

Decade at a Glance (the 1980s)

President Reagan signed extensive budget- and tax-cutting legislation in 1981 and sweeping tax-reform legislation in 1986. The "Black Monday" stock market crash of October 19, 1987 became the largest one-day stock market decline on record, as the Dow Jones Industrial Average fell an astounding 508.32 points.

Index	Average annual total return
Standard & Poor's 500 Index	17.6%
Long-term U.S. government bonds	12.6%
U.S. Treasury bills	8.9%
	Average for the decade
Short-term interest rates	11.8%
Annual inflation rate	5.1%
Unemployment rate	7.3%

Decade at a Glance (the 1990s)

From November 1990 through the end of 1999, stock market investors were rewarded by the longest bull market in history, which added about $7.2 trillion to households' balance sheets. The Asian economic crisis briefly shook U.S. investor confidence as the Dow Jones Industrial Average experienced the single-biggest point loss ever on October 27, 1997. The decade ended with technology stocks fueling the NASDAQ Index to its highest close ever on December 31, 1999.

Index	Average annual total return
Standard & Poor's 500 Index	18.2%
Long-term U.S. government bonds	8.8%
U.S. Treasury bills	4.9%
	Average for the decade
Short-term interest rates	8.0%
Annual inflation rate	2.9%
Unemployment rate	5.8%

Appendix O
Individual Stocks Versus Mutual Funds

If you believe recent headlines in the media, you might think that mutual funds are a thing of the past and that today's investors prefer to choose individual stocks for their portfolio. However, as you will see in the table below, funds are more relevant now than they were in 1924, when MFS invented the mutual fund. Unlike individual stocks, funds provide active management with the risk-reduction benefit of diversification. Perhaps no other investment has provided a better balance of risk and return.

Did you know that:

- Over the past five years ended December 31, 1999, **39 percent** of stocks produced negative annualized total returns as compared to **less than one-half of 1 percent** of equity mutual funds
- In 1999, the standard deviation of individual stocks was **229**, while it was only **37.3** for equity mutual funds
- Historically, individual stocks have had higher annualized average returns over the 1-year period, but equity mutual funds produced higher returns over the **3-, 5-, *and* 10-year periods** ending 9/30/00

Individual U.S. Stocks	1 year (2000)	3 years (1998–00)	5 years (1996–00)	10 years (1991–00)
# of stocks in existence	6,375	5,424	4,408	2,524
average annualized return	32%	-3%	5%	12%
highest return	5,569%	395%	179%	94%
lowest return	-97%	-83%	-76%	-35%
% of stocks with negative annualized return	49%	57%	39%	17%

U.S. Equity Mutual Funds	1 year (2000)	3 years (1998–00)	5 years (1996–00)	10 years (1991–00)
# of funds in existence	2,683	2,110	1,565	778
average annualized return	28%	14.4%	17.4%	17%
highest return	264%	88%	56%	41%
lowest return	-75	-18%	-17%	-8%
# of funds with negative annualized return	116	140	13	1
% of funds with negative annualized return	2%	3%	0%	0%

About the Author

Gordon K. Williamson, JD, MBA, MS, CFS, CLU, ChFC, RP, is one of the most highly trained investment counselors in the United States. Williamson, a former tax attorney, is a Certified Fund Specialist and branch manager of a national brokerage firm. He has been admitted to the Registry of Financial Planning Practitioners, the highest honor one can attain as a financial planner. He holds the two highest designations in the life insurance industry—Chartered Life Underwriter and Chartered Financial Consultant. He is also a real estate broker with an MBA in real estate.

Mr. Williamson is the founder and executive director of the Institute of Business & Finance, a professional education program that leads to the designations "CFS" and "Board Certified" (800-848-2029).

He is also the author of more than thirty books, including *First Time Investor, Building & Managing an Investment Portfolio, Making the Most of Your 401(k), The 100 Best Annuities You Can Buy, All About Annuities, How You Can Survive and Prosper in the Clinton Years, Investment Strategies under Clinton/Gore, The Longman Investment Companion, Investment Strategies, Survey of Financial Planning, Tax Shelters, Advanced Investment Vehicles and Techniques, Your Living Trust, Sooner Than You Think, Getting Started in Annuities, Big Decisions—Small Investor, Building and Managing an Investment Portfolio,* and *Low Risk Investing.* He has been the financial editor of various magazines and newspapers and a stock market consultant for a television station.

Gordon K. Williamson is located in La Jolla, California. The firm specializes in financial planning and investments for individuals and institutions ($100,000 minimum account size). Additional information can be obtained by phoning (800) 748-5552 or (858) 454-3938.